C000186240

Victory in
LONDON

The Inside Story of the Boris campaign

By Alex Crowley

For Robyn, the rock upon which
I am fortunate to lean

All rights reserved. No reproduction of any part of this
publication is permitted without the prior written
permission of the publisher:

First Published 2012
Copyright © Alex Crowley 2012

Bretwalda Books
Unit 8, Fir Tree Close, Epsom, Surrey KT17 3LD
www.BretwaldaBooks.com

To receive an e-catalogue of our complete range of books
send an email to info@BretwaldaBooks.com

ISBN 978-1-909099-25-8

Bretwalda Books Ltd

Contents

PROLOGUE

So you've bought the book. You've settled down into your chair, or maybe your bed. Or you're sitting bolt upright on the 8.15 to Waterloo, trying not to touch knees with the commuter opposite. Either way, as you open the cover for the first time you're thinking; what am I about to read?

Well obviously, you're going to read about Boris Johnson. That bloke with the blonde hair who is Mayor of London. The bloke that makes you laugh, says what he thinks and gets stuck on a zip wire. You may have found yourself asking more than once, just how did he get elected as Mayor – twice? I suspect that's why you're reading this. Well let me tell you you're in for a ripper. Not because of any particular skill on my part, but because the story of how Boris went from lovable buffoon to major political player is unlike any you'll ever read. At least when it comes to politics.

I've had the privilege of working for Boris, on and off, for five years. I was plucked from obscurity to work on his first election campaign for Mayor in 2007/08 and went on to be his political adviser in City Hall before working on his re-election campaign in 2011/12.

People always ask me; what was it like working for him? Is it all just an act, hiding an inner ruthlessness, or is he really that crazy? How did he win two elections in a Labour-voting city? Was it just his personality, or something more? This book is an attempt to answer those questions.

Because of his success and seemingly inexorable rise, this is not the first book about Boris nor, I suspect will it be the last. But it is the first book that looks at Boris the Mayor – how he was first elected, the challenges he faced in what is an important and difficult job and how he got re-elected in the face of voter disillusionment and a ferocious challenge from Ken Livingstone, that other great maverick of British politics. Parts of this story have been told, but never completely, and never by someone who was there virtually every step of the way.

Through these pages, you will see the many sides to Boris that add up to the man we see today. Sides that are seemingly conflicting yet are more like the layers of a croissant – adding up to something rich and substantial.

You will see that he is the same in private as he is in public, as capable of reducing sombre officials to hysterical laughter as a paying audience. You will see a serious thinker with a thirst for knowledge and understanding. A man who thinks at twice the speed of most other people. You will see a man who seeks and enjoys power, a man that can be utterly ruthless yet endearingly compassionate in equal measure. He has sacked a police commissioner, despite having no official power to do so. To deliver taxpayer value, he has taken tough decisions resulting in job losses. At the same time, he cares deeply about the victims in society – whether they are of inequality, crime or prejudice. Once, when travelling through Bond Street tube station during the re-election campaign, he spotted a beggar with severe facial scars. Boris immediately gave the man money and then politely introduced himself to a staff member, asking him to make sure the man was looked after. This, as we scuttled between campaign events on a tight schedule. For all of Ken Livingstone's posturing, you could never imagine him doing the same. Whatever else is written and said about Boris, that incident sums up the man for me.

You will also see a man who delights and frustrates in equal measure. The man who doesn't try because he knows he's brilliant, and the man who makes Margaret Thatcher look like a shirker.

Above all you will be immersed in the great political debate that Boris provokes. Is his fame and sparkle the secret of his electoral success, or a hindrance to it? Can he only succeed by moderating his eccentricities? Is he destined to become Prime Minister? And if he is, will he be a Berlusconi or a Churchill? You will see the debate play fiercely out among his closest advisers in the high-pressure atmosphere of one of the most high profile and closely contested elections in recent history.

I have tried to tell this story in a relatively even-handed way. Of course that's virtually impossible. I was in the trench with a point of view. Trying to float above that position after the event and see both sides isn't easy. As I did at the time, where I felt strongly about something, I've said so. Where I felt colleagues (including Boris) were wrong, I've said so. I have tried to put across their point of view, informed by how they expressed it to me at the time. In doing so, I hope mis-representation is minimal. If there are any errors they are my own.

You will see, in particular, that I have a strongly held view about how politics and election campaigns should be conducted. It is a view thoroughly masticated over the following pages, so I will merely summarise it here by saying that, in the end, you cannot change anything if you don't win. And you cannot win on instinct alone.

I am a Londoner who believes that the mayoralty is an important institution and uniquely placed to solve some of the deep rooted and intractable problems this city faces. I believe someone like Boris, who is bolder and more principled than most other politicians, is what the mayoralty was designed for. I believe the mayoralty is one of the best and most influential positions in politics because the mayor is free to make the tough calls. It is one of the biggest prizes in British politics. I hope in years to come, it will attract other talented politicians (not necessarily high profile) who would otherwise be lost in the sterile Westminster bubble.

I also believe that the manner in which the two election campaigns were fought and won contain important insights for future Conservative election campaigns. Boris beat the toughest opponent in British politics twice because he combined his supreme talents with innovative and highly disciplined campaigns. In these pages you will read how this was achieved.

Just before you turn to the action, a brief word about how the mayoralty is structured. The position of Mayor of London was created in 1999 and the mayor is in charge of something called the Greater London Authority (GLA). His main powers are in planning, transport, housing and policing. He raises money from a share of council tax bills, as well as tube and bus fares, and Government grant. The GLA oversees other bodies that run various services in London, such as Transport for London (TfL) and the Metropolitan Police. Also within the GLA is something called the London Assembly, an elected body of 25 members whose purpose is to hold the Mayor to account (although they have few powers to do so). Elections are held every four years, and at the time of writing there have been two Mayors, Ken Livingstone (2000 – 2008) and Boris Johnson (2008 – present).

7

I make clear distinctions between those who were campaign staff and those who were part of the mayoral team. I refer to the latter, in general, with the shorthand 'City Hall' and this usually refers to the team of deputy mayors and advisers that surround Boris.

Finally my thanks must go to Boris, Lynton Crosby, Mark Fullbrook, Sam Lyon, Sir Edward Lister, Dan Ritterband and Richard Blakeway for their generous help, advice and support. It is a general rule of the best practitioners of election campaigns to keep what happens in them private, often for very good reasons. I am therefore grateful to all for trusting me to write this book and shining a light on what happened. Above all, I would like to thank my wife, Robyn for her endless patience and incisive and candid assessment of the manuscript as it evolved. I couldn't have done it (as with so many other endeavours in my life) without her love and support.

And now you can turn over the page and begin....

CHAPTER ONE

FROM CELEBRITY TO MAYOR

JULY 2007 – MAY 2008

The hat goes swirling into the ring....

"Boris?! Boris?!" The squeaking voice of the highly-strung, well dressed, slightly portly Conservative London Assembly member rang out through the 6th floor of London's City Hall. Staffers like me had become used to histrionics from this particular member. Yet, for once, his outburst broadly resonated.

The date was 16th July 2007. After a desperate search for viable candidates and months of speculation, Boris Johnson had finally confirmed he was going to run for London Mayor.

The subject had been hotly debated within the London Conservative party for weeks. It would be great fun, most felt, but he was obviously doing it for nothing more than that.

Particularly sceptical were the Conservative members of the London Assembly. The Assembly is the elected body that scrutinises the Mayor of London. There's no reason why you should have heard of it. It is a largely toothless, faceless entity. After almost 8 years of being utterly dominated by Ken Livingstone, there was a certain resignation amongst the long serving Conservative members. They had tried to lay numerous gloves on Red Ken – with very little success. The truth was they had been pummelled into submission. A sort of institutionalised fog had descended and wrapped them in a cloak of defeatism – Ken could never be beaten, they reasoned, even though they would love it to be by someone like Boris.

Despite this, members and staffers like myself rushed down from the 6th floor and took our place among a sizeable crowd that had gathered outside the 'glass testicle' by the Thames – as Ken Livingstone once dubbed London's City Hall.

It was the sort of welcoming committee someone graduating from B-list to A-list might expect. Not quite Beckham, but enough to make you more intimate with the people around you than strictly necessary. It was a glorious day. The sunlight hit the glass panels of Norman Foster's creation, scrunched up into a ball of sparkle and

10

broke up into flares that shot down and danced on the River Thames.

I wasn't to know it then, but this moment marked the start of a remarkable journey that took me from being an office junior to a double mayoral election winner and senior mayoral adviser within the space of five years. A journey that would see me witness, first hand, the incredible political rise of one of the most high profile politicians in the country. A rise that, at the time of writing, seems set to continue.

I watched, bemused as two minders barked orders at the assembled media, bunching the journalists into a huddle – their huddle, to do with as they pleased. The crowd waited expectantly; the press and Boris's aides played a thrilling game of cat and mouse. As they were distracted with phone calls, the huddle would creep forward, before being caught and ordered back. This Flanders Field-esque move and counter move continued for several minutes as the usual jokes about Boris being late did the rounds.

And then, from behind the curve of the building, a dishevelled blonde mop suddenly appeared. The hacks surged forward, as Boris Johnson walked out, wheeling his bicycle in one hand, waving with the other. He was quickly enveloped in a chaotic scrum of journalists that pushed, cajoled and circled around him. There were no preliminaries. Just a hailstorm of machine-gunned questions. As the scrum veered this way and that, Boris breathlessly declared he was "thrilled and excited" to be standing.

Through the noise (and interruption) eventually emerged the following words:

"London is an outstandingly varied and beautiful place and it deserves a proper debate. I want to bring fresh ideas to the capital and offer a new direction for Londoners.
"Even the greatest cities have further greatness in them. I will stand for a greater London and for putting the smile back on London's face."[1]

It wasn't quite St Francis of Assisi, but it was Boris.

I stood on the periphery of the rather surreal scene quietly observing this group of grizzled hacks shed their cynicism and inhibitions to display a kind of infectious, childlike excitement. Boris hadn't even been selected as the official Tory candidate, yet he was already being treated as an election winner. In the first twenty minutes of Boris's mayoral journey, he was demonstrating his most powerful weapon – an ability to connect with people and make them happy. A skill other politicians would chew off their own feet for.

Of course, I was a huge fan. I had read his books, seen him on TV and generally considered him a top class human being. I was genuinely excited to see him in the flesh. As I stood there in the sun, I contemplated the possibility of him actually making a go of it.

I had been a junior staffer at City Hall for two years, and in that time I had grown immensely frustrated at the Tory party's inability to defeat Ken Livingstone. I longed for them to take the mayoral contest seriously – but until this moment, it seemed like they had already given up on the race.

Various candidates had been talked about; radio shock jock Nick Ferrari, Big Issue founder John Bird, even former BBC Director General Greg Dyke. All had passed up the opportunity. Instead, it looked like the party would choose from the usual assortment of non-entity councillors and wannabe MPs, any one of which would be easily swatted aside by Ken.

Now, finally, did we have a potential winner on the ticket?

Also there that day from Boris's future inner circle was Guto Harri – in his then guise as the BBC political correspondent. He summed up the media verdict perfectly. In his report that day, he described Boris as having "a rare combination of qualities. Man of the people and toff, classical scholar and buffoon, much loved celebrity and politician." He concluded with the question on everyone's minds; "but is he actually qualified for the job?"[2]

Boris eventually fought his way through the scrum and with a somewhat implausible nimbleness, hopped on his bike and tottered away. Like a school of migrating tuna, the hacks had dispersed as quickly as they had formed.

The verdict among the gathered Assembly members was instant – there was no way bumbling Boris had the discipline to match such a consummate pro as Ken Livingstone.

It was a view unsurprisingly shared by Ken. Just a few days after the announcement, at Mayor's Question Time, he entered the nasal octave he reserves for objects of special derision (the sort of deep base nasal tone that wakes hibernating voles); "I can't see Boris Johnson concentrating on the minutia of the PPP contracts! All you would have got by now is, 'I am sorry' and he would be off to a TV show!"[3]

This was one thing Livingstone and the bulk of the Tory Assembly members wholeheartedly agreed on.

I took a different view, however. I was quietly positive that if he took this seriously, he could beat Ken. When I aired this view I was greeted with hearty, derisive laughter. He's very funny, but he hasn't got a clue, they would chortle. Only we know London, the Assembly members gravely intoned. Anyone else will come unstuck within weeks, they dismissed.

Part of the problem was that the Conservatives had little interest in the London mayoralty. They opposed its creation from the start and had lost the two elections there had already been. Thus, they had come to view the mayoralty with weary pragmatism. Ken Livingstone served a very useful purpose, noisily defying the then Labour Government. As long as Ken kept being the fly in their ointment, the Tories were content to let him be.

To me, the 2008 contest had to be treated differently. Gordon Brown had just become Prime Minister, and speculation was already mounting he would call an early election in order to secure his own mandate. Either way, with an election due by 2010 at the latest, the party needed to demonstrate momentum, particularly in places like London. Victory in London would prove they could do it nationwide.

More importantly, Ken Livingstone was doing immense damage to London's reputation. Allowing him to run for re-election without a serious challenger was simply not an option. Londoners deserved a proper contest.

I saw at first hand the all-powerful court of Ken and the personal fiefdom that he had created at City Hall. The mayoralty was designed to be strong. Although there is an elected body to keep an eye on the Mayor (the London Assembly) they have little real power to block anything. This meant that Ken could do what he liked – from striking oil deals with South American dictators to doling out public money to every pet political cause he felt like. He behaved appallingly at times, and he did so because he knew no one had the power or the guts to challenge him. He had to be stopped. And my view was that he could be stopped.

However, the prevailing view in the Conservative Party at the time was that the voting system would always disadvantage them. London's mayor is elected by a system known as the 'supplementary vote'. This means that voters are given two choices – a first and second preference. The winner is decided by counting first preference votes and then adding second preference votes if no one gets over half of all votes cast. In practice, the contest has always gone to second preferences.

The Tories believed that even if they could get more first preference votes than Ken, the natural leftie-ness of the capital would always provide enough second preferences to push Livingstone over the line. And in previous elections, many voters who supported the Lib Dems voted tactically against the Conservatives and gave Ken their second preferences. The Tories believed this would always be the case. However, even a cursory analysis of the electoral arithmetic showed that the problem wasn't the voting system. The truth was that in the 2004 mayoral election, previous Tory candidate Steve Norris had underperformed the 'normal' Conservative vote in key areas of London that he needed to win. Places like Croydon, Wandsworth and Barnet. If he had simply turned out all the people who usually voted Conservative in these places, he could have beaten Livingstone.

And the subsequent local elections in 2006 returned Conservative councils in many outer London boroughs that voted for Ken in 2004 and would be key battlegrounds in 2008.

The numbers didn't lie. If the 2008 Conservative mayoral candidate merely polled at the same level the party polled in recent elections, they could beat Ken just by getting the vote out (and suppressing Labour turnout sufficiently).

Yes, London was a Labour leaning city – but enough votes were there to run a tired Ken Livingstone mighty close in his bid for a third term.

From that day on, I was determined to help Boris win in any way I could.

"He's a wanker!"

A few weeks later, Boris's application to be on the Conservative shortlist was accepted. His application form was leaked to the *Daily Telegraph*, and in it we got the first glimpse of how he intended to conduct himself. In the section asking candidates to list the challenges they had faced, he listed the following:

"1. Trying to help raise 4 children in inner London. Outcome: too early to call, but looking promising.

"2. Taking on Blair and Campbell in the battle of Black Rod's Memorandum on the Queen Mother's lying-in-state. Outcome: Total victory.

"3. Negotiating Hyde Park Corner by bicycle. Outcome: survival."[4]

I remember reading about it in the now-defunct *London Paper*. Boris was portrayed as a bumbling idiot who wasn't serious about the job. And I must confess, that was my reaction at the time too. My biggest fear was he was just doing this for a laugh, and couldn't care less about actually doing the job. I nursed a hope that this tomfoolery was a façade, hiding a ruthless politician quietly planning his assault on the summit.

Few had taken the idea of Boris running as anything more than something that would provide a good laugh. David Cameron and the team around him had become increasingly worried that the party would end up with a non-entity mayoral candidate. They realized how bad this would look, particularly as this would be Cameron's first big electoral test as leader. Cameron and his then communications director Andy Coulson had tried to persuade Boris to stand with little success. Perhaps Boris could detect the half-heartedness in their voices. Privately, the team around Cameron barely concealed their belief that Boris would lose. Nevertheless, they wanted a big name to stand and Boris fitted the bill. After the failed attempts to persuade Boris directly, they turned to a man who believed that Boris could win.

Dan Ritterband was a former advertising man turned politico who had helped get David Cameron elected as Tory leader in 2005. Ritterband didn't fit the usual mould of a Tory adviser. As he liked to put it, he was a "fully paid up member of the human race". He entered politics working for previous Tory leader Michael Howard during the 2005 General Election. He really got the political bug when he worked on Cameron's successful leadership campaign. After that, he had worked on the abortive mayoral bid of Nick Boles, who subsequently withdrew due to illness.

Although the party higher ups thought a Boris candidacy was a bit of a joke, Ritterband thought otherwise. He had done the work and felt Ken could be beaten. Moreover, in Boris, he saw someone who could appeal beyond party loyalty and provide enough media interest to compete effectively with Ken Livingstone. Ritterband had his own powerful reasons for stopping Livingstone – he was one of many Jewish Londoners who had had enough of Livingstone's calculated insults against the community. The time Ken compared a Jewish reporter to a concentration camp guard was just one of many examples.

Just days before the official deadline for candidates to register, Ritterband cornered Boris at *The Spectator* summer party and pitched him the idea. He sold it to him on the basis that a successful mayoral bid would re-ignite Boris's career and establish him as the natural successor to Cameron. More convinced by this pitch, Boris asked Ritterband to his house the following day to discuss it properly. After thinking about it for two days, Boris decided to take the plunge, handing in his application on the day of the deadline.

A few years later, I asked Boris why he decided to run. He told me it was the moment he was almost knocked off his bike by a bendy bus.

The rest, as they say, is history.

The early group around Boris consisted of Ritterband and two formidable former Tory press officers, Katie Perrior and Jo Tanner. Then Bexley Council Leader Ian Clement (later a Deputy Mayor) also provided help with the Boroughs. Ritterband was in charge of the campaign and was chief ideas man. Perrior and Tanner would cajole the media with a velvet gloved clenched fist. They guided Boris through the Tory open primary election, which to no-one's surprise, he successfully negotiated to become the official Conservative candidate.

It was a team that fitted Boris perfectly. All three were gloriously irreverent. They had the same heart on your sleeve, say what you think personalities that Boris responded well to. All of them reveled in the early 'us vs. the world' atmosphere – determined to prove the sceptics wrong without diluting the uniqueness of brand Boris.

Soon after Boris had been officially nominated in September 2007, Ritterband came to City Hall to meet the Tory members and their support staff. He was very candid – the campaign team knew little about how the mayoralty and City Hall worked. They had researchers in Parliament looking at some ideas, but nothing more than that. They were seeking help and advice from the people who had lived and breathed the organization for eight years.

After the meeting I was fired up. I saw it as a massive opportunity to help shape and influence the platform Boris would run on. The Tory group had developed numerous ideas over the years, and this was the opportunity to push them to the top of the agenda.

However, most of the staff and members took the opposite view. Very soon after the meeting I was told by a senior staffer that we were not to offer anything other than basic help to the Boris campaign. It was an inexplicable position. They clearly needed help, and we had a major incentive to provide it. But the unanimous view was that Boris would prove an embarrassment, and they wanted nothing to do with a campaign that would almost certainly lose.

Rebelling, I made contact with the campaign and offered as much help as they could stomach. It turned out to be a wise decision. Within weeks, Dan Ritterband had invited me in to see Boris in his Westminster office (he being the MP for Henley at the time).

On the appointed day I will happily admit I instantly descended into chronic star-struck-ness. As I walked down the plush corridor in the Palace of Westminster, I could scarcely believe that I was about to meet the man himself. I involuntarily gave it the full treatment – hand shaking, stomach churning, and brow sweating nerves. I was 23 years old and I was about to brief Boris Johnson about the London mayoralty. Cripes, as he might put it.

I was met by a very polite woman and asked to kindly wait outside his office. The corridor was eerily quiet, and a long row of faded wooden doors stared me down as if I were an intruder. Or an errant schoolchild.

Some time later (yes, he was running behind schedule) the woman re-emerged from the end of the corridor and told me he was ready. She disappeared, and I had to summon the spirit to cross the patch of green carpet and knock on the door.

Knuckles white, I took a deep breath and gave two sharp raps against the door. From inside, a noise that sounded like a cross between a bark and a Tuvan throat singer rang out. I dared to poke my head behind the door. Boris looked up from his desk, leapt up and bounded over to me offering his hand.

It took a good ten minutes at the start of the meeting to stop myself from laughing every time he spoke. Not because what he was saying was inherently funny or unserious, it was just his manner of speaking – as if every word was an answer to an embarrassing question. He was no different in this private setting to how he appeared on *Have I Got News For You.*

We talked for over two hours, the conversation galloping across a vast expanse of policies, ideas and questions. No sooner had I finished one answer than Boris had leapt upon a new question or idea, before quickly discarding it and spotting a more interesting subject. It was dialectic on steroids. Many people accuse Boris of not being able to concentrate in discussion – the reality is his mind is spinning much faster than anyone else in the room.

At one point, as I was explaining yet another example of Ken's arrogance, Boris fixed me with a fearsome stare, banged the table and roared; "He's a wanker!" He briefly paused, before his face lit up; "That's it! I know what I'll say! I'll just say vote for me because Ken's a wanker!"

Unsure of how to respond, I diplomatically replied that the

sentiment was right but needed a little refining. It's amazing to think now that this was just the emotional response we would need in getting the vote out.

The meeting must have gone well, because shortly after Ritterband invited me into his office and offered me a job. I was to join the campaign to oversee the research and policy work. An amazing journey had begun.

'You've got the wrong candidate'

London's old County Hall stands by the River Thames opposite the Houses of Parliament. A towering monument to municipal socialism turned tourist destination and keeper of such capitalist monoliths as McDonalds. But ascend the still grand marble staircase, past the wood paneled debating chamber, down a corridor that smells like an old library and you find a suite of offices untouched from the days of the old Greater London Council, which Ken Livingstone led in the 1980's.

The ornate fixtures and fittings were stripped out years ago, but on a clear day tall windows throw magnificent sunlight on these large wood paneled rooms, hinting at their former glory. It was in this suite of three interconnected offices that the 2008 Boris campaign began in earnest. We were to mount our assault on Red Ken's empire from his old stomping ground.

The suite of offices was tucked behind a Star Wars exhibition. In order to get to the offices, you had to walk through a prop store. Each day, staffers and visitors alike were greeted with giant Darth Vaders, model aeroplanes and clown costumes.

At particularly stressful moments of the campaign, Boris would occasionally disappear. At first, no one knew where he went. But then one day, someone discovered his guilty secret – he would hide behind a giant coffin in the prop store like a naughty cat.

As if the grave importance of our work were not apparent enough, the theme from Star Wars played on a loop, seven hours a day. They say campaigns can drive you mad, but this was something else.

Boris came under pressure right from the start. The media and other Tory politicians were clamoring to know more: what was his pitch to the London electorate? Why did he want the job? What would he do as Mayor? These were questions we were asking too. The trouble was, he hadn't yet come up with the answers.

Soon after I joined the campaign, Boris called me to discuss how things were going. He was being overwhelmed with advice about everything – what his message should be, what policies he should prioritise, how he should attack Ken. It was apparent he was starting to realize what a mammoth enterprise he was letting himself in for.

I told him we needed a clear steer from him as to what he wanted his priorities to be. We had less than two months to develop a whole policy platform from nothing, so we needed him to engage early so we didn't waste time going down blind alleys. We needed to establish what his position was on the things Livingstone had already done, and what the new initiatives would be. Above all, Boris needed to do some serious swatting up on what the Mayor was actually responsible for.

Right from the start, I felt the biggest threat was the charge that Boris wasn't serious about the job. Therefore, this had to be neutralized by getting him up to speed quickly on the basics. He was never going to become an expert on London government overnight, but by demonstrating a basic grasp of certain things we could at least show people that he was really committed to making it work.

Boris was agitating for 'big ideas'. He enthused about a new Routemaster bus at length. The idea contained perfect political symmetry for him – it was something to get excited about, and it was a way to highlight Ken's 'miserablist' attitude to "elf and safety'.

I told him the big ideas would come – but first he needed to do the hard grind of knowing the boring details and having strong arguments on the issues Londoners cared most about. It was like I had pricked a bubble. You could almost hear the air deflating on the other end of the line. But people are expecting big ideas, he appealed. I retorted with a challenge; "Ok then, if you were Mayor for a week, what is the one thing you would do?" The line went silent for a moment, before he went into full Boris mode; "Uuuh, errrmm, gosh….." After a few more silences and spluttered noises, he eventually said; "Can I get back to you on that?"

As would later become clear, Boris has another quality other politicians lack – he genuinely wants to answer a question with a proper answer. It's why, if he hasn't thought of one that's good enough, he tends to bluster in this way. He would rather do that than try and make something up.

The early conversation highlighted the biggest source of tension between Boris and the campaign team in the early days. The team shared the same view – Boris was undoubtedly brilliant, but he couldn't chance his way through this election. In a way, his brilliance was his biggest enemy. He was the child in the class whose homework would always be late, but the best. And he knew it.

He thrived on spontaneity and living in the moment – it's why people like him. He is a man who grabs opportunity when it presents itself, he doesn't plot and scheme for years. Our biggest challenge was to convince him that in order to beat someone as ruthless as Ken Livingstone, he needed a campaign that was well ordered. Otherwise, we would all be overwhelmed.

It didn't help that in those early days Boris still had a large number of other commitments to fulfill. In fact, some weeks the campaign team only had access to him one day a week. He was still an MP, as well as writing, doing speaking engagements and filming a TV series. Combined with a woeful lack of campaign resources (I had a very small group of mostly part-time researchers) we were sitting ducks for the well-oiled Livingstone machine.

Ken had wasted no time in getting stuck in. Almost as soon as Boris announced he was running, his allies in the left-wing campaign group Compass had released a dossier entitled; *'Boris Johnson: A member of the hard Tory right'*. Authored by Chukka Umunna, it purported to demonstrate that Boris was 'Norman Tebbit in a clown's uniform'[5] by listing a series of highly selective quotes from his humorous writings.

Umunna – who at the time of writing had risen to become a senior Labour politician – fired the opening salvo in what would turn out to be a very dirty Labour campaign by pronouncing at the launch:

> *"Boris Johnson represents the type of out-of-touch public school Toryism that thinks it's acceptable to refer to black people as 'piccaninnies' and as having 'water melon smiles' - remarks for which he has been strongly attacked within the black community."*[6]

That particular quote would prove to be the most damaging, and by December it had kicked off a race row of such ferocity that it almost sunk our entire campaign. Indeed, Boris still has a bad reputation amongst many black Londoners to this day – quite unfairly when you consider how much he cares about tackling gang violence, something that disproportionately affects the black community.

There was no doubt the words were ripe to be ripped out of context, but then Boris was never one to censor himself. They were used in an article lampooning Tony Blair's penchant for self-aggrandising foreign tours. The tone of the article was plainly satirical – mocking Blair as a wildly out of touch Emperor, reveling in the entirely false cheers of submissive natives.

The offending paragraph is worth re-producing in full. Only then do you get the crucial sense of context:

'What a relief it must be for Blair to get out of England. It is said that the Queen has come to love the Commonwealth, partly because it supplies her with regular cheering crowds of flag-waving piccaninnies; and one can imagine that Blair, twice victor abroad but enmired at home, is similarly seduced by foreign politeness. They say he is shortly off to the Congo. No doubt the AK47s will fall silent, and the pangas will stop their hacking of human flesh, and the tribal warriors will all break out in watermelon smiles to see the big white chief touch down in his big white British taxpayer-funded bird.'[7]

Of course, we knew context was irrelevant when it came to scoring political points. And the words were what Sir Humphrey might call 'unfortunate'. The tactic was typical Ken – below the belt, ruthless and precisely calibrated to fire up his base. It was designed to set one group of Londoners against another, in stark contrast to Boris, who tries to unite Londoners. I remember sitting in the Chamber of City Hall at one Mayor's Question Time in early September where Ken, with a twinkle in his eye, sinisterly drooled; "I have to say to you I have already read more of Boris Johnson's original writings than I ever hoped or intended...."[8]

To those familiar with his 'play the man not the ball' approach to politics, he was clearly giving notice that he was going to have some fun.

Even though the Compass attack had been launched in August, Ken's allies had refused to relinquish the bone and by December 2007 they had persuaded the media to give the race angle a run. The *London Paper* splashed on it and everyone else followed. For almost a week, Boris was suddenly portrayed as a racist bigot unfit to lead as diverse a city as London. Livingstone had worked up his usual suspects into a frenzy to keep the story alive. Stoking the fires that fuel racial and religious division is a tactic he had used to good effect in the past.

Boris was utterly bemused and irritated. He was personally stung and appalled by the suggestion that he was a racist. Even though the quote is close to the bone, he genuinely felt it was way below the belt to 'wrench' it out of context and use it to suggest something that isn't in his heart. And he didn't hide his irritation in public – which of course only encouraged his opponents and the media.

He also (perhaps naively) felt betrayed by his opponent. Boris had previously defended Ken when he got into trouble for comparing a Jewish reporter to a concentration camp guard. In a later note to the senior team he complained; "he (Livingstone) is a sly old tosser who plays dirty, calling his opponents racists without any foundation (and when they have gone out of their way, I might say, to stick up for him when he has got into hot water)."[9]

I was angry too – but not surprised. To me, this was standard issue Ken. And in a way, I think Boris needed to feel the full force of a Ken attack in order to let him know that he was in a real fight.

The pressure was starting to get to everyone. Newspaper articles had started appearing criticizing Boris and the team for not performing. One article in particular had Boris seething. On 14th December 2007, the journalist Peter Oborne reported in the *Daily Mail* that; 'David Cameron is "tearing his hair out" at Boris's lazy campaign.' He went on; 'at the moment, his lazy (and according to critics, selfish) approach is allowing Ken Livingstone's Labour Party in London to get away with an outrageous abuse of power. Even more importantly, it is threatening to derail the chances of David Cameron becoming Prime Minister.'[10]

Boris was used to being attacked, but such criticism coming from one of his journalistic peers really hurt. It was certainly true we were struggling, and the campaign team felt Oborne had a point. We had virtually no support in terms of manpower from Tory HQ, a patchy organization on the ground and a candidate who was reluctant to change his style. Indeed, this was a major dilemma for the team.

We felt that his trademark act – spontaneous and ruffled – simply wasn't going to cut it if he was going to be taken seriously in the election campaign. To us, it wasn't just the hair (we were resigned to that). It was how he could sometimes come across on TV: slouching in his chair, mumbling incoherent noises to straightforward questions, not having a clear message.

To Boris, it was a style that had made him successful. He knew all too well that people liked him because he was not just another robotic politician. He felt very strongly that, as the late Christopher Hitchens put it: 'The people who must never have power are the humourless.' Boris knew that the more he spluttered to simple questions, the more people would laugh. It was his brand, and it worked. So when it was suggested he undergo a process of gentle refinement, naturally he refused.

At a meeting to discuss the issue, Tanner and Perrior outlined their concerns. They felt that he couldn't afford to appear like he had done on *Have I Got News For You*. Londoners were looking for more than a quiz show host. In an election where he had to convince people he was serious, he had to come across as sharper and less bumbling. It wasn't a case of performing a lobotomy – the rough edges just needed a little sanding.

Boris disagreed. He argued that it would be a fraud for him to pretend to be something he wasn't. They tried to re-assure him that we weren't expecting him to suddenly turn into a smooth talking politician – they just needed him to be a bit sharper. What he heard was an appeal to be boring and Boris will accept being called many things – but boring is where he draws the line.

As the debate dragged on, he slouched into his chair – which had been placed, Mastermind style, in the centre of the room. Tanner snapped at him; "Look! You're even doing it now!" Boris snapped back: "Well maybe you've got the wrong candidate!"

Dan Ritterband diplomatically adjourned the meeting. It was a subject to which we would all return and indeed, it remains the central dilemma for all those who advise him. As we would see later, Boris is at his most electorally potent when he combines his personality with a clear message.

As Christmas 2007 approached, the mood was gloomy. The race row had really shaken Boris, and the close scrutiny of his candidacy so early in its existence had thrown him off guard.

The sniping and whispering about how he and the team were performing was also denting morale. Dan Ritterband was under intolerable pressure. He knew what needed to be done, but he had a candidate who had to learn on the job and a party machine that was more interested in briefing against him than lending a hand. There was still a blank sheet where policy should have been – all we had was a very long list of options, with more questions than answers. He had intended the period between September and December 2007 to be 'policy lockdown', used for Boris to get to grips with his brief and come out fighting in January. It was a sensible approach but such was the huge interest in Boris's candidacy, it didn't satisfy either the media or the party. The reality was that Boris wasn't a Ken Livingstone style machine politician, who had been assiduously preparing for years. He was a unique character who believed that – at that moment – he had something positive to offer Londoners.

We entered the holidays full of uncertainty. Would Boris have enough time to focus his mind? Would the party finally agree to provide more resources? Could we turn things around in time? Would Dan Ritterband still be the campaign manager? We had no answers. But it was clear that something had to change.

Knuckling down

Over the Christmas holiday, Boris was finally afforded the time and space to do some serious thinking. He reflected on why he wanted the job and what he wanted to do with it. Behind the scenes moves were afoot to shake up the campaign team. Unbeknown to me at the time, the Tory hierarchy had become so concerned at the campaign's lack of direction they decided to force a change. Overtures were made to the Australian strategist Lynton Crosby.

Crosby had established an international reputation as Federal Director of the Australian Liberal Party – guiding Prime Minister John Howard to successive election victories. Since then, he had run election campaigns the world over.

He was well known to this generation of Tory politicians, having run the Tories 2005 General Election campaign. Both Cameron and Osborne held him in very high regard. Although the Tories lost the 2005 election, it was widely acknowledged to be one of the most professional and effective campaigns the party had run in years. This was attributed almost solely to Crosby, whose tough, no nonsense style had fired up the long dormant Tory machine to achieve levels of activity previously unheard of.

The deal to bring him over from Australia and run the remainder of the campaign was done relatively quickly. I was told over the holidays to expect a new campaign manager when we returned. The news wasn't a complete surprise. There had been open whispers for weeks, as well as half-baked and very unsubtle attempts to replace Ritterband. Before Christmas, at least two other individuals turned up uninvited having been asked to provide help, before being swiftly dispatched. When it eventually came, he was sanguine about the coup. Although he was happy to defer to Crosby's experience, he felt that he hadn't been given the time or support to make it work. He agreed to stay on the campaign, although he felt increasingly marginalized.

Meanwhile, the time off was clearly doing wonders for Boris. He was beginning to articulate his vision and motivation to run.

Before Christmas, the researchers and I had put together a detailed document that outlined all the major issues and presented policy options for him to decide between. The day before we all departed for our holidays, we gathered in County Hall and sipped champagne in plastic cups. Boris was looking more relaxed, relieved that the spotlight would be momentarily dimmed. As we said our goodbyes, I handed him the 146-page dossier for his holiday homework. If eyes could groan, believe me, his would have done.

The dossier hadn't crushed his spirit too much because in between Boxing Day and New Year's Eve a document dropped in our inboxes entitled; 'Why I Want To Be Mayor'.

The 5,000 word missive laid out his thoughts on the policies he wanted, the positions he felt we should take on the major issues and what he wanted to campaign on. It opened with his big picture vision, and then went into each major policy area, outlining what our attack on Livingstone should be, and what we should be proposing as an alternative. It was incredibly detailed and dripping with clarity. It was Boris the policy thinker and political strategist rolled in one. It showed his determination to control his own destiny and silence his critics.

It was – essentially – what would become the manifesto. Indeed, looking back on the document now, it's amazing to see how many of the positions he outlined went on to become core parts of his agenda. It was all there; a focus on tackling gangs, scrapping the £25 congestion charge and the western extension, scrapping the bendy buses, introducing a bike hire scheme, championing a new airport in the Thames Estuary, a new Routemaster, fining utility companies who dig up the roads and his desire to shake up the Metropolitan Police. It was a serious agenda, and it showed he had a clear view as to what he wanted his mayoralty to be about.

It was also a thoughtful, heartfelt outline of what really drove Boris to want to do the job. And in it emerged a personal priority that would become a major theme in the election.

In the run up to Christmas, there had been a wave of tragic youth murders that belied the overall drop in crime figures. At one point, a teenager was being murdered virtually every week and the issue dominated the media. By the end of the year, 27 teenagers had lost their lives.

Boris was genuinely moved by these murders. To him, it was unacceptable that London could be a city where the young had no future. In the faces that stared hauntingly out from the police 'murder' posters, he saw hope for young Londoners extinguished. He saw the appalling prospect of a whole generation of kids condemned to a life in the gangs. It was a situation he knew would take root unless something was done.

He felt strongly that it was the personal responsibility of the Mayor to take action. He was so appalled because he felt, above all, that London should be a place where the young prosper. London should be a place that championed and nurtured ambition:

> *'I want to be the mayor who CHAMPIONS AMBITION, and that means helping young kids cheat the dreadful fate of being sucked into a gang. This is where I think I can make the biggest difference to London, and I want as many policies as possible to be aimed at ending the INEQUALITY OF AMBITION. I have had a very privileged and very lucky life – and I want kids across London to have the kinds of chances I have had. I will use sport, and art, and whatever powers I have over education and skills to help achieve this. That is the chief objective of my mayoralty.'*

It was the insight into what was driving him that we wanted. He wasn't trying to be clever, or funny. His only audience was the campaign team. This was no newspaper column. It was genuinely what he wanted to do as Mayor.

The document also showed just how much a loathing of Livingstone was motivating him:

'he is no longer sticking up for the little guy against the system. He is the system. He has morphed into the ruling class like the pigs in Animal Farm he sits like Smaug on the great heap of GOLD he has accumulated from his FINES (why don't we have a poster of a giant newt coiled avariciously around our dosh – contrast my more generous regime, which will give people more time to pay and will be less brutal and fascistic and dictatorial)'

Boris had suddenly locked into gear and decided that he really, really wanted to win. It was a pivotal turning point in his transition from lovable rogue to serious politician, and he was making that transition in his own way. Beneath the entertaining exterior was a man who had something to say, something to achieve. The pressure, it seemed, was just the medicine he needed.

Rescue from Down Under

Lynton Crosby and his business partner, the expert pollster Mark Textor ('call me Tex, mate') got to work straight away after the New Year. The situation they walked into wasn't perfect, but they quickly saw that the fundamentals were there.

The public polls were close, with never more than a few points in it. The Westminster village chatter about the deficiencies of the campaign mattered little to ordinary Londoners. The focus group findings were also encouraging.

People acknowledged that Livingstone had a good record, but he was becoming arrogant and out of touch. They felt that whilst London had moved on, Livingstone was stuck in the past – more interested in his own political obsessions than the issues they cared about. In the past, they liked his feistiness because he was using it to help Londoners. Now, he was just unpleasant. There was a growing 'time for change' sentiment. That Boris was liked was never in doubt. People felt that the Mayor of London should have a big personality, and that Boris was in this respect well qualified for the job. But they also worried that he wouldn't take it seriously. Although they understood little of what the Mayor did, they felt it was an important role that needed to be taken seriously. They were looking for re-assurance that Boris was committed and focused.

Over January and February, Crosby and Tex commissioned further research to dig deep into what was driving the vote. It was a level of analysis that went beyond what the Conservative Party usually commissioned. Yet it was vital in pinpointing the specific issues that would drive our target voters to come out and vote for Boris. It would also help us understand where to direct our meager resources.

By mid-February they were ready to present their findings. Crosby, Tex, Boris and the team gathered in County Hall. The presentation got off to a shaky start when Tex stood up and starting talking about 'Kevin' Livingstone. As he flicked to the next slide, the words 'Kevin' Livingstone flashed up on the screen. Boris looked around, bemused. Yet Tex ploughed on. After a very uncomfortable few minutes, the error was eventually pointed out, much to everyone's amusement. Crosby and Tex took it in good spirit – they had been advising an Australian campaign whose opponent was Kevin Rudd, and got the names mixed up. Boris still roars with laughter about it to this day.

The mistake didn't undermine their point. Their analysis was that Boris had to prove to the voters that he was serious about the job and competent to do it. The only way a challenger can do this, they explained, is to run a disciplined and focused campaign.

Part of the problem was that Boris and the campaign were talking about too much. We were responding to the day-to-day concerns of the media – who wanted something 'new' every time – rather than the concerns of ordinary Londoners, who wanted clarity and consistency. Boris was thinking like a columnist – wanting to produce something new and exciting every day. This approach didn't give people the chance to hear his message, because it was always changing. The result was people had no idea what he stood for, even though he had a clear agenda he wanted to enact. We needed to talk about fewer issues, and only those that really mattered to our target voters: crime, council tax, green spaces and transport.

They had identified the key voters in outer London we would need to turn out. This has subsequently been referred to as Crosby's 'doughnut strategy'. Others like to denigrate it as a 'core-vote' strategy, echoing the criticism of the 2005 General Election campaign Crosby ran.

The truth is that Crosby doesn't run 'core-vote' campaigns, because that is never enough. You always need to convince new people.

A more accurate term would be the doughnut plus jam strategy. It was true that many of our target voters were in a ring of outer London boroughs. But it was clear this would not be enough to secure victory – we needed a mix of core and swing voters. This meant reaching out to parts of inner London as well in boroughs such as Wandsworth, which had voted Livingstone in 2004. We also needed to appeal to Lib Dem leaning voters in south west London, whose 2nd preference votes would be vital.

Boris was skeptical at first. He is a politician who distrusts fixed ways of doing things. He prefers spontaneity and flexibility. He questioned whether 'boring people to death' was going to work. On the contrary, Crosby and Tex argued, focusing on what the voters want isn't boring – it's how you win elections. And they knew.

They laid out the stark reality facing Boris. Although Livingstone had plenty of negatives, he was still the most likely winner. We were facing a massive hurdle: the people who were most likely to vote for Boris were the least likely to turn out. Whereas the people most likely to vote for Ken were the most likely to turn out. Therefore, our campaign had to be about motivating our people to participate. We had to define the election, and the important choice facing Londoners, in very clear terms. And this message had to be re-enforced with ruthless consistency. Anything else, and Ken would win.

Our campaign would rely on a mix of positive and negative messages. We would seek to re-assure Londoners that Boris had the energy, focus and fresh thinking to fix the problems of the past. And we would re-enforce Ken's negatives as tired and out of touch, wasteful with public money and dangerously obsessed with his pet political causes.

It was the kind of razor sharp analysis and clarity of purpose we needed. We left the meeting in a reflective mood – and in no doubt as to what needed to happen.

Days later, Crosby and Tex had produced the Boris story 'in 8 lines' and plastered every available office wall space with it. It summarized the narrative that would inform every piece of communication that went out from February to May, no matter how minor. The narrative finished with the big pitch:

'This election is a choice between a Mayor who's out of touch and had his day and Boris who will bring fresh thinking, energy and commitment to the forgotten issues that matter to Greater London and it's people. Whereas Ken will simply revert to his old self after the election, Boris offers the hope of a change to something better.'

With the strategy and message in place, the final task was to get Conservative HQ to commit the extra resources we needed. After weeks of behind the scenes talks, Boris and the senior team were summoned to see David Cameron, George Osborne and their senior staff to seal the deal.

It was a bitter winter's evening, and the yellow lights of Westminster shimmered on the deathly still Thames. The senior team filed into the Shadow Cabinet room in the Norman Shaw South building on the Parliamentary estate. The room looked out to the

River, and beyond, the neon lights of the touristified County Hall. It was like the ghost of Ken was hovering outside the window, mischievously peering in.

The lighting was conspiratorially low, even though we had nothing sinister to discuss. A moment later, David Cameron strode in purposefully and took his seat at the head of the table. George Osborne crept in behind, almost unnoticed, slipping into a seat that was just to the left of and marginally behind Cameron. Boris was to Cameron's right.

The demeanor of the three men was fascinating. Cameron was sat with a perfectly straight back, exuding freshness and razor sharp concentration despite this being the end of a busy day. He chaired the meeting briskly and efficiently. Boris was slouched in his chair, hair messy, shoelaces undone. He seemed to exaggerate his slouch more than usual, almost as a direct riposte to Cameron's sleekness. Osborne sat in the shadows, with his head tilted to one side, carefully listening to the exchanges but never interrupting. He wore an utterly inscrutable expression. I found myself wondering if he ever played poker.

Crosby outlined the strategy and what the campaign needed in terms of manpower and resources. Cameron stressed how important the mayoral election was to their overall strategy and insisted that, for the good of London, Ken Livingstone must be beaten.

Cameron was particularly keen to scrutinise the overall message and theme of the campaign. Crosby summarized it perfectly, but Cameron wanted to hear it from Boris himself. He wanted to know what Boris was offering the London electorate – the 'retail offer' as political pundits refer to it.

I soon noticed that Boris was becoming increasingly defensive, saying something along the lines of; 'don't worry, it's going be fantastic Dave'. The more Cameron and then Osborne pressed, the more Boris obfuscated. It seemed like he was playing a game of hide and seek with his old school chums. He seemed to revel in their exasperation.

Their behaviour around each other was fascinating. Much is made of their 'bitter' rivalry, even though they've never directly competed for a political job. It's more a clash of styles. If Boris was the schoolboy who handed his essay in late, Cameron was the schoolboy who always handed his essay in on time. Both would know that Boris got higher marks. Cameron seemed irritated by Boris's haphazardness. Boris seemed irritated by Cameron's smoothness.

This was perfectly demonstrated when later, Cameron attempted to straighten Boris's tie before the main campaign launch in Edmonton, as if he were his mother. And just like a child, Boris successfully squirmed his way free from the interference.

Seeing his interrogations were getting nowhere, Cameron broke off pursuit and succinctly summarized the meeting – indicating its conclusion. He agreed that the party would provide whatever support was required. He thanked Crosby and the team for their efforts, and then Dear Leader was gone, Osborne not far behind.

The meeting was a decisive point in the campaign. With Cameron and Osborne fully signed up, resources flooded in. Within days, senior staffers from Tory HQ had arrived and set up camp. James McGrath, another Aussie blade that cut straight through to the bone, took charge of the ground operation. He had worked with Crosby on 2005 General Election campaign, and they knew each other well. He was joined by a team of people who would co-ordinate the volunteers and organize Boris's campaign schedule. Among them was Sara Argent (nee Cadisch), who would go on to run Boris's operations team in City Hall.

McGrath was the kind of political staffer that worked hard and played hard. He re-named Fridays 'cocktail Fridays', and he would pad around the office in his socks drinking his favourite 'Bundie and coke' from a plastic cup while barking orders at staffers – who'd be wondering if they'd see another Friday night again. Despite his quirkiness, he was hugely respected for his ability to deliver.

Several of the party's best policy and media people joined too. Suddenly, our suite of offices was jam packed with people. For the first time, there was an energy and buzz in the place. Even the Star Wars theme on loop became tolerable.

And into the fire...

By the beginning of March, Crosby had the machine purring. Each morning and afternoon, he would hold a meeting with the entire campaign staff announced by the shriek of a bugle. The bugle was to become his campaign trademark, blasting the ears of campaign workers. These meetings were a chance for people to come up for air. Crosby would use them not just to impart information, but to re-energise the troops and make everyone feel involved.

Each morning, at 7am, Crosby and the senior staff would gather to discuss the previous days media, and what the plan was for the forthcoming day of campaigning. We would run through the campaign grid and discuss all the major calls. By 7.30am, we all knew what our priorities were, which we then communicated to our respective teams.

By 8am, the whole campaign team had met and been instructed. The day would then accelerate towards the evening news bulletins on BBC and ITV London. The core team would crowd around the small TV in the management office – someone always holding the aerial in the right position lest the very poor signal be lost completely.

This moment was always the most nerve racking of the day. On most days, we had come to terms with the fact that BBC London would portray Boris in a negative light. We always complained, but the BBC never accepted there was ever any hint of bias. Ever. It just so happened to be the case that Ken's word was always accepted without challenge, and Boris was always questioned with the assumption he was lying.

It was in the newspapers that the battle was more evenly matched. Under the editorship of Veronica Wadley, the *Evening Standard* had taken a broadly pro-Boris position. This was most famously demonstrated by the extensive space given to Andrew Gilligan's long running story uncovering grants given by Ken Livingstone's London Development Agency to organisations that appeared to have very close links with his Policing and Equalities adviser Lee Jasper.

Gilligan alleged that at least £2.5 million of Londoners' money had been given to; 'a shadowy network of businesses and NGOs directly linked to Mr. Jasper and his close friends and associates, many of them supposedly operating out of the same small room in Kennington. Hundreds of thousands of pounds are unaccounted for or have disappeared, while several of the companies have gone bust or are dormant.[11]' The investigation raised legitimate questions about Jasper's role in the award of the grants, given his apparent closeness to the people involved. Jasper was a long-standing friend and ally of Livingstone and a powerful figure at City Hall. Was he using public money to help out his friends? If he was, did Livingstone know about it?

By late January, the story was gaining real traction. Ken took a typically robust stance – angrily denouncing it as a racist smear campaign against his adviser. No matter what compelling evidence Gilligan produced, Ken maintained that there was no charge to answer. Even when the police were called in to investigate the potential fraud, Ken stuck to his line. He also stuck with Jasper for what seemed like an eternity, as fresh allegations emerged. It was the first time in the campaign that Ken was put under serious, sustained pressure. And it would drag on right up until polling day, 1st May.

As we watched the story unfold, we couldn't believe our luck. Gilligan clearly wasn't going to let it go, and he was being given as much space in the paper as Wadley could get away with. The ferocity of the attack was to cement a bitter feud between Livingstone and Gilligan that persists to this day.

It was the perfect story for us. The minutia mattered little to the electorate – what they saw was something not quite right about the whole affair. This was made worse by Ken's aggressive response to it. We couldn't believe he was showing such poor judgement. All he had needed to do was sack Jasper immediately and announce a full enquiry. Instead, he clung on to Jasper and tried to fob everyone off with a half-baked 'internal investigation' that – surprise surprise – concluded there was no wrongdoing.

City Hall officials told me after the election how disgusted they were with the way Ken and Jasper had behaved. Despite strong advice that Ken remove Jasper and investigate properly, the cabal around Livingstone had closed ranks and decided they knew best.

Evidently, someone decided to take matters into their own hands, because Jasper was eventually forced to resign after his salacious emails to a married woman were splashed all over the *Evening Standard*.

The story uncovered a deeper malaise at City Hall that we sought to take full advantage of. People already believed that Ken had lost his way. Now, a bright light had been shone on the 'ken-ocray' at City Hall. It emerged that many were part of a secretive organization called 'Socialist Action'. Journalist Martin Bright (no friend of the Tories), in a Dispatches documentary for Channel Four, revealed evidence that Ken's staff were abusing public resources to run political campaigns – including a smear campaign against respected former Labour politician Trevor Phillips. Londoners were being reminded – in a way they hadn't been in years – that behind the cheeky chappy image was a ruthless politician who was prepared to do anything to get his own way. It also alleged that Ken would occasionally drink on the job, including sipping whiskey at Mayor's Question Time – an important regular meeting that usually started at 10am.

A very bad smell was starting to envelope Livingstone. The story rumbled on through February, March and April 2008. As the clock ticked down to polling day, he found it increasingly difficult to move the agenda back to his positive issues. Every time he was attacked, he would react badly and waste time on rebuttals. His campaign even went to war with pollsters who had the temerity to put Boris in front, issuing lengthy press releases denouncing their methodology.

But perhaps Livingstone's biggest mistake was his response to the youth murders. To everyone's horror, the gruesome pattern of 2007 was continuing into 2008. Ken's response was sadly familiar. He insisted that London was the safest it had been for years, and accused the media of blowing the story out of all proportion. When he quipped on 27th March 2008, "if it bleeds it leads"[12], we wasted no time savaging Ken's calculated heartlessness. He became defensive, insisting that he didn't feel any responsibility for tackling the issue and sticking to his line that London was safer on his watch.

It was a woefully tin-eared response. He had fallen into the trap that had claimed many incumbents before him – believing your record is enough. Yes, the overall crime figures had shown an improvement, as had police numbers. But Londoners were scared and looking for a Mayor who would acknowledge this specific problem and deal with it. What they got from Livingstone was an arrogance that seemed to say; 'what's all the fuss about?'

Again, we found ourselves astonished at his lack of judgement. What he should have done was acknowledge the problem and take immediate action. He should have used his incumbency; he was able to enact new ideas immediately – we had to get elected first. But he did none of this, and it hurt him badly.

By April, Boris was well into his stride. He showed real passion about the issue and talked enthusiastically about how he was going to tackle the problem. It became the number one issue of our campaign. The early analysis Crosby and Tex had done showed that crime was an issue that Boris had a big advantage on, and it was most likely to motivate our voters. For the remaining weeks of the campaign, this became our priority.

'There's a swing on'

Polling day rapidly approached. Ken had spent the crucial months of March and April bogged down in the Jasper affair and his disastrous response to the youth murders. But things weren't perfect for us either. Boris's policy to introduce a new Routemaster bus had, at one stage, threatened to derail the campaign. Ken's team had very effectively exposed our costings on the plan, and they were using the lack of detail as evidence that Boris was a risk Londoners couldn't afford to take. It again tapped into genuine concerns about Boris, and kept Ken in the game.

Our biggest fear was turnout. We knew that Ken would easily get his core vote out in high numbers. His proxies in places like Tower Hamlets had run ruthless scare campaigns, accusing Boris of wanting to ban the Koran and running his 'piccaninnies' quote in areas with large black populations. He stopped at nothing to whip up fear. He would regularly assert that Boris would scrap the Freedom Pass for the elderly, and free travel for kids on buses. None of it was true, but his conviction created doubt.

Our own vote was less certain. Many lived in areas, such as Romford and Bexleyheath, that didn't consider themselves part of London. They didn't feel the mayoralty was relevant to them. We knew that if they stayed at home, Ken would win. In the last few days, everything had to be geared towards getting them out and voting.

One of the defining moments of the campaign was the last community debate, two days before polling day. It was hosted by London Citizens, who represent a network of church and voluntary groups. They were certainly good at organizing events – they had filled the 2,000 capacity Methodist Central Hall in Westminster to the rafters.

We knew it would be a tough gig for Boris, especially as many of the groups represented were black churches. When Crosby and I took our seats at the back, we were totally unprepared for what happened next. As soon as Boris was invited to give his opening speech, virtually the entire hall erupted into a chorus of boos. The noise was deafening and intimidating. This was no ordinary political heckling – this was real hatred. At first, Boris was shocked. But never one to shy away from a fight, he persevered – shouting to make himself heard.

We watched in horror – willing an escape hatch to appear in the ground. Then something remarkable happened. Boris cast aside his notes and made a direct appeal to the audience to be heard. He cut straight to the issue of gang violence, speaking from the heart about how moved he had been and how we must prevent kids making 'catastrophic choices' with their lives. He spoke about how the real outrage was that the majority of victims were from the black community, and how all communities needed to come together to fix the problem. Gradually, as he spoke, the boos began to subside.

The more passionately he spoke about how he wanted to make London safe for young people, and give them the opportunities he had, the more the boos started to turn to cheers. Astonishingly, by the end of his speech, people were cheering and clapping thunderously. He was again demonstrating his main strength – an ability to unite and connect with even the most hostile of audiences.

After the event, Boris was mobbed by young people wanting to speak to him and have their photo taken with him. As we struggled out of the venue, Boris turned to Crosby and said; "There's a swing on. I can feel it."

And he was right.

The first time I truly felt that we could win was on polling day itself. I was dispatched to Bromley to help get the vote out. We had started with a 'dawn raid' at 4am, delivering leaflets reminding people to vote on their way to work. Richard Blakeway (housing adviser and future Deputy Mayor) and I walked up and down the long driveways leafleting and knocking on doors throughout the day.

It was perfect polling day weather: dry, warm and sunny. The response we were getting was amazing. People were coming out in their droves and we got regular reports of queues at polling stations. Almost everyone we spoke to throughout the day were not only voting for Boris, but were excited about doing so.

Meanwhile, reports flooded in of low turnout in Ken's strongholds. And most importantly, the vital swing areas in inner London and southwest London were reporting good turnouts.

We had billed it all along as a change election. And that feeling was evident on the ground.

After the polling stations had closed, the team gathered at the Century Club near Piccadilly Circus for a well-deserved drink. The mood was electric, as we swapped stories of high turnout and good responses. Boris gave a short speech thanking everyone, before we were treated to a compilation of his out-takes from the campaign videos. Boris liked to give little comic monologues in between serious takes, and the video had the room in convulsions of laughter.

The following day, Boris, his family and the senior team gathered at the Park Plaza Hotel in Westminster to await the results. There were fourteen GLA constituencies to declare before the final result would be known.

It was an agonizing wait, and we knew that the important numbers wouldn't be in until the evening. Mid afternoon, we left Boris alone to write his speech. He was so confident, that he only wrote a victory speech.

After Boris and his family had eaten dinner, we gathered in a quiet waiting area by the bar. It was a surreal scene, as hotel guests occasionally wondered past this group of people, some standing, and some sitting on the floor, staring hypnotically at laptops. Boris had gone quiet as each result was confirmed. The early ones were all Ken's strongholds, and turnout had surpassed expectations. He was piling up the votes in his good areas, and at one point Boris turned to me and nervously enquired; "Do I need a concession speech?"

We held our collective breath for our good areas and we weren't disappointed. Our turnout was magnificent, and we quickly established a very healthy lead on 1st preference votes. The *Evening Standard* released a special edition to call the election for Boris. Close to midnight, we got the call to depart for City Hall and the final declaration. As we were leaving the hotel, guests kept approaching Boris and congratulating him, believing he had already won. He kept telling them he hadn't – yet.

Fifteen minutes later we arrived in the bowels of City Hall. Security led us through a maze of corridors. Boris was ushered off in a different direction, and the senior team was ushered into the Chamber, where the result would be announced. Right up until just before the candidates were brought out on stage we didn't know the final result. We knew Boris led on 1st preferences, but we had no idea how the 2nd preferences had broken. Our worst nightmare was Ken getting many more 2nd preference votes and sneaking into first place.

30 seconds before Boris emerged on stage, Ian Sanderson (the official election agent for the Tories) bounded down the auditorium steps to where we were sitting. By the look on his face, we guessed we had little to worry about.

In the end, the victory was relatively comfortable. Over a million Londoners had voted for Boris, and we had beaten Ken by 139,772 votes. It was exactly as we had planned. We had got more votes in a single election than previous Tory candidate Steve Norris managed in two. Turnout in Tory areas had increased massively, and there was a substantial swing in the southwest. Later analysis would show that the biggest single swing was amongst Lib Dem voters.

The victory party was held on the 29th floor of Millbank Tower. As Boris arrived, a beaming David Cameron, who grabbed his hand and held it aloft, greeted him. Looking over the city they had just captured, Mayor Boris and the team partied late into the night.

And then the hard work began.

CHAPTER TWO

BEING MAYOR

MAY 2008 – SEPTEMBER 2010

The new challenge

The morning after the dramatic night before, bleary-eyed campaign staff and supporters shuffled into London's City Hall for the swearing in ceremony. We were tired, but excited; eager to claim our prize. It happened on the top floor in the grandly named 'London's Living Room' that provides panoramic views of the city. The audience was an odd mix of campaign volunteers wearing the same clothes from the night before and smartly dressed GLA officials.

The event felt hastily arranged, with confused City Hall security guards turning many campaign staffers away. Even campaign director Lynton Crosby – the man who delivered victory – wasn't invited. The order and focus of the campaign had evaporated in the space of 12 hours. Boris was now in the hands of the officials.

Press officers who had spun aggressively for Ken Livingstone now cajoled the media on behalf of the man they had been fighting. It was a surreal situation.

When Boris eventually emerged, the room erupted into loud applause and cheering. The buzz and enthusiasm of the campaign team had rudely intruded an otherwise sombre local government atmosphere. For those of us who had been there from the start, it was a proud moment to see Boris in his first official act as Mayor. In his acceptance speech, he assumed a statesmanlike tone. He spoke passionately about his plans to tackle youth crime and how the problem of kids growing up without boundaries and getting lost in catastrophic, self –destructive choices was the number one issue the city faced. He would govern as he had campaigned and deliver on his promises.

He finished off by joking that; "If there are any dogs in the manger, I will have those dogs humanely euthanased." The quip pre-figured the scale of the challenge he faced.

As has been well documented, the early stages of his

administration were difficult, as they would have been for any new Mayor taking over an unfamiliar and unknown organisation. The transition from one Mayor to another had never happened before. When the office was first created in 2000, Ken Livingstone was given two months to set up his administration. In 2004, he simply continued with many of the same people and structures. It was new territory for everyone.

It was particularly difficult because the institution had been created in Ken Livingstone's own image. So much so, that he had come to believe the mayoralty was his by right. Many officials had, in turn, come to believe that Ken would always be mayor. It was always, therefore, going to be tough for any new mayor to come in and set a new agenda.

Boris had been declared the winner around midnight on Friday 2nd May. He officially became Mayor on Sunday 4th May. And although that Monday was a Bank Holiday, everyone expected the mayoral administration to be up and running. To all intents and purposes, Boris had 48 hours to install a new, fully functioning team from scratch.

When a new national Government takes office the speed is similar but the team is already largely in place. An opposition party will always have had a Shadow Cabinet for a number of years, and its members will have been elected in their own right and subjected to the invasive scrutiny of the nation's media. Boris did not have this luxury.

As an emotional Ken Livingstone and his advisers cleared out their offices on the 8th floor on the Saturday morning, Boris and his transition team were given temporary offices on the 6th floor to begin planning.

Some weeks before the election, then Tory Chairman Francis Maude had tasked Nick Boles with putting together a team to run the administration if Boris won. Boles ran the Conservative 'implementation unit', which was responsible for planning a smooth transition to Government. He was considered to be something of a rising star. He had run David Cameron's favourite think tank, Policy Exchange, and had even briefly been a mayoral candidate himself, before he withdrew due to illness.

He went about his work quietly – lest any sense of complacency creep in. Very few people on the campaign knew what he was planning. A man who could walk into any Westminster cocktail party and know most faces, he headhunted amongst a relatively small group of political friends and contacts.

Those of us who knew City Hall made clear to Boles our biggest concern; how to deal with the 'Ken-ocrats' who populated the building – a small cadre of technically neutral officials that were nothing more than Ken's stooges. We were all aware of the huge challenge Boris would face in getting a building teeming with people that had only ever known Ken to deliver for him.

The task, therefore, was to put together a strong, loyal, united team that would help Boris be a successful Mayor and deliver on his campaign promises. It was the least he deserved, given he had a serious agenda that he was passionate about.

It had long been understood that Lynton Crosby would return to Australia after the campaign. So that weekend, Boris named Boles his interim Chief of Staff. Boles had come prepared with a list of names for most of the key positions and a clear idea of how the administration should be structured.

The Conservative leadership's biggest worry about Boris was that he would crash and burn as Mayor. It became clear that they simply didn't trust him to discharge his duties with the diligence and discipline that would be required. To those who had seen Boris fight a tough election campaign and win, this view was grossly unfair. He had proved himself to be disciplined and competent, and Londoners had clearly endorsed him. However, it seemed that the party wasn't willing to entertain any risk with a General Election potentially only two years away.

Therefore, Boles' idea was to create a team of powerful 'deputy mayors' around Boris, led by a 'first deputy mayor' who would, in effect, be the chief executive to Boris' chairman. This would leave Boris to be the face of the administration, while the actual work would be left to his deputy mayors. It was an idea that jarred with the campaign's message to Londoners. Boris won because he convinced people he was the right man for the job. To then bring in a group of powerful people around him suggested he couldn't manage and this simply wasn't true. It was a situation that Boris became gradually unhappy with.

A team of deputy mayors and advisers – including respected figures like then Westminster Council leader Sir Simon Milton, his former deputy Kit Malthouse and then BBC Political Correspondent Guto Harri – were appointed. Despite being capable people in their own right, subsequent events proved that the plan was too hastily executed and fundamentally flawed.

It was based on the assumption that Boris would find the day-to-day grind of running a large bureaucracy 'boring'. However, the assumption failed to take account of one thing; Boris had put his career and reputation on the line to gain power, and he wasn't about to hand it over to other people. More importantly, he had earned the right to govern in his own way. He didn't want a group of (as he saw it) Cameron stooges keeping him on a tight leash. He didn't need babysitting.

The subsequent resignations and scandals brutally demonstrated the truth of this. They also did much to bolster Boris's critics, and distract him from the important and clear agenda he wanted to pursue. He was a spring set into a prolonged and unwanted coil; all he wanted to do was get on with the job. Although damaging at the time, with hindsight the shaky start was, in many ways, the making of Boris the mayor. It gave him the opportunity to stamp his authority on the organisation and make clear that things were going to be done his way.

At one early team meeting, he made clear what he wanted to see happen. He told the gathered advisors that he didn't want anything to distract what they were trying to achieve. He ran through the priorities he wanted people to concentrate on: youth crime, Olympic legacy, electric vehicles and transport. He was focused and determined. He concluded the meeting by quipping; "Oh, and if none of you could resign for a few months, that would be great!" It was greeted with nervous laughter.

Boris was starting to assert himself, and fast realized that he had to demonstrate his authority if he was to be taken seriously. Because he was so jovial, people relaxed around him. But sometimes they relaxed too much. He was the man who had the guts to put his name on the ballot paper in the first place, and that alone deserved respect.

One incident above all proved beyond doubt that Boris was no pushover. It was one of many examples where Boris confounded his critics and demonstrated his zeal for reform. It established his credibility as a strong Mayor, a perception that held through to his re-election campaign in 2012.

Of all the recent Commissioners of the Metropolitan Police, Sir Ian Blair was perhaps the most controversial. He had earned a reputation as 'New Labour's favourite copper', allowing himself to be seen as too close to successive Labour governments. The Conservatives had already declared that they had no confidence in Blair. During the campaign, Boris came to the same conclusion, telling the campaign team; 'I have already called for him to go, and it is therefore hard to see how I can work with him.'[13]

The campaign team had discussed many times how Boris could credibly follow through on his threat. We knew that the Mayor had no power to sack the Commissioner. And we had wanted to give a manifesto commitment that the Mayor would lobby for that power. But the then Shadow Home Secretary David Davis had refused to endorse such a policy on the morning of the crime manifesto launch, meaning we had to remove it. So it was a stalemate. Boris wanted Blair out, but had no power to do anything about it.

Instead of accepting this uneasy situation, however, Boris decided to take a huge gamble. The Government had recently changed the law, so that the Mayor had the right to Chair the body that oversaw the Met police – the Metropolitan Police Authority (MPA). We had made it a manifesto commitment that Boris would exercise this right.

When we got in, officials advised that the earliest date Boris could legally take over would be 1st October 2008. As he discussed the issue with his deputy, Kit Malthouse, a delicious idea began to take shape. The Mayor couldn't sack the Commissioner, even as chair of the MPA. But surely the Commissioner could not realistically continue if the directly elected Mayor made clear he had no confidence in him? And this time, the elected Mayor would also be speaking for the MPA. Surely no Chief Constable (as they are in the rest of the country) could carry on when the police authority expresses no confidence?

They were entering uncharted waters. If he got it wrong, Boris would bring the Met to a grinding halt as he fought out a Mexican stand off with the Commissioner. With youth crime top of Boris's agenda, he had to have a cooperative commissioner.

Growing in confidence and authority, Boris decided to go for broke. On the morning of Wednesday 1st October 2008, Boris sat down with Sir Ian Blair, Kit Malthouse and MPA Chief Executive Catherine Crawford in his office in City Hall. Blair had no idea what was about to hit him. He had believed they were to discuss the agenda for the following week's MPA meeting. Instead, Boris cut to the chase.

He informed the Commissioner that he felt it was time for a change of leadership. He made it plain that he could not work with him. And then he delivered the coup de grace: as the new Chairman of the MPA, he would move a motion of no confidence at his first public meeting if Blair didn't agree to resign.

Blair had no choice. Even though an exasperated Home Secretary, Jacqui Smith, pleaded with him to stay, Blair concluded that clinging on without the public support of the Mayor would irrevocably damage the police. Labour Ministers were furious that Boris had taken such unilateral action. But they could do nothing about it.

On Thursday 2nd October, dressed in a normal suit, Sir Ian Blair gave his resignation statement to the media. In the private office at City Hall, Boris, Malthouse and the political team gathered to watch. As Blair spoke, Boris looked reflective. When it was finished, I asked Boris how he was feeling. He replied; "I hate doing this stuff," before disappearing into his office alone with his thoughts.

Boris did what needed to be done, but he certainly didn't feel happy about it. Nevertheless, he had shown everyone what he was capable of and established an important principle of the mayoralty. The mandate Londoners give you often has far more influence that mere official powers. The precedent had been set. In future, no Met Commissioner will be able to serve without the explicit support of the Mayor, whoever they are.

Boris's political supporters were delighted. This surgical strike had shown that Boris meant business. It was a demonstration of the kind of leadership that would prove invaluable in the battle for re-election in 2012.

Although the first year had been challenging, Boris was still able to drive through his political priorities. In a relatively short space of time, he was delivering on the promises he made to Londoners during the 2008 campaign. He had ended the madness of King Ken, freezing the mayor's share of council tax for the first time in eight years – after years of successive increases. Gone was Livingstone's propaganda sheet '*The Londoner*', saving the taxpayer almost £3 million a year. Ken's 'embassies' in places like Venezuela were shut down and the murky oil deal with Venezuelan President Hugo Chavez was ended.

Most importantly, Boris had begun to get a grip on the violent crime and low level disorder that Livingstone had ignored for so long. Drinking alcohol on public transport was banned, almost 5,000 knives were recovered from the streets through the sensitive use of stop and search, as well as knife amnesties. For the first time, there was a proper long-term strategy in place to deal with violent youth crime. This involved pioneering new ideas, such as the specialist Heron Unit at the Feltham Young Offenders Institute. This was where first time offenders were segregated from hardened, repeat offenders. In doing so, studies showed they became less likely to fall under the sinister tutelage of their peers and were prevented from entering the cycle of re-offending.

Progress was also being made on policies that Livingstone had failed to deliver for years, despite continually promising action. Boris agreed a deal with borough councils to deliver a 24-hour Freedom Pass, enabling pensioners to use public transport before 9.30am for the first time. Deals had been struck with the train companies to introduce the Oyster payment system on suburban rail services, making it cheaper and easier for millions of commuters. A plan was also in place to deliver London's first ever bike hire scheme (where previously there had not even been so much as a blank sheet of paper) and the loathed bendy buses were subject to a timetable of doom. They would all be retired to Scandinavian airports by the end of the first term, paving the way for the brand new Routemaster to make its debut.

As Boris's effectiveness and confidence grew, thoughts among the team turned to re-election relatively early in his administration. Many of us had assumed Boris would run for re-election regardless, even though he always insisted he would only do so if he felt he had delivered on his promises and had more to offer.

By mid-term, it was clear that Boris's own criteria had been met.

Governing vs. campaigning

The near certainty of Boris running gave rise to the traditional dilemma faced by all first term incumbents. In office, it is often difficult to have as disciplined a message as during an election campaign. Attention is diverted by the issue of the day and it's easy to lose sight of why the voters put you there in the first place. In essence, the question is always the same: do you pursue a narrow agenda that speaks only to your voters' concerns, or do you go much broader and focus on initiatives that (although the right things to do in the long term) may have no immediate electoral payback? That was the dilemma facing the City Hall team.

A meeting early in late 2008 demonstrated how hard it was to resolve this dilemma. Boris gave an inspiring speech to open proceedings, describing in vivid detail his vision for what a future Mayor of Beijing would see in London as he visited for the Olympics in 2012. He spoke of the journey from the new 'Malthouse International' Thames Estuary airport (christened after his Deputy Mayor, Kit Malthouse, who led on the project at the time) to the Olympic Park in Stratford. It encompassed the hire bikes, mobile phones that worked on the tube, a new Routemaster and much more.

It was uplifting, optimistic and ambitious – Boris at his best. The challenge for the team was to deliver the big picture vision, without losing sight of the bread and butter issues Londoners voted on in the first place.

Boris was predominantly elected by Londoners living in the outer suburbs. He would need those voters again in 2012, especially as 2008 would prove to be the high point for the Conservative vote in London.

They voted for him the first time because he spoke to their concerns; crime, green spaces and a sense that City Hall couldn't care less about outer London. This meant ensuring these issues weren't forgotten about and ensuring that City Hall was for Zone 6 as well as Zone 1. Our job was to ensure Boris's ambitious vision would mean something in voters' everyday lives.

A debate ensued about where the balance should be struck, and very different viewpoints emerged. Some advisers argued that we needed to have a clear set of political messages and priorities to anchor and enhance the natural Boris fizz. After all, Champagne works best in a flute. What would ultimately matter was a clear plan about the things of most impact to the electorate, on fares and council tax, for example. What was needed was a plan to get re-elected. As Crosby had once put it; "You can't fatten the pig on market day."

However, other advisers argued that because you cannot predict the future, it was pointless being doctrinaire and sticking to a rigid plan or having 'repetitive' and 'dull' messages. Boris's biggest strength was his unpredictability and effervescence. If he were shackled with dry spin, he would undermine his biggest selling point. Why take the bubbles out of the champagne?

The issue was difficult to resolve, as both approaches had merit. Ultimately, Boris's biggest fear was that in getting too 'professional', he could become too predictable, samey, systematic and dull. He preferred to err on the side of excitement and unpredictability. He reasoned that, either way, voters would reward him if he delivered on his promises. He didn't want endless debates – he wanted the team to get on with delivering his agenda and be judged on the results.

However, the difficulties of simply getting your head down and not looking up again until election day were amply demonstrated by evidence that showed Boris's achievements – frustratingly – were not cutting through to the electorate.

The little polling public funds gave us access to confirmed a picture that was to remain consistent throughout Boris's first term. He was a popular figure – we knew that well enough just from walking down the street with him. But when asked if they knew what the Mayor does for London, the number saying they knew dropped from 51% in 2007 (the last comparable year) to 39% in 2009. The number saying they had no opinion of how well or badly the Mayor was doing his job had almost doubled from 17% in 2002 (when Livingstone was new in the job) to 32%[14].

The numbers reflected unfairly on Boris. On the contrary, he had brought much needed focus to City Hall after years of Ken Livingstone's waste and flirtations with South American presidents.

However, the numbers didn't lie and they demonstrated the scale of the challenge. It was clear that in order to get re-elected, Boris needed to be seen to have delivered on the issues that mattered to our voters, as well as remain popular. As subsequent events would show, it was extremely difficult to get the balance right. He would remain popular – even in the teeth of a recession and a plunging Conservative poll rating – but the challenges of maintaining a consistent message meant his achievements did not spring readily to voters' minds. This would prove a major barrier to overcome as 2012 crept nearer, particularly as he was likely to have a stubborn and difficult opponent.

The ghost of Ken

Ken Livingstone had never expected the London electorate to hand him his P45 in 2008. He thought it inconceivable that the voters would entrust a celebrity with the serious task of running London. Moreover, he felt that a man with Boris's history would be too easy to shoot down. It was precisely that arrogance that led many Londoners to conclude that Ken's time was over.

After his defeat, some of us were expecting him to slink off into the shadows, do some gardening, give after dinner speeches and write the standard self-justificatory memoir. Instead, he treated us to the far more bizarre spectacle of hanging around City Hall as if he had never lost.

Once a month, the Mayor has to answer questions from the elected members of the London Assembly in the Chamber at City Hall. The Chamber is in the same circular shape as the rest of the building. A squirming staircase rises above it, disappearing to the top of the building in an unnatural lean. The public gallery looks down, as 25 politicians, arranged in a horseshoe formation, shout at one politician in the middle about bus routes for two hours – all in the name of transparency.

This Socratic wonder is not the hottest ticket in town. It is mostly watched by a smattering of other City Hall staff, press, interest groups and a small number of London government fanatics, and now Ken Livingstone. For most of Boris's early years in office Livingstone would shuffle into the front row of the public gallery in a cream linen suit, directly in Boris's eye line and watch Mayor's Question Time from start to finish. We would watch him, bemused, as he listened earnestly and took notes. Desperate for a taste of the action, he would occasionally pass notes to the Labour Assembly members, urging them down particular avenues of attack.

After staying for the full two hours, Ken would stay behind chatting to journalists and others, before heading down to the public café and having a cup of tea. It was like no one had told granddad he didn't live here any more.

Boris found the whole spectacle highly amusing, perfecting his impression of Ken in the briefing meetings prior to each question time. He thought Livingstone was pathetic, clinging on to his former glories instead of gracefully departing the stage. But he also found it motivating. Each time that Ken would glare at him, Boris was reminded that someone else wanted his job.

A popular parlour game at City Hall was to discuss who Labour would select as their mayoral candidate in 2012. Many simply couldn't believe that the Labour Party would let Ken go for it again. Surely it would be electoral suicide to put up a man who had so clearly been rejected by Londoners?

There had been much press speculation, including the delicious but absurd suggestion that Alan Sugar would be tempted into running. But no matter who was suggested, it was clear that Ken had started planning to run again the moment he lost the election. In an interview with the *Evening Standard* on 24th February 2009, Livingstone confirmed the worst kept secret in London; "I would love to stand for Mayor against Boris in what will be the Olympics year[15]."

This seemed to galvanise Boris. It was clear no one else could seriously challenge Ken for the Labour nomination. They had plenty of interesting options, but none with the profile or wiliness of Ken. Moreover, many in the Labour Party felt like they had no choice but go for Ken, in the fear he would simply run as an independent if they didn't choose him.

Those of us who had fought the last election knew just how dangerous Ken could be. However, many in the Mayor's Office felt that if Ken were the candidate, he would be a walkover – why would Londoners want to go back? This view overlooked the fact that he was able to do something few other politicians could. He had, over many years, cultivated deep pockets of electoral support that rewarded him with unswerving loyalty at virtually every election. He clearly worked on the basis that you only need to win 51%, and that it didn't matter if the other 49% hated you.

It was a tactic that had proved remarkably successful over the years. The last time Livingstone had lost an election prior to 2008 was in 1979. As a result he had spent virtually his entire adult life in some kind of elected position.

Ken would now spend the next few years re-charging his support base. Indeed, he had already established a quasi-re-elect Ken organization called 'Progressive London'. It was clear that we would need to re-charge our own machine if we were to be competitive in 2012. As the ghost of Ken materialized into something more real, the arms race had begun.

The General Election, in May 2010, was to demonstrate the scale of the challenge Boris would face in order to get re-elected.

Re-starting the machine

The Conservatives (then in opposition) had spent most of 2009 and the early part of 2010 with a very healthy poll lead over the Labour Government. Then Prime Minister Gordon Brown was losing control, as his Government lurched from crisis to crisis. Everyone confidently predicted that David Cameron's Conservatives would comfortably win the election.

But their General Election campaign looked, from the outside, as if it was suffering from a form of political ADHD. Across the entire campaign, they had no consistent message other than the untested, electorally numbing 'Big Society' – still a mystery to most people. In their desire to prove to the media elite they had changed, they lost sight of the concerns of ordinary voters who were fearful about the future and wanted to know what the Conservatives would do for them in specific terms.

The failure of Cameron to win an outright majority dismayed Boris. As the result sunk in, Boris's sister, the journalist Rachel Johnson tweeted; 'It's all gone tits up. Call for Boris.' A joke, to be sure. But it reflected the feelings of many Conservative activists. David Cameron, the man who they thought could deliver victory after so many years in the wilderness, had fallen short. They were back in Government, but only thanks to a coalition with the Liberal Democrats – a party they distrusted and despised.

What concerned Boris most about the 2010 General Election were the results in London. The capital had stubbornly clung to the Labour nurse for fear of something worse. On a night of mixed results across the country, Labour performed far better in London than they did in the rest of the country.

Prior to the election, it was London marginal seats like Tooting and Westminster North that were judged as the barometer of success for David Cameron. He needed seats like those in order to win a majority in Parliament. In the event, both voted to keep their incumbent Labour MPs, despite the Conservatives pouring money and time into efforts to remove them.

There were also local council elections held on the same day. The higher than usual turnout saw Labour snatching Ealing, Enfield and Harrow from the Tories. They also gained Brent, Camden, Hounslow, Islington, Southwark and Waltham Forest where previously no single party was in control.

Labour had succeeded in getting their vote out at a time when they had the most unpopular leader in their history and the Conservatives were at their strongest. As one Labour activist told me at the time, the plan was to cling on by dragging their supporters out by hook or by crook – and it worked.

The big concern for Boris was that Labour had made gains in many areas that had voted for him in 2008. Ken Livingstone had been given a major boost. Not only was the Labour inner London vote still solid, it appeared that they were also making serious inroads into Boris's outer London heartland. It was a deeply sobering moment. If the General Election result were repeated in 2012, Boris would lose City Hall.

It was the moment Boris realised he would need to start serious preparations for the re-election campaign. Lynton Crosby – who had returned from Australia – began coaxing the Boris election machine from its hibernation.

Crosby knew right from the start who the core team would be. Running the campaign with him would be his U.K business partner Mark Fullbrook. Amiable and hugely respected, Fullbrook was a veteran of political campaigns the world over. He had started his political career as an election agent, rapidly rising through the ranks to be part of the team that ran the marginal seats operation in the Conservatives 1992 General Election campaign. It was this work that was to bring him to international attention in political circles, particularly in America and future Republican Presidential hopeful Newt Gingrich. The Conservatives had won the 1992 General Election by only 21 seats and it was the marginal seats team that helped make the difference. He also had experience of fighting Ken Livingstone, having run the unsuccessful campaign for the Conservative candidate Steve Norris in the first London mayoral election of 2000. He had built a successful business of his own advising candidates in America and the U.K on running election campaigns and had now joined with Lynton Crosby. Now, he wanted another chance to defeat Livingstone.

Also later to join in January 2011 would be Sam Lyon, the then Deputy News Editor of the *Evening Standard*. Idealistic, sharp and with a fondness for accelerating straight to the point, Lyon had grown tired of journalism. He was looking for a new challenge, and Crosby provided it.

I was to join in November 2011.

By September 2010, a campaign office had been established, polling was in the field and a website was ready to launch. On 10th September, Boris finally ended the speculation and confirmed that he was seeking the Conservative nomination once again.

In making his announcement he said; "With every day that passes I have come to love and understand the complexities and challenges of this job – and I also see how much more there is to do….. I always said that if I felt things were going well – and if I thought my team had more to deliver for London – then it would be crazy not to put myself forward for the party to consider[16]."

The Godfather

Ken Livingstone has cited *The Godfather* as his favourite film, principally because he identified with the political manoeuvrings of the Corleone family and how Al Pacino's character gained the ascendency after his father's death. It was very much the style in which he conducted himself. In the 1980's, Livingstone had pulled off a coup similar to Michael Corleone at the Greater London Council, usurping the then elected Labour leader Andrew McIntosh just after the elections to run the Council himself.

In 2010, Livingstone and his allies were getting up to the same old tricks.

Ken's determination for a re-match with Boris had sparked a lively debate within the Labour Party. Many felt that his 2008 campaign had been too divisive and had ignored crucial parts of outer London. After his defeat, there was a feeling that the candidate in 2012 should be someone younger who could appeal to a broader range of Londoners. Big names, such as then Cabinet Minister and popular former postman Alan Johnson were frequently touted.

But the General Election and Labour's subsequent defeat had diverted everyone's attention from the looming mayoral contest. As Labour licked their wounds, adjusting to life in opposition after thirteen years, Ken Livingstone moved quickly.

Gordon Brown resigned as Prime Minister and Labour leader after it became clear he couldn't form a government. His deputy, Harriet Harman, became Acting Leader whilst the party organised an election for a new leader – the result of which would be announced at the Labour Party conference in September 2010.

Behind the scenes, Livingstone and his long-time ally (and former City Hall Chief of Staff) Simon Fletcher executed a plan that was as ruthless as it was brazen. Their plan was simple; if they could ensure the mayoral selection contest was brought forward to coincide with the leadership election, it would leave little time for any other candidates to build up enough support. Major contenders, such as Alan Johnson, wouldn't have the energy or resources to set up a campaign that quickly. Everyone would be focused on the battle for leader.

This would be important for another reason. By having the mayoral selection contest at the same time as the contest for Labour Leader, it would mean whoever became Leader would have to accept Ken as the candidate whether they liked it or not.

They also sought to change the voting rules to give greater weight to the party members and trade unions, sidelining the many Labour MPs in London who were expected to vote against Ken.

Simon Fletcher had positioned himself well. In January 2010, he had got a job in the Labour Party as London Regional coordinator. Many felt it was as the result of an implicit deal between Livingstone and the Labour hierarchy. Fletcher would ensure the Ken machine delivered for Labour in crucial London marginal seats at the General Election. And in return, Labour would ensure that the mayoral selection would be run in the way Livingstone wanted[17]. Fletcher had certainly delivered on his side of the bargain; London was one of Labour's best performing regions in the General Election.

Taking advantage of the leadership vacuum, and the weakness of their enemies, they successfully pressured Labour's powerful National Executive Committee (NEC) to deliver what they wanted. It was later reported that 'a lot of Ken allies march[ed] into the NEC sub-committee that agreed the rushed timetable and made his victory certain[18]'.

It was a decision that left Ken's only challenger, former east London MP Oona King, with no chance. It was even subsequently reported that Ken's union backers (apart from the GMB union) refused to put her leaflets in their pack to union voters[19]. The selection contest left, in the words of one Labour activist, the 'choice of the candidate in the hands of eight union leaders[20]'.

When the result of the selection contest was announced at the Labour Party conference in September 2010, it surprised no one. Ken Livingstone had won convincingly and the re-match with Boris was well and truly on.

CHAPTER THREE

ANNUS HORRIBILIS

OCTOBER 2010 – NOVEMBER 2011

As 2010 withered and the fresh shoots of 2011 appeared, Boris and his team were feeling good. He was firmly grasping the slippery entity that is the mayoralty and was making it his own. Officials were getting used to his unique style and things were getting done. Brand Boris was still alive and well, but now it came with a clear sheen of administrative competence. By confirming his intention to go for re-election relatively early, he would be no 'lame duck'. His mayoralty was a two-term project. And with the challenges London faced, in his mind, it had to be.

Boris's office on the 8th floor of City Hall overlooks Tower Bridge, towards east London. It is dominated by a large conference table in the middle, where after a long day, Boris is to be found using it as a makeshift table tennis (or 'whiff whaff') table. There is a giant map of London at one end, and a desk and computer at the other. The back wall heaves with books. The fridge and wine rack unit Ken Livingstone installed under the desk held bottles from the impressive collection he built up at London taxpayers' expense (served personally by Boris; "Have some of Ken's wine!")

Often, he would sit at his desk and in a quiet moment allow his eye to be caught by cranes in the distance. Beyond the Victorian splendour of Tower Bridge and the Thatcherian might of Canary Wharf, the Olympic Park was steadily changing the face of east London. To Boris, this represented London's future and getting it right was more important than anything else.

Early opinion research conducted by Crosby and Fullbrook (who had nicknamed Boris 'Socrates') showed that he was in a relatively strong position. Although the economic downturn and national narrative about cuts had left voters in a gloomy mood, they remained positive towards Boris. He had exceeded their original expectations and they saw him as a strong and credible Mayor. They liked his strong independent streak, and thought he was a good advocate for the city. Now they wanted to see him press on and deliver on the issues they cared about. This was quite a turnaround from 2008, when many people who voted for Boris did so not quite knowing what to expect. Many had voted for him purely because they wanted Ken out. Two years out from the next election, Boris's performance in office was being judged favourably, and many felt vindicated in their decision to vote for him.

To further cheer City Hall, people retained a dismal view of Ken Livingstone's time in office. They gave him credit from being competent and committed to the job, but they did not want to go back to Ken again. This sentiment was to inspire Crosby's idea for a separate anti-Ken campaign named; 'Not Ken Again', which was to prove pivotal in the effort to win back City Hall. Despite the downturn and emerging unpopularity of the Conservatives, were the election held tomorrow they would overwhelmingly vote for Boris.

Boris and those around him were thus feeling confident, not least because he had successfully overcome two major challenges in 2010. Both challenges were to demonstrate the best and worst of Boris. One was the survival of a personal crisis; the other was a political triumph for London.

On 18th July 2010, the *Daily Mirror* broke the story of an alleged affair. Coming at the traditionally awkward mid-term point, the story had the potential to scuttle Boris's chances of re-election.

Indeed, right from the start, the campaign team's biggest fear in 2007/08 was an unforeseen scandal. Indeed, the Saturday night before polling day, Katie Perrior and Jo Tanner were so worried that they had waited at Victoria station for the first edition of the now defunct *News of The World* just in case. To their relief, there was nothing about Boris.

However, the media storm that followed was more like a gentle breeze. The tone was mockery rather than outrage. It was greeted with nothing more than a mild chuckle. City Hall breathed a sigh of relief. The last time Boris's private life was in the news, in 2003, he was effectively sacked from the Conservative Shadow Cabinet.

This time, the situation demonstrated one of the advantages of being Mayor – your fate isn't in the hands of your political party or even Parliament. Your party leader can't touch you. The London Assembly is weak and has little power to sanction you. You can only be sacked by the voters at election time. And the verdict seemed to be that Londoners were less interested in what Boris got up to in his private life than what he was doing for London. Indeed, one focus group respondent around this time said; "Why should I worry about that? I just want him to do a good job for London."

The tabloid leering was more than balanced by perhaps his biggest political triumph as Mayor; a triumph that decisively addressed the worries that some voters had about him. After the coalition Government took office in late May 2010, they were faced with a dire economic situation. The outgoing Labour Treasury Minister Liam Byrne had left a note behind for his successor that simply read; 'I'm afraid to tell you, there's no money left'. [21]

The coalition was faced with an impossible scenario. The previous Labour government had left the country saddled with debt and had run up a huge budget deficit at a time of recession and stagnation.

The reality was brutal in its simplicity. If the U.K kept spending money at the rate that was planned, the deficit would get bigger and we would be at risk of being dragged under with the likes of Greece. The markets would pass a harsh verdict, pushing up the cost of Government borrowing and this, in turn, would result in swingeing cuts and savage tax increases.

All the options were bad. The least bad was to cut back immediately, in order to reduce the budget deficit. The coalition decided that they had no choice, they had to make cuts. Nothing was safe from the axe.

London is hugely reliant on funding from the Government for investment, in transport infrastructure in particular. Unlike many other major world cities, the Mayor has very few direct fund raising powers (apart from fares and a proportion of council tax bills) to pay for the investment that's needed.

The previous Government had committed to a plan to invest billions in a creaking transport system over the next decade. The tube was in the process of a huge upgrade programme, and a major new east-west rail link, Crossrail, was planned.

As anyone who has found themselves wedged into the armpit of their neighbour in a sweltering tube carriage knows, these improvements were long overdue. But suddenly, the funding needed to see the programme through was under threat from the coalition axe.

The spending needed in London presented a juicy target for the men with the red pen. Crossrail had a bill of around £17 billion and the tube upgrades had a bill of around £6 billion. Prior to the General Election, there was a growing view within the senior ranks of the Conservative Party that London would have to choose. They could have either Crossrail, or the tube upgrades. But they could not have both.

Boris was having none of it – London needed both projects to be funded in full if the city was to be able to compete on a global stage. Ever a keen student of history, Boris knew that London was always the victim of cuts in hard times and so always had to settle for a second-class transport system. He was determined that London would not lose out again.

Boris set about persuading David Cameron and George Osborne that London's budgets should be protected. And it wasn't just transport. Police budgets nationwide were also under threat, and the Metropolitan Police had one of the biggest budgets. Funding for policing would become a major issue at the 2012 election, and Boris fought hard to protect the numbers.

In his speech to the Conservative Party conference in October

2010, just weeks before a decision was due to be made, Boris made a direct appeal to the faithful. He devoted a large section of his speech to describing, in detail, how the rest of the country benefits from investment in London transport. He reeled off a dozen or more towns and cities that made components of tube trains and buses, urging the MPs from those areas to back him. It was a compelling argument, and he had the economics on his side. The numbers were big, but so was the return, not just for London but the whole country.

Despite pressure to protect other parts of the budget, and to distribute money more evenly in the regions outside London, on 20th October 2010 Chancellor George Osborne announced that Crossrail and the tube upgrades would be protected. It was a significant political victory for Boris, his Chief of Staff Sir Simon Milton and TfL Deputy Chair Daniel Moylan, who had worked tirelessly behind the scenes. Those who accused Boris of not delivering, or not doing the necessary detail, had to feast on humble pie with a generous side serving of boiled hat.

The victory was to give Boris a significant edge in the 2012 election campaign. Ken Livingstone had built his reputation as the man who could bang the table and get a good deal for London. But over the years, Londoners remembered the rows, not the results. Boris had delivered, in a calm constructive way. He had patiently made his argument and won, in a way that Livingstone could never have done. It caused a shift in voters' attitudes, as more viewed Boris as being able to get a better deal for London than Ken. This was to prove a decisive factor when it came to framing the choice between the two men.

All this added up to one verdict in the pundit's minds; in 2012, Boris would have no trouble dispatching yesterday's man, Ken Livingstone.

Indeed, Boris was brimming with confidence when he addressed a rally at the Conservative Party conference in October 2010.

Assuming a slightly haughty tone, he declared with faux gravitas; "The Labour Party has responded to the challenge of finding a new mayoral candidate with a stupefying lack of originality! They have found..... a piece of DNA.... preserved in the tar pits of Cricklewood...[22]" Never happier than when he has an audience in rapturous laughter, Boris returned the compliment and chuckled along with the gleeful activists.

Above all, he was relishing the drama of the fight with Livingstone; "Like Holmes and Moriarty, like Harry Potter and Voldemort, it seems that this contest is feted to continue for more than one episode." He was in no doubt as to which side he was on.

The manner of the mocking revealed the risk of complacency. Boris talked about Ken as if he were a laughing stock, a crusty old dinosaur almost to be pitied. He didn't feel compelled to attack his policies, or even his previous record. To what sensible question was Ken Livingstone the answer?

But a YouGov poll released a few days after the speech showed that Ken's return was no laughing matter. And it would set the scene for a difficult 2011, the crucial year before the election.

The headline voting intention was neck and neck; Boris led Ken by a slender 46% to 44%. Within that, Ken narrowly led among men and every age group except over 55s. Things got slightly better when people were asked whom they would rather have as Mayor. This saw Boris's lead increase to 46% versus 41%; comforting City Hall that Boris was at least still more popular. Also encouraging was the 17% of Labour voters who said they would rather have Boris as Mayor, despite the Tories being four points behind Labour in London.

This seemed to suggest that Ken was struggling to attract Labour voters. And it fed a narrative that said Ken couldn't win, because he was losing too many Labour voters to Boris. But a closer reading of the detail showed that Ken was actually more likely to make people vote Labour than his supposedly less toxic party rival, Oona King (by 24% to 11%). When it came down to it, slightly more people said they would vote for Ken (44%) than would vote for Labour in a General Election (42%).

People also saw Ken's record as Mayor in a positive light, agreeing that he had performed well as Mayor by 56% to 36%. It had long been assumed that Ken's Achilles Heal would be his record. Not on this evidence. This was compounded by the fact that they saw Livingstone as more competent than Boris, by 52% to 45%.

But perhaps the most worrying finding was that more voters saw Livingstone as 'in touch with the concerns of Londoners' than Boris by 44% to 40%. This was to prove a major advantage for Ken during the election campaign, particularly at a time when Londoners were facing tough times.

City Hall advisers greeted the findings with incredulity and disbelief. They were mystified as to why Ken was coming out much better than anyone expected. Boris was disappointed that he wasn't getting the credit for his achievements in office. But to Lynton Crosby and the campaign team, the results echoed their own findings about the state of opinion.

Focus groups conducted in November 2010 were broadly positive towards Boris – in the sense that he was liked and had performed above expectations. The voters weren't exactly clamouring for a return back to Ken. But two major themes were emerging that provided Livingstone with an opportunity to be competitive and erode Boris's popularity. There was a growing sense that – as the cost of living started to bite – tube and bus fares were too high and the service wasn't showing enough signs of improvement. This was coupled with the perception that although Boris had done some good things (such as scrap the bendy buses and the western extension of the congestion charge) he wasn't focusing on the really important issues, like the cost and reliability of transport.

City Hall had found it difficult to maintain a consistent political message, which meant the progress Boris was making on transport (and other important issues) wasn't getting through to voters. Livingstone had taken full advantage of this and campaigned hard on the issue, highlighting virtually every signal failure. He shamefacedly attacked Boris for tube strikes, even though his campaign was briefly based in the offices of one of the agitating unions. It wasn't the first or last example of such hypocrisy.

The traditional challenges of incumbency were undoubtedly contributing to the problem. Because Boris was relatively hyperactive, City Hall struggled to establish an underlying consistency in their communications. Boris's leadership style was energetic, tending to regularly switch focus between exciting and unorthodox initiatives. It reflected his enormous capacity to concentrate on several issues at once. This meant that equal priority – at least in communications terms – tended to be given to issues that had less electoral relevance than, say, the performance of the tube. Even though in reality Boris would devote the majority of his time addressing transport (in diary terms, meetings with TfL would dominate most weeks) and other big issues, what voters heard and saw of him didn't necessarily reflect this.

The cumulative effect was that Boris was likeable and popular, but not seen as particularly focused or effective – despite his substantial record of achievement. This was heightened when contrasted with Livingstone, who for all his flaws, was still seen as someone who got things done. Londoners saw the mayoralty as a serious job in serious times and there was a perception that Boris wasn't fully meeting those expectations.

The challenge was amply demonstrated by the difference between what had been achieved, and what was being communicated. By mid 2011, Boris had among other things delivered his cycle hire scheme, secured the funding for the tube upgrades and Crossrail, cut crime (particularly on transport) and kept council tax at the level it had been in 2008. Yet these were etiolated by other schemes that tended to be pushed with the media, such as initiatives to: save London's bees, encourage kids to read with Peter Andre, encourage more street parties with Barbara Windsor, build a floating river park and a cable car across the Thames. Boris's 2nd term 'vision' became about trying to build the 'village in the city'. All worthy initiatives that few could disagree with and generated plenty of press coverage. But they risked the impression that Boris wasn't focusing on what voters really cared about, when the reality was that he had.

The political consequence was that the field was left clear for Ken to campaign hard on popular issues, slowly building the unfair perception that Boris was failing on crime and failing to deliver any transport improvements. Although Ken didn't appear to be making waves, he was building a very solid foundation that would see him put Boris under severe pressure when it mattered most.

The private polling conducted by the campaign later in the year confirmed this analysis. It found that an election that was about who was better able to knuckle down and deliver on the issues that really mattered would result – were it held there and then – in a Livingstone victory. With just over a year to go, it would take significant changes to get Boris back in the game.

And two tragic events in 2011 would soon pull Boris out of his comfort zone and provide the unexpected opportunity to make those changes.

'A grievous loss'

Politics is often talked about in hyperbolic terms. Relatively minor changes are described as the movement of tectonic plates. Amusing indiscretions are crises. And grubby power grabs are performed by those 'wielding the knife'.

But just occasionally, something happens that is genuinely worthy of the words to describe it. On 11th April 2011, Sir Simon Milton died after the recurrence of a previous serious illness at the age of 49. It was, as his close friend and Tory MP Mark Field put it at the time; "A very grievous loss".

Twenty years before, Milton had survived Leukaemia. He developed pneumonia while he was recovering from the bone marrow transplant and ever since he was left with weaker lungs, making even a small flight of stairs a breathless and dangerous experience.

Nevertheless, he displayed no overt signs of ill health during most of his time at City Hall. Looking back, he would walk a little slower than others and avoid the stairs if he could. But that was entirely in keeping with a style that was deliberative instead of rushed. Most of us knew about his Leukaemia, but since he clearly felt strong enough to take the role at City Hall in the first place, we assumed the worst was over.

However, on Thursday 8th April 2011, Milton was taken into hospital having developed pnuemonia. By Sunday he had been transferred to intensive care. He never regained consciousness.

That night, Milton passed away with Boris and his close family by his side.

It was a bitter personal and political shock. Boris had come to like, respect and rely on Milton. They worked extremely well together because they shared the same political outlook. And Boris is at his most successful when he has someone by his side to balance his extrovert nature. Milton was one such person. His calm and razor sharp analysis would frequently bring a lengthy meeting to a productive end. Often, he would sit quietly at Boris's right hand and make only a single intervention. But it would always be the decisive one. And Boris knew that no problem was too thorny with Milton at hand.

He also appreciated Milton's dry sense of humour and sharp wit, flashes of which he would show at just the right time. In his article for the *Evening Standard* paying tribute to Milton, Boris recalled the time when they were both watching news footage of Boris falling into a river in Catford. With impeccable timing and delivery, Milton turned to Boris and said: "I've got the Standard their headline. River Crisis: Mayor steps in." I was there at the time, and I've never heard Boris laugh so much.

Milton was well regarded by his political opponents too. As leader of Westminster Council, Milton had developed a reputation as a 'compassionate Conservative', showing as much care and attention to the poorer parts of the area as the richer. He approached City Hall in the same way, quietly squirreling more affordable housing from hard-nosed developers. But he also managed to simultaneously cultivate respect among the more Thatcherite Conservatives.

I'll never forget, during my time at City Hall, he briefly allowed a glimpse of his political steel. It was early 2009, and we were embroiled in a row with the City Hall branch of the union Unison. They were trying to use City Hall's facilities to host political meetings about Palestine and the problems in the Middle East. We felt it was completely unacceptable to allow London's resources to be used in this way. Their role was to stand up for their members, not use London's resources pontificating about geo-political issues over which they had no control. As we were discussing the issue in the private office, Milton overheard and came over. With a quiet voice and glint in his eye he said; "People of your generation won't appreciate this, but there are some people who are evil and must be destroyed." Even though it was partly said in jest, it showed how Milton had managed to combine ruthless Thatcherism with social concern. It is a blend that Boris appreciated and understood. Not least because it reflects where he stands too.

As City Hall went into mourning, Boris had an uncomfortable decision to make. He had lost his Chief of Staff and point of stability. Guto Harri took over as Acting Chief of Staff, while Boris considered the floods of offers and suggestions. As ever in politics, things move on very quickly and the rumour mill soon went into overdrive as to who would take over.

It was a very sad time. But it also presented an unexpected opportunity to re-shuffle the mayoral team so that it was fighting fit for the election.

Boris moved to end the speculation and internal positioning quickly. A week later, on 18th April, he announced that he had appointed Sir Edward Lister as his Chief of Staff and Deputy Mayor for Planning & Policy.

Lister is something of a legend in Conservative circles. He was the longest serving Council leader in the country, having led Wandsworth from 1992 to 2011. He was truly Wandsworth's servant, having been first elected to the council in 1976. The administration he led was ground breaking, leaving Wandsworth with the lowest council tax in the country and rated as one of the highest performing. To Conservatives who believed in low tax and a small state, Lister's Wandsworth was the poster child of how it could be done.

With bright white hair and collegiate manner Lister looked a little like he had mistakenly wondered off the set of a Werthers Original advert. But he was no fuddy duddy. In fact, he was the perfect choice to follow in the substantial shoes of Sir Simon Milton. Known as 'slasher' Lister by his critics, he is uncompromising when it comes to dealing with a recalcitrant bureaucracy. It was precisely what City Hall needed with a year to go until the election and he was to play a crucial role in getting Boris fighting fit.

For many years he viewed City Hall and Transport for London in particular as serial wasters of public money whose bluff needed to be called. Now, he was gagging to get his hands on the purse strings. And to Lynton Crosby's delight, as a serial election winner himself, Lister was as ruthlessly political as he was.

Lister immediately understood what needed to be done to give

Boris the edge. He arrived to find a team that was not as focused on re-election as it should have been. He was amazed at the scattergun manner of some City Hall initiatives. Almost from the start, he would regularly complain about his District Line journey into City Hall to remind Boris of where his priorities should lie.

The truth was, despite Milton's formidable abilities, he had never entirely got to grips with the weaknesses in the mayoral team that remained following the upheavals of 2008/09.

A day after Lister was appointed Boris made a decisive move to address the issue. Kulveer Ranger was moved from Transport – the most demanding policy area – to Environment and the person he replaced was made Deputy Mayor for Transport. Isabel Dedring was eminently qualified to do the job. A hyper energetic, sharp New York lawyer, she had served as TfL's policy director when Ken Livingstone was Mayor. After Boris won, she was appointed Environment Director in the Mayor's Office – considered suitably non-partisan to make the jump. Over time, she had built a reputation as highly effective scrutineer.

When she took over the transport brief, she was billed as the no nonsense American that was going to march into TfL and 'bust some balls'. It was an approach that was sorely needed given the importance of transport in the context of the election.

Another crucial change was the removal of Anthony Browne as Economic Adviser. With the economy likely to be a major issue at the election, Boris wanted more firepower in the role and turned to the respected Sir Peter Rogers, who was the outgoing Chief Executive of the soon to be defunct London Development Agency. Rogers had also been Chief Executive of Westminster Council when Milton was leader, and he had impeccable regeneration credentials.

These were surprising moves. Boris is a man who avoids personal conflict at virtually any price. He prefers to play the medieval monarch, majestically presiding over a court battling to gain his favour. But once every so often, he descends from on high and performs the kind of clinical surgery that makes him far more ruthless than many other politicians. This was one of those moments.

He could now look forward to the election confident he had the right team and leadership in place. Lynton Crosby and Mark Fullbrook were carefully preparing the ground behind the scenes; raising money, building an organisation and doing the extensive homework on Ken Livingstone that would prove so lethal during the election. They were determined that this campaign would be much better prepared, organised and effective than Ken's.

The new sense of focus and energy seemed to have paid an immediate dividend. In a series of polls, Boris started to pull clear of Ken Livingstone. One poll put him seven points in front. As the summer break began, the media assumed the election was in the bag and began turning their attention to a time when Boris would run for leader of the Conservative Party. For weeks, it was all anyone in political circles could talk about.

And then a man was shot dead in Tottenham. It changed everything.

Flipping over the rock

On Thursday 4th August 2011, the police shot a man named Mark Duggan in Tottenham. The officers were from the 'Trident' unit – the unit that deals with gun crime in the African and Caribbean communities. It was reported that they were attempting to intercept the car Duggan was travelling in. What happened between the interception and Duggan falling dead to the floor remains disputed.[23] What we do know is what happened next.

Around 5pm on Saturday 6th August, it was reported that 300 people had gathered outside Tottenham police station to protest against the shooting and demanding 'justice' for Mark Duggan and his family.

At around 8pm violence broke out, with protesters throwing bottles at police and setting cars alight.

Meanwhile, approximately 1,000 miles to the south, several members of Boris's team past and present were settling into drinking a delicious Sherry cocktail in the pretty Spanish resort of Arcos. They were there to celebrate the wedding of Sara Argent (nee Cadisch), a trusted member of the team who handled all Boris's public appearances. The sun set on a perfect day and music boomed out across the resort. The guests were in a very relaxed mood. The members of the Mayor's team who were there, including Kulveer Ranger, Guto Harri and Dan Ritterband were glad for the break before the serious work of re-election would begin in earnest. They could afford to relax. Their boss was four thousand miles away in Canada on his family holiday.

'Shop talk' was explicitly banned. As the evening wore on and the dancing became more epileptic, someone mentioned that something was happening back in London. A former member of Boris's team had briefly checked their messages and seen that Tottenham was, apparently, on fire. Glad to be away from grim old blighty, the conversation soon moved on, and glasses were topped up.

Now and then, Guto Harri would break away from a conversation to check his Blackberry. As the party powered late into the night, the faint outline of Harri could be seen pacing up and down the field behind the venue, trying to make sense of it all amid the fog of the party.

It seemed like there had been a minor criminal disturbance and all that was needed was to issue a statement condemning the violence and allowing the police to get on with the job. Calls for Boris to return to London seemed overblown. He was advised not to come back.

The next day, the line had been briefed – Boris would not be returning to London because to do so would be 'rewarding' the criminals.

By Sunday evening, however, it was clear the situation had escalated beyond an isolated incident. Rioters ran amok in several town centres across the city. Hooded youths poured through broken windows like some kind of liquid anarchy. Gangs put aside their differences and joined forces to devastating effect. Even the sons and daughters of respectable parents happily strolled down high streets with widescreen TVs tucked under each arm. One girl even stopped to commandeer trainers in the correct size. It was Dark Knight Rises meets Supermarket Sweep.

The initial police response was to try and isolate the disturbances and keep the perpetrators in one place, as if policing a Millwall FC game. This led to a widespread perception that the police had held back from arresting the perpetrators. What was never in doubt was that the police soon found themselves outnumbered and unable to prevent the spread of violence.

The situation was considered serious enough for Home Secretary Theresa May to cut short her holiday and return to London. But Boris was initially reluctant to return. It didn't help that it was almost impossible to get hold of him. He had chosen as his holiday location a DIY camper van trip around the Rocky Mountains. Mobile phone reception was extremely patchy and both his phones were rapidly running out of battery.

Nevertheless he was in touch with the police and the Government, receiving as many updates as the patchy mobile reception allowed. There was little he could personally do to improve the situation, he reasoned. Not to mention he was 300 miles from the nearest airport, so far away from civilisation was he.

Lynton Crosby and the campaign team saw the political danger very clearly indeed. In their view, Boris needed to return to London immediately. Londoners would expect their Mayor to be seen to be taking charge at a time of crisis. They needed re-assurance and action.

As the situation got markedly worse on the Monday, with police fighting running battles with rioters and most of Croydon ablaze, Boris decided to return to London. As he waited in the airport departure lounge, the TV screens relayed live pictures of London seemingly falling apart. Boris was powerless to do anything about it. As he watched, he overheard a fellow passenger say: "Isn't that the Mayor of London?"

Boris touched down at Heathrow airport on Tuesday morning. Having had barely any sleep, and desperate to regain the initiative, he headed straight to the most affected areas. His first stop was Clapham, where the damage was particularly bad.

The local residents had very quickly come together and begun a clean-up operation. Clean-ups were being organised for many other areas too, with Londoners from all over the city volunteering their time. The volunteer with a broom soon became the symbol of defiance against the yobs. It was an amazing display of solidarity in a city where community usually ends at your front door.

When Boris arrived, he was greeted with taunts of "Where's your broom?" It was a tone Boris was unfamiliar with. As the crowd grew louder and angrier, he cut off the live TV interview he was giving, grabbed a broom and walked down Clapham High Street holding it aloft.

There was a brief cheer. But it very quickly subsided. The local community was angry – as were most other Londoners – at the inadequate police response. People couldn't understand why the police had seemingly stood by and allowed the rioters to cause so much damage. There was a widespread assumption that the Met hierarchy had been afraid of being seen as too 'heavy handed'. But heavy handed was exactly the approach Londoners wanted. People were hugely admiring of the individual officers but scathing of the leadership.

As Boris stood alongside Home Secretary Theresa May praising the police for their work, it very quickly became apparent that he had misjudged the mood of the crowd. Local residents loudly heckled him, demanding to know why the police didn't intervene sooner. He manfully tried to continue with his speech, but the shouting was too much. One woman stood directly in front of him and demanded to know – in a quiet and determined way – why there were no police in Clapham the previous night. As the shouting intensified, behind him, Theresa May quietly slipped away, leaving Boris alone to face the angry locals.

He looked tired, overwhelmed and bemused. He simply had never experienced such a reaction before. People needed re-assurance and specifics but nothing Boris said could satisfy them. In the end, he had no choice but to let his minder guide him away from the crowd and into the safety of a neighbouring street.

It was one of the few times in his political career that the magic had deserted him. I'd seen him in a hundred crowd scenarios, and every time he eventually had them eating out of the palm of his hand. Even at the initially hostile London Citizens debate in the 2008 campaign, Boris performed what amounted to alchemy on the chorus of boos. This time, it didn't work and it made for uncomfortable viewing.

The one saving grace was that Ken Livingstone had also struggled to handle the situation. As mindless thugs were destroying people's homes and businesses, Livingstone was gravely pronouncing that this was a justified response to the 'Tory cuts'. At one stage, he even blamed Margaret Thatcher. It was like he had just stepped out of a time machine, sent here from some point in the mid-1980's. Londoners quickly rejected Ken's opportunism. Even the Labour Party knew it couldn't pin this one on the Government.

The giant, lumbering elephant in the room was the issue of how Londoners viewed police tactics. It was not an issue of national police cuts (although the lack of officers on the ground on the first night was an issue). It was the reality that many Londoners believed the leadership of the Metropolitan Police called it wrong. They were angry at seeing TV footage of police in full riot gear, but doing nothing to intervene as yobs ransacked homes and businesses.

People felt that if the police had been tougher earlier on, the situation might not have escalated as it did. It was clear that the second and third nights of rioting occurred, in part, because the gangs realised that the police couldn't stop them. It was a pernicious mindset that was allowed to take hold, and once it did, the thin blue line between order and chaos melted away.

This was a thorny dilemma for Boris. As Mayor, he could hardly criticise the police so soon. But as a candidate running in a very tight election, he needed to acknowledge what Londoners were feeling. Electorally, he needed to say what everyone was thinking: the initial police response could and should have been firmer.

Boris, however, was extremely reluctant. He felt that this wasn't the time to criticise the police, particularly given the pressure they were under. Understandably, the last thing he wanted to do was undermine the police at what was a delicate time (an entirely reasonable and responsible position).

Not wanting to rush into making the wrong call, I was one of the people he phoned after the riots asking for advice, at a time when I wasn't officially working for him (although I would join the campaign a few months later). I told him that Londoners wanted to see their Mayor restore order, support the victims and be honest about where the police had gone wrong. There was a clear distinction between the brave officers on the ground, and the men in dress uniform who give press conferences. I reminded him that he was elected on a promise to change the culture of policing. He had promised he would move them away from political correctness and back on Londoners' side, always ready to intervene and protect them from thugs. He was responsible and he had to acknowledge what had gone wrong.

He was reluctant to go any further than he had already done. I responded by saying he didn't have to dump on the police, just say what they had already admitted – that it was an extraordinary situation and they were unprepared. In the end, he settled on a form of words that began with "In hindsight…"

His public acceptance of what Londoners were feeling helped the storm to die down. As the Government juddered into action and Parliament was recalled, order was restored to the streets and the focus swung away from Boris. To everyone's relief, in the days and weeks that followed, there was no repeat of the violence.

In the ensuing debate about the causes of the riots, Boris seemed to find his voice in a way few other politicians could. He spoke about how a "big flat rock has been flipped up and we've seen all sorts of creepy crawlies come out." He told how police commanders had informed him that 60% of the rioters had previous convictions. What was the point of sending these kids into an unreformed prison system that was merely a university of crime?

To show understanding of the sociological problems that underpinned their actions was not to excuse them. It was just common sense. His analysis was neither hang 'em and flog 'em or feel sorry for them. It was about giving these kids some hope that they had a future, and intervening early in order to prevent them falling into the hands of the gangs. And it was also about restoring a sense of faith in the criminal justice system. His measured analysis and prompt actions to secure money from Government to help the damaged parts of London went a very long way to repairing the situation.

Long after the media had lost interest, Boris was still visiting the most affected areas (some several times) to see the impact first hand, talk to those who had suffered and help the re-building process.

By the time the party political conference season had started, in late September, the sound and fury from the riots had dissipated. But in the process, Boris had taken a big political hit so close to the election. It would take the combined talents of Boris, his City Hall and campaign teams to get the show back on the road.

CHAPTER FOUR

THE
DILEMMA

OCTOBER 2011 – DECEMBER 2012

"Mate, there's a lot of fuckwits in the world, but you can't go around telling them they're fuckwits." Lynton Crosby took a sip of his whiskey – Jonny Walker Black, lots of ice, soda water – and remained leaning forward. We had met for an early evening drink to discuss my role on the campaign. It was the beginning of October 2011, and after a period away from the action, I had taken up his offer to be Political Director of the re election campaign.

Crosby is well capable of out clowning Boris, but on this occasion he was deadly serious. Our biggest challenge, he said, was to avoid a 'them and us' situation developing between the campaign team and City Hall. He knew that even with the best of intentions, political operatives had a natural talent for falling out with one another. We were all under strict orders to get on well with our counterparts, despite our frustration with some of the compromises they had to make. We had to remember we were on the same side, and that they had a very clear interest in success – their jobs depended on it.

The relationship between the two camps had become delicate since the summer. Boris's City Hall team had always wrestled with the central dilemma of an incumbent; how much to govern, how much to campaign? Boris had made clear right from the start that he would only deserve to be re-elected if he delivered on his promises. He wanted to fight the 2012 campaign on a strong record, and he felt that Londoners would judge him on that basis. It was the right call in the sense that he had delivered. But – to all our frustration – his wasn't always given the credit he deserved. Deep down he knew it was about repeating achievements until raspingly hoarse, but the entertainer in him refused to inflict such boredom on his audience.

As the pressures of governing had consumed City Hall's energy and attention, the dilemma was never really satisfactorily resolved. This was manageable in the early years, but just seven months before the election it was clear – to the campaign team at least – that the dilemma needed resolving.

Crosby had been here before. From his years of experience, he knew all too well what it was like trying to get an incumbent administration to focus on the 'dirty' work of re-election. Incumbency is a bubble in which you feel that you're delivering what you were elected to do. Outside the bubble, however, this may not be evident to the voters.

Crosby knew it was a very fine line he was treading. He had a duty to tell Boris what he really thought, but he also knew that if tensions between the two teams were allowed to develop, it would only serve to undermine the re-election effort with possibly disastrous results. The only person that would benefit from 'Tory wars' would be Ken Livingstone.

In reality, however, the theological arguments were academic. By early October 2011 the evidence from the internal polling was undeniable. Despite a substantial body of achievement, after three and a half years, Londoners were still asking; "What's Boris actually done?" It was immensely frustrating for Boris, as he felt that he achieved great things for London.

The reason for ambiguity around Boris's record was demonstrated in a meeting of all the mayoral advisers on 17th January 2012 to consider the manifesto ideas. The team had gathered in the Tower Hotel – the vile building that despoils the otherwise glorious aesthetic of Tower Bridge. In a lively session, it was obvious that many of Boris's own team, like the public, could not recall what had been achieved. Frequently, one person would suggest an idea only for someone else to say it had already happened before someone else would promptly disagree. No one could agree on what had been achieved.

People argued and several conversations were had at once. One of the Deputy Mayors spent most of the meeting buzzing around the room trying to adjust the air conditioning. All the while the Mayor of London and his new Chief of Staff Sir Edward Lister grew increasingly exasperated at the advisers' lack of knowledge about the administration in which they served. If they didn't know what had been achieved, how could Londoners be expected to? A sad indictment of how City Hall had communicated over the years.

Moreover, internal polling showed that Ken Livingstone was more popular than anyone thought. Despite everything, he was the second most popular politician in London – only a whisker away from Boris. In fact, they were the only two politicians in London with a positive rating. It really wasn't campaign mind games to say that Ken stood a very, very good chance of winning and was easily Labour's strongest candidate.

What was most astonishing is that nothing much had changed since 2007, in terms of whom the candidates most appealed to. Outer London voters still preferred Boris over Ken, with the reverse true for Inner London voters. There was still a sharp divide between white voters, who overwhelmingly preferred Boris and black voters, who overwhelmingly preferred Ken. It was the same for housing tenure. Homeowners were voting for Boris, council tenants were voting for Ken. Older voters were for Boris, younger for Ken. City Hall's early strategy of trying to broaden Boris's appeal and win the support of the likes of *The Guardian* had evidently not paid off.

The picture was comforting, in a way. It meant we knew precisely what we needed to do; simply turn out the same people as last time. The issues hadn't changed either. The top three were still transport, crime and the economy. Everything else was irrelevant. And the issues that Boris talked about, like the Thames Estuary airport, a cable car and the notion of creating the 'village in the city' didn't resonate as much as City Hall believed.

These initiatives were the subject of the fiercest debate. Crosby's analysis was that by constantly talking about them, Boris was simply alienating the voters he needed on his side. This was exacerbated by Ken Livingstone's relentless focus on the bread and butter issues.

However, Boris felt that these projects were genuinely important things for the good of London. And some members of the mayoral team felt that the campaign team had underestimated their electoral value. It wasn't that the initiatives were unpopular, it was simply a case of priorities. At a time when voters are too busy getting on with their lives to follow the minutiae of politics, consistency on the issues that matter is what counts.

Just before I started the campaign, in October 2011, in a meeting with Guto Harri, he explained why many in the City Hall team didn't agree with the campaign internal poll findings. He said that things like the cable car, Thames Estuary airport and the statue in the Olympic Park (the Orbit, as it's now known) were vital in shaping voter perceptions of Boris. They showed a depth and breadth to Boris that would impress them. As I noted in my diary at the time, he acknowledged that the 'core' issues were important, but added; "I think most voters have higher aspirations. I know I certainly do."

Preparing the ground

Despite the unresolved issues behind the scenes, the position in early October 2011 – on the outside at least – was that the re-election bid seemed to be in very good shape. Boris still led in the public polls and the bookies made him the clear favourite to win.

Tucked into a small suite of offices in Mayfair, in the same building as Max Clifford's PR firm, the campaign team was quietly preparing for the war to come. Every day, z-list celebrities and bemused campaign staffers would populate the small lift that served the building. At this stage, there were just seven permanent staffers and a handful of volunteers.

I had joined the campaign at the beginning of November. One of the advantages of having worked on the 2008 campaign was that I knew exactly what needed to be done (a far cry from how I had felt the first time). The campaign had been going for over a year. In that time, a lot of work had been done to try and make sense of Boris's record, so it could be communicated and defended across London. This was no easy task, especially when it came to breaking down achievements in individual boroughs, of which there were 32. They had also done much to wade through Ken's record. Throughout 2011, volunteers would take turns searching the British Library press archive looking for the original press clippings of every Livingstone story published during his time as Mayor.

We were far better prepared than at the same stage in 2007. But there was almost too much information, which made it difficult to respond to political attacks quickly and effectively. I had experienced just how ruthless Ken's operation could be, and – as the incumbent – we were up against a more hostile media. There was also more to rebut. In 2008, Twitter was still an unknown quantity in campaigning terms (one press officer who used it was roundly and repeatedly mocked for doing so), but now it was ubiquitous with attacks coming in almost by the minute. We had a record to defend, and no shortage of politicians and interest groups trying to take it apart. It meant we had to have the systems in place to deal with this effectively. I knew from my previous experience that failing to respond to attacks could see whole days of campaigning lost.

I also knew that we had to take advantage of the sackfuls of baggage that came with Ken. We were in a rare position for an incumbent – our opponent had a long and often ignominious record. This meant detailed investigative work on everything that Ken had ever said and done that was controversial, every penny of public money he spent and every instance of hypocrisy. Hours were spent trawling through the transcripts of obscure City Hall sub-committees, searching and cataloguing answers to mayoral questions and scouring old budget documents for anything we could use.

It was a mammoth task, particularly given that everything had to be robust and fully sourced. We had to be sure that in the heat of battle a particular fact or quote was 100% accurate and backed up by an official document or newspaper article. Otherwise, mistakes would be ruthlessly punished.

Therefore, I set about creating a political unit furnished with a library of every fact about Boris and Ken that would be used in the campaign. Thanks to the wholehearted support from Conservative Party Chairman Andrew Feldman, Director of the Conservative Research Department Nick Park, Oliver Dowden and Stephen Gilbert at No.10, the unit was soon populated by some of the Party's brightest researchers.

Everything was driven by a document I christened the 'Book of Truth'. Updated daily, it catalogued every fact and argument in short bullet points, structured around the main campaign narrative. Stretching to 64 pages and 20,000 words, it was truly the bible of the campaign. Although it took months to compile, it was invaluable, enabling any staffer to quickly find a fact and use it in rebuttal. My stock response to most questions of fact became; "Read the Book of Truth".

We had expected Ken's team – at some point in the campaign – to issue a dossier taking every 2008 manifesto commitment and claiming to show how each had been broken. Working on the basis of knowing yourself better than the enemy, Crosby asked the team to look back at the old manifestos and do our own audit of what happened, taking every promise and giving an honest assessment of the outcome. We did the same for Ken, taking his 2000 and 2004 manifestos, and comparing it to his record in office. It transpired that Boris had kept 91% of his promises, whereas Ken had only met 53% of his. Both documents were incredibly detailed, the former stretching to 68 pages and the latter to 74. Both were based on the facts and measured in tone, which is principally why we were able to get good media stories out of them. Indeed, Sam Lyon and I felt strongly that every fact had to be nailed in order to build trust with the media – this would be critical to winning. This was particularly important given trust would be a major issue of the campaign. By contrast (and to my surprise) Ken's team often produced short, flimsy and hysterically worded dossiers that rarely got media coverage because of their transparent amateurishness. Amazingly, they never thought to issue their own credible audit of Boris's election promises versus his record.

To complete the library was a document that kept track of every commitment Ken had made on the campaign trail since early 2010 and how much it would cost. Transcripts of every public meeting Ken had spoken at since he was officially selected, which had been recorded by campaign team members who attended, aided this. The final 'cost of Ken' would total over £2 billion and enabled us to get a good run in the media accusing Ken of wanting to put up council tax.

All this detailed work was critical in giving us the edge when it mattered, because defeating Ken Livingstone would prove to be no cupcake party.

Extensive work had been done on researching Ken's campaign team and understanding their potential strategy. Nick Dines, also a former staffer for the London Assembly Conservatives, was in charge of opposition research and had painstakingly constructed a mock up of what Ken's campaign 'war book' might contain. It analysed in detail the electoral maths and pin pointed what Ken's strengths and weaknesses were. The document highlighted three major advantages: Ken only needed 70,000 votes to change hands to win (or a 3.1% swing), there were 820,000 union members in London they could tap into (to put into context, Ken got 893,877 first preference votes in 2008) and Boris was popular but seen as out of touch. It demonstrated just how winnable the election was for Ken.

A big challenge was dealing with the fact that the Conservative

Party had a limited 'machine' on the ground in London. This was in stark contrast to the Labour Party who showed in the 2010 General Election just how effective they could be. The difference was that there had been, for many years, a 'London Labour Party' – treating the capital as a single entity in which the party's resources should be pooled to fight the numerous elections that take place in the city. This is partly why London has historically been a Labour city. By contrast, the Conservative Party has never treated London as a single entity. Thus, it is fragmented into many different 'associations', each of which cares principally about the parliamentary seat or council they contest.

This difference in approach mattered hugely because a mayoral election is about delivering a large volume of votes in 'safe' areas. Usually, a political party gives most effort to 'marginal seats', where sometimes a handful of votes can make the difference between defeat and victory in a General Election. Therefore, there is a real incentive to reach out to new people and maintain a well-oiled machine in those areas. However, this means that resources are often drawn away from the 'safe seats' because these are areas that will vote Conservative come what may.

The requirement in a mayoral election is completely different. The idea is to turbo charge areas considered 'safe' because the result is decided on the absolute number of votes – not how many seats you can win. Our strategy was about turning out large numbers of Conservative voters in these 'safe' areas. The trouble was that the Conservative Party organisation in such areas was not used to intense campaign activity. This meant that Crosby and Fullbrook had to make some very smart decisions about where to focus limited resources. They scouted bright volunteers who, within the space of three months, built a sophisticated database that pinpointed the specific postcodes that were most likely to vote for Boris. It meant we could target resources where they would be most effective.

It was a scientific approach that left nothing to chance. In an election that eventually came down to tens of thousands of votes out of an electorate of millions, it was an approach that would make all the difference.

Ken Livingstone's campaign had, by late October 2011, been relatively underwhelming. He had doggedly kept hammering away at the major issues, but he hadn't made the breakthrough. He had also failed to take clear advantage of Boris's troubles during and immediately after the riots. His own response was very poorly received, and he gave the impression that he was excusing the rioters' behaviour. It was precisely the wrong moment to flip open his well-worn left-wing songbook.

He had also been distracted by needless political rows. By making a series of controversial and offensive public remarks, he was reminding Londoners of what a divisive politician he was. For example, he told a Conservative councillor to "burn in hell"[24], called Sir Edward Lister the "Ratko Mladic of local government"[25] and asked a public meeting how many audience members would like to see George Osborne hanged.[26] We got a lot of media coverage out of his nasty, divisive attacks.

He also sent a very clear signal to London's Jewish community by accepting a paid presenting role on *Press TV*, an Iranian funded satellite channel widely acknowledged to be the propaganda arm of the fiercely anti-Semitic Iranian government. So much so that the channel was subsequently banned by OFCOM (the broadcasting regulator) because of their lax editorial standards.

Most damagingly, he had no new tune to play. He had lots to say on why Boris was failing, but not a great deal on why he would be better. His policy platform was mostly about re- hashing parts of his old agenda – such as the £25 congestion charge for large family vehicles. There was no compelling new idea or offer that would make people sit up and take notice. All he seemed to be doing was launching ever more hysterical attacks on Boris. He didn't seem to be answering the most fundamental question of all; if you didn't vote for him last time, why are you going to this time?

This bred an atmosphere of increasing complacency not just within City Hall, but the wider Conservative Party and Westminster pundit-ocracy. As parts of the Labour Party began to openly question whether Ken was the right candidate, most Tories openly scoffed that the race was already over.

But Ken Livingstone's political career is replete with examples of his opponents underestimating him. Because as the campaign team knew very well, all Livingstone had to do was provide a compelling alternative offer and we would be in real trouble.

Which is precisely what he did on 26th September 2011. At the Labour Party conference in Birmingham, he unveiled a bold promise to reverse Boris's fare increases and instead cut tube and bus fares by 5%. It was typical Ken: brash and nakedly populist. It got him the splash he wanted.

No one within the mayoral or campaign teams believed he would have the gall to promise a fare cut, such was the parlous state of public finances. We all believed that such a commitment would backfire spectacularly, as he wouldn't be able to answer the most important question of all; where's the money to fund the cut coming from? We had, however, badly underestimated its potential impact.

Fares fair?

Tube and bus fares are one of the few direct charges that the Mayor controls. Thus, they attain huge political significance. They're also something of a political straightjacket. They were to dominate the 2012 campaign.

When the mayoralty was created in 2000, the then Labour Government knew what it was doing. London's transport network has always been reliant on fare income not just to keep the system running but also to fund the investment that brings improvements. The problem was that politicians had in the past frequently played politics with fares, extremely reluctant to increase them any more than necessary and usually cutting them at election time. This meant that, over the years, there was less money for improvements than there ought to have been.

Indeed, part of the reason that the tube still has major problems today is that it was starved of investment in the 1980's, which we are now only just making up for. This is thanks in no small part to Ken Livingstone, who as leader of the former Greater London Council (GLC) in the 1980's enacted a bold election promise to cut fares by up to 30%. The cuts were so damaging to London's finances they were subsequently ruled illegal by the Law Lords, following a legal challenge by Bromley council. The huge debt this created, combined with subsequent recessions, meant the tube did not get the investment it needed.

When the mayoralty was created, the Government made sure that a significant chunk of London's transport funding would come from fares. They strictly limited borrowing and in the financial settlements that followed, the money was virtually conditional on rising fare income. It meant that whoever was Mayor would have to increase fares, or face severe financial consequences.

Of course, when Livingstone was Mayor, he didn't let this reality bother him too much. He simply promised a fare cut at election time and went back on his word when the votes were safely counted. He would convince people he was serious by offering limited fare cuts just before the election, and then whacking them up again straight after. But the effect was to leave a ticking time bomb in the finances that would – sooner or later – have to be rectified.

When Boris took over in 2008, he was presented with a TfL business plan that didn't balance. By playing politics with fares, Livingstone had reduced the amount of money coming in. Yet at the same time he had committed to spend more money on transport projects. To try and plug the gap, Boris had to scrap the unfunded projects that Livingstone had promised and increase fares in 2009. He had also ordered TfL bosses to make significant savings, worth billions over several years. But this wasn't enough.

By September 2009, the recession had exacerbated the funding shortfall and TfL had a 'black hole' of around £800 million[27]. Officials believed that the recession would significantly reduce fare income, as fewer people would use the tube in particular. Coupled with a wide expectation that a new Government would take over in 2010 and make cuts, Boris was presented with a nightmare list of cuts and fare increases that would fix the 'black hole' and protect vital investment. But they would also spell political disaster.

Some of the options were dire. Officials recommended scrapping free bus travel for children, increasing the congestion charge, delaying the removal of the Western Extension of the congestion charge, drastically cutting back bus services, increasing fares by as much as 25%, obliterating the cycle superhighways programme and gutting the plan to make tube stations accessible for wheelchairs.

They may as well have called it the 'one-term' plan.

At the meeting where the proposals were first raised, Boris was so downhearted he compared the gathering to the "last days in the fuhrer bunker" and asked TfL Commissioner Peter Hendy; "How many panzer tanks are left?"

What had made the situation infinitely worse was that the Labour Government's 'Public Private Partnership' (PPP) deal to upgrade the tube was costing a fortune. The idea behind the PPP was to pay private companies to do the work, in the belief they would do it faster and cheaper than London Underground. In reality, the contracts were so complicated that it took a King's ransom to work out if the companies were doing what they said they would. One company (Metronet) performed so badly it went bust, leaving the taxpayer on the hook for hundreds of millions. The result was that the work cost far more than it should have done, and in most cases it was late.

And it wasn't just a case of getting TfL to save more money. The most expensive part – the London Underground – was in the grip of the RMT union and was thus the most resistant to the kind of changes that would produce significant savings.

It was the perfect financial storm at the worst possible time. Boris had to reach a politically painful compromise that would severely handicap him in the race to be re-elected. His priority was protecting the investment that he believed would serve Londoners well for years to come. In speeches, he would often use the line; "when you're in a hole the size of Crossrail, you keep digging". He felt it was vital to the future economic health of London that transport investment be protected from cuts. Therefore, he agreed to a policy of increasing fares every year by inflation plus 2%, as well as closing tube station ticket offices, cutting back the wheelchair access programme and increasing the congestion charge (despite an election promise not to). These were painful cuts to make, but they were the right ones for London and Londoners.

However, he didn't accept every cut offered by the bureaucracy. He outright refused to scrap free travel for children, cutting back the bus service and any delay to the cycle superhighways programme.

Boris and his team knew that this would be an open goal for Livingstone. But they also felt that Ken was in a corner too. The political compromises meant the budget was on a knife-edge. TfL wanted Boris to cut more than he agreed to, so it meant finding even more savings than they had planned. No Mayor, whoever they were, would be able to afford to cut fares without cutting investment. It just wouldn't be credible.

But Livingstone knew all the tricks. He claimed he had 'discovered' a vast mountain of cash that TfL had been sitting on and not using. He pointed to official figures apparently showing there was a £700m-odd 'surplus' in the TfL accounts that he would now use to cut fares by 5%. This number was the so-called 'operating surplus' – the difference between what TfL thought they would spend on running the system and what they actually did, combined with the difference between what they thought they would get in fare revenue and what they actually did.

Livingstone knew very well that this 'surplus' had existed for years, particularly when he was Mayor. He also knew that it was allocated to investment projects, just like it was when he was Mayor. It was money that appeared spare, but was in fact earmarked for things that would improve the system. It was why he never once used it to cut fares himself.

It was a common tactic to claim this was 'unspent' money, just as the Conservatives on the London Assembly had tried in 2007. Back then, Mayor Ken explained why it couldn't be used:

"There has been some fascinating speculation in the press that I have a £500 million slush fund that I can spend between now and the election. You know me; if I had it I would, but I do not. There is the small matter of the need for TfL to balance its budget in law, and the balances we carry are all allocated against the range of projects coming forward.[28]"

Moreover, Livingstone was equally clear about the choice between cutting fares and cutting investment. When it was proposed he use this money to fund fare cuts in 2007, he replied:

"That is fine as long as it also has the honesty to go on and say what I should cut whilst cutting the fare increase.[29]"

In the heat of an election campaign, these fine distinctions were irrelevant and Livingstone knew it. It was a simple calculation. Voters would understand a proposal to cut their cost of living a lot better than a complicated argument about surpluses and allocated investment. And people were feeling the squeeze, so much so they were more than willing to accept a cut to future investment if it meant immediate relief.

November and December 2011 saw Ken wage a guerrilla campaign against Boris, using every opportunity to justify and re-enforce his policy. He suddenly had his compelling offer, and it would prove to be almost irresistible to voters. It would put us in an awkward position.

"Stop talking about fuckin' fares"

Boris's initial response to Livingstone's fares pledge was to dismiss it as an electoral bribe that was based on fantasy economics. He had done the grinding work of studying the numbers and closely scrutinising TfL officials. The choices were limited and simple – cut fares and stop investment, or modestly increase fares and guarantee investment that would enable London to compete in a global marketplace. He felt that Livingstone's sums were so obviously fraudulent, the pledge would have the survival chances of a trout on dry land.

However, to Boris's frustration, the media took Ken's pledge seriously. Each time a new financial estimate was published by TfL, Ken would attack hard and the media would inevitably give it a run. City Hall would hit back, explaining in ever lengthening terms why Ken's figures didn't add up and theirs did.

This move and counter move was precisely what Ken wanted. He had taken a big gamble, and he needed this issue to dominate the early political news coverage. The only way he could do this was to create a row. By so brazenly challenging the official figures, he did just that. And each time he did, we felt obliged to respond in detail. Yet each time we engaged in this tit for tat, we unwittingly pushed the issue higher and higher up the agenda.

In mid November, Crosby had spotted an alarming trend in the latest round of research and conveyed his concerns to Ed Lister and the campaign team. In a note of 12th November 2011 he wrote:

'Transport is cited as (the) most important issue……Transport is cited as the biggest single hesitation in voting for Boris….Ken's strongest positive positioning over Boris is 'will keep fares low'…… More people believe it is time to give a new person a go than Boris deserves to be re-elected…. It is the perfect storm for an election to be won on transport…. We must re frame the election away from transport fares whilst neutralising on transport where possible.'

His view was that by arguing about the numbers behind Ken's fares pledge, all we risked doing was raising the salience of Ken's strongest issue and letting him set the terms of the debate. The election was in danger of becoming a referendum on fares, which the research showed Boris would lose every time. Boris wanted to win the argument about fares and investment precisely because he felt he was in the right. He felt passionately that the policy advocated by Ken would do irreparable damage to London, and he was determined not to let that happen. Moreover, he was exasperated that the media and voters couldn't see that Ken's prospectus was so fraudulent and damaging to the London economy. But in Crosby's experience, it was entirely possible to win the argument but lose the election.

He cited a national example; during the 2010 General Election the Conservatives devoted a lot of time to talking about the NHS, in an attempt to win the argument that they could be trusted on the issue. But every time they did, although the media would give them credit, they would lose electoral ground to Labour. This is because the reality was (and is) that the Conservatives are not trusted on the NHS. The more they talked about it, the more the election became about the NHS. And if the question was about who was trusted to run the NHS, the voters' answer was almost always Labour. In Crosby's view, it was one of the reasons why the Conservatives failed to win a majority – they spent too much time talking about issues they weren't trusted on and too little about issues they were.

The same thing was happening to Boris and City Hall over transport fares. Crosby's advice was clear; "Stop talking about fuckin' fares." Like all good conviction politicians, Boris wasn't willing to shy away from an argument where he believed he was in the right. But he gradually accepted Crosby's point that when it comes to elections, it's not enough to be right. Crosby felt that Boris needed to make as forceful an argument about other parts of his agenda where he was in the right, on the economy, tax and crime. City Hall had to take advantage of incumbency and focus on these issues.

Boris himself wasn't yet fully in campaign mode. He felt that getting embroiled in a slanging match with Ken Livingstone so early wouldn't benefit anyone. He is a relentlessly optimistic character, and he felt that stooping to Ken's level would shroud the campaign in a heavy cloak of negativity. His focus was on being Mayor and getting on with the job of delivery. He still believed that as long as he delivered his promises, Londoners would reward him with a second term.

At the beginning of November 2011, he launched his new book; '*Johnson's Life of London*'. It was his musings on the people who have made London the city it is. He was in extremely good spirits at the launch on 9th November, the famous author being lauded for his efforts. It was a setting he felt truly at home in. He excels as a politician because he is a great communicator, stemming from his ability with the written word. For that reason, he is understandably proud of his accomplishments as a writer. You see this in his reaction to anyone who tries to persuade him to allow others to write his speeches and articles for him. Once, when I did, he gave his standard polite refusal and then pointed out; "I can't, it's my livelihood."

As he held court at the launch, I was able to observe just what a curious mixture of people he has picked up in his slipstream over the years. Politicos and campaign staffers like myself shared the space of the Marylebone bookshop with very proper City Hall officials; on their best behaviour lest conversation stray into matters electoral. I could have sworn one was taking minutes, just in case. Interspersed with us was what can only be described as the literary 'dahlings' set. Mainly, it has to be said, glamorous bone achingly thin and posh young women. It was a world away from the daily grind of politics.

After his speech, Boris, his publishers and I chatted in the corner. He was delighted to see one of his old books on the bookshelf. I dared him to sign a copy as a nice surprise for whoever bought it. Always game for mischief, he duly obliged, giving that wicked smile he does when rule breaking is not only afoot, but consented to.

His publishers were full of talk of new books and TV series after the Olympics. Boris was enthralled with the seemingly endless possibilities. I gently reminded him he had to win an election first, and a look came over him as if his schoolmaster had reminded him of upcoming exams. I told him to wake up every morning hearing Ken Livingstone's victory speech in his head, that incessantly whiny voice enjoying the spoils of war ("As I was saying before I was ruuuudely interrupted…."). This seemed to focus his mind and he nodded reluctantly. Then, he looked at me and said; "after this, I never want to run for anything again." The modest Englishman in him instinctively shied away from brash electioneering.

On 28th November 2011 the headline in the *Evening Standard* was unequivocal: 'Four more years of Boris, says poll.' A Com Res poll had put Boris eight points clear of Livingstone. It cheered Boris up immensely, but the campaign team was more circumspect. We were of the view that it was much better to be marginally behind – all the better to fight complacency with. Complacency was a big problem; it would mean Conservative voters staying at home in the belief that

Boris would win, allowing Ken to sneak in by the back door by turning out his own supporters in huge numbers. Our own internal polling had already uncovered a big expectation that Boris would win. In an election where turnout was everything, that was a problem. Equally, we were anxious that the sense of complacency within City Hall was reduced as much as possible. Crosby stressed that the headline voting intention should be taken with a pinch of salt – it was based on an unrealistically high turnout of 51% (turnout at the last mayoral election was a record 45%).

We looked at the detail of the poll, and it confirmed Crosby's earlier analysis that an election about transport could only benefit Ken. Unsurprisingly, Livingstone's policy of cutting fares was far more popular than Boris's policy of increasing them. The argument that higher fares are worth paying for better services fell on deaf ears, with only 17% agreeing and a massive 70% opposed. 59% felt that the priority should be keeping fares low, even if it meant stopping upgrade work. Ken was more trusted on transport, and a clear majority of Londoners felt that the tube had not improved under Boris (by 37% to 30%).

The good news was that Boris led in the poll on all the other major issues, particularly the economy and crime. There was also an interesting finding that we would seek to capitalise on. An overwhelming majority preferred Boris open the Olympics than Ken, by 41% to 33%. This was echoed in the focus groups, where people felt that having such a divisive politician like Ken would send a negative message to the rest of the world.

The campaign had to stop talking about transport, and start talking about the other issues where Boris was stronger. However, Boris was very unhappy about the fares situation. He hates doing anything unpopular and he was really starting to see just how bad this issue was for him. You couldn't blame him – what politician would want to go into an election defending (in effect) tax increases? He was desperately looking for a way to mitigate the pain Londoners were feeling.

Fares had taken on a national dimension as well; with a lot of campaigning by Labour and the unions against the planned national rail fare increases due in January 2012. Chancellor George Osborne was coming under pressure and he could see the damage the issue was doing to Boris. Cameron and Osborne had made clear to Boris from the start that they would do as much as they could to help him get re-elected, understanding the impact a defeat would have on Conservative fortunes. As rumours circulated that Osborne might be able to limit the damage with spare cash, Boris lobbied hard to make sure London would be included in any relief.

Over the weekend of 26th and 27th November, it was confirmed that in the forthcoming Autumn Statement extra money had been found to limit the national and London fare increases. This meant Boris would be able to limit the fare increase to inflation plus 1% instead of 2%. We greeted the news with mixed feelings. It was a good way of emphasising one of Boris's main strengths – bringing home the bacon from the Treasury. But on the other hand, it wouldn't make that much difference and it was nothing compared to what Ken was offering. It would only prolong a conversation we didn't want to have. And again, it risked allowing Ken to set the agenda.

Boris remained downbeat. He felt it was a pathetic concession to offer, even though he was grateful for the extra money. Crosby's advice was not to try and make it sound bigger than it was, and to carefully frame it in terms of a statement of principle. It showed that Boris was an instinctive tax cutter, reducing charges wherever and whenever he could. The most important thing was not to get into a bidding war with Ken.

The night before the announcement was made, Boris had a wobble. As he had done throughout the first term, he once again pushed TfL officials on the question of whether the fare increases could be palliated without hurting investment, using the Government's money as a starting point. As he scrutinised the budget reports he regularly received, he saw a glimmer of hope. The recession had not caused a decline in passenger numbers (and thus revenue) – a major assumption when the doomsday list was presented to Boris in 2009. In addition, TfL Deputy Chair Daniel Moylan had been driving a relentless savings programme that was working, ending the chronic waste of the Livingstone years. On this evidence Boris came to believe that money might be there to ease the burden on Londoners without hurting investment.

As it turned out, the rising costs of fuel along with fallout from Labour's failed Public Private Partnership deal for the tube meant that the choice remained the same. You couldn't cut fares without hurting investment. Although Boris believed that his policy was the right thing to do, like any other politician in this situation, he would continue to feel unhappy about it.

"Mate, he's back in the game"

A week after the Autumn Statement, Ken Livingstone went for broke. On 5th December 2011 he upped the ante and announced that he would be cutting fares by 7% not 5% as he had originally promised. He claimed that extra money from the government combined with a bigger TfL 'surplus' meant he had the money to cut further. The Labour campaign had concluded that the only way of beating Boris was to make the election a referendum on fares and the cost of living. The announcement got him very good coverage and Boris was again on the back foot. As Crosby observed to me; "Mate, he's back in the game".

The Labour machine was very impressive. The sheer ruthlessness with which they hammered home the message about fares at all levels was causing our campaign some concern. Every time Ken or any Labour politician appeared in public, on any issue, all they would talk about was fares. They never missed an opportunity to repeat their story, always finding a new comment or new set of figures as a hook to get more coverage. It was single-minded and crystal clear. And it was working.

Meanwhile, the competing demands of trying to govern and campaign were causing frustration for both City Hall and the campaign team.

One incident – although small in the grand scheme of things – typified how these competing demands affected the political strategy. The campaign had targeted Monday 9th December 2011 for some time, as it was the day when the last ever bendy bus would be in service before departing to a comfortable retirement in Malta. It was a huge symbol of delivery and a perfect contrast with Ken. Our voters hated the bendy buses and this would remind them that Boris had delivered the promise he made three and a half years ago. It was the perfect opportunity to do something pro-active.

It was also a big day in the national political calendar. As the euro-zone crisis deepened, David Cameron was due at an emergency summit to discuss the future of the Euro with the other leaders of the European Union. In the run up to the summit, Cameron was under intense pressure to offer a referendum on any new treaty that emerged from the talks. It was the classic routine – Tory Prime Minister goes to European summit, Tory Party goes into meltdown, demanding all sorts of table banging, handbag waving concessions. Anything short of donning a blonde wig and pearls, and returning home with a sack load full of cash is deemed a terrible failure.

On Friday 7th December, Boris had got in on the act telling BBC Radio 4's *World at One* programme that the Government should put any new treaty to a referendum – echoing what many rebel Tory MPs had said and what many activists felt. His intervention had caused the predictable storm in Westminster and in the media. That evening, as I accompanied him to a student rally, he spent most of his time tapping away on his phone muttering; "George [Osborne] isn't happy…" I cheekily asked him if he was causing trouble again and he replied with exasperation; "They're just wrong!" He had his views on important national issues, and he was going to use his national platform to convey them.

The campaign was less excited about the Euro summit story. It was another classic example of Westminster politicians working themselves into a frenzy about something that mattered little to the voters. We had pushed hard for a good media event on the Monday where Boris theatrically waved the last bendy bus goodbye. It was exactly the type of activity that would resonate with our voters. Boris was initially keen. However, on the Sunday night news emerged from Brussels that Cameron had dramatically exercised the British veto and rejected a plan by other countries to bind everyone into tougher budget rules. On the Monday, Boris was drawn into media interviews about the story and the bendy bus event was cancelled.

The result was good national coverage for Boris, but little London coverage about the demise of the bendy buses and in particular, his role in their execution. This would not have been an issue in mid term, but six months from an election that would be decided on the bread and butter issues it was too risky.

In an attempt to relieve the tension, the two teams had Christmas drinks together. Staffers from both camps shuffled into the swanky Brompton Club in Chelsea. The booze flowed unashamedly, while in the function room next door there was an Agent Provocateur party. Alcohol, lingerie models and Boris. What could possibly go wrong?

Boris, to his credit, was resolutely sticking to his booze free diet and on his best behaviour. Sensing a bit of tension in the room, he gave a short speech that urged the two teams to work together and "mate like pandas". Later, I asked him how he was feeling about things. He spoke about how difficult the last campaign had been, and how much better prepared he felt this time. The main difference, he said, was; "I know what I'm doing now!" He looked and sounded relaxed, utterly confident that things would work out in the end.

The other City Hall staffers were equally upbeat. There was no way that nasty old Ken would come out on top. He was tired, they said. And his fares policy was so transparent a con that nobody would believe it. The best thing, they said, was for Boris to rise above the fray and ignore the petulant whiner in the corner. Guto Harri sketched out what he thought would happen; Boris would win easily and go on to become Prime Minister. He shared the infectious enthusiasm of his boss. Boris shared hearty belly laughs with his City Hall staffers as they merrily supped – each content that Livingstone couldn't possibly win.

Meanwhile, Crosby and the campaign team were becoming increasingly worried about where things stood.

Livingstone had dominated November and December with his fares policy, taking advantage of his freedom to campaign and make irresponsible promises. In doing so, he got right back into contention even if the public polls weren't showing it yet. Up until this point, Boris didn't feel the time was right to go into campaigning mode and would rarely mention Ken or anything he was proposing. He felt it was beneath the dignity of office to directly engage Ken in a daily tit for tat. There was an official election period (from 20th March when City Hall would go into an enforced hibernation) and that was the time to take the gloves off. Until then, he was determined to use the time he (potentially) had left as Mayor to deliver what was right for Londoners. Doing a good job would ultimately determine how Londoners voted, and would demonstrate that he was by far the better choice. He would not make short term, uncosted promises just for the sake of matching Ken.

Boris had always accepted, however, that there would come a point when he had to change gear. He knew that the realities of campaigning meant that he would have to start framing the choice and engaging with Ken directly. No one expected Ken to be so competitive so early, and we all had to re-examine our assumptions about when the gear change needed to occur.

Boris knew that the pressure would continue in the New Year. On 3rd January, Londoners would return to work to find their fares had increased again. Ken wouldn't waste the opportunity to go on the attack.

Crosby's advice was that our strategy had to be to try and move the agenda onto our stronger issues. It meant focusing on council tax, crime and the economy and, let's face it, the negative aspects of Ken's character. We had to use the remaining months of incumbency to our full advantage. We also had to neutralise the fares issue as much as possible, by raising the issue of trust in the election. Despite Ken's populist stance, we knew that voters didn't trust him. The only way we could undermine Ken's most effective policy was to convince people that it was just another broken promise in waiting.

Boris had always felt that the gear change from Mayor to candidate shouldn't happen too early, but over the Christmas holidays he reflected that Ken's strong start to the campaign would mean that gear change would have to happen a lot earlier than planned.

CHAPTER FIVE

BORIS ENTERS THE RING

JANUARY 2012 – FEBRUARY 2012

The campaign team started the New Year by moving into their new larger, open plan office in Savile Row. The former stock trading floor was swiftly transformed into a war room, with large maps of key constituencies in London and campaign posters. Crosby ordered that not a single bit of empty wall space should remain. He wanted to instil in us a sense of urgency and excitement to reflect the gear change that Boris was going to make. In a matter of weeks, the offices would be stuffed full of people as resources and volunteers flooded in.

The office was entirely open, except for one segregated office in the corner. This is where Crosby and his business partner Mark Fullbrook sat. From there Crosby merely had to thump on the wall to get our attention. They had a genuinely open door policy and they made it clear to directors and volunteers alike that they could speak to them any time they wanted. The only time the door would be closed was when confidential discussions were had with Boris and the management team. The rest of the time, Boris mingled freely with the campaign staff building an excellent rapport with them.

Crosby and Fullbrook liked a structure that was as flat as possible. They knew all too well how campaigns could disintegrate because of internal tensions. The layout of the physical space and the clear demarcation of responsibilities was key to designing out tension from the start. A political campaign brings together people with a potentially toxic mix of ambition, strong mindedness and cunning. Combining those elements can be dangerous. But, just like the internal combustion engine, explosiveness can be harnessed to drive the whole vehicle forward provided it's done correctly. In their experience, as long as people had the security of knowing where they stood and shared the same space, they would work harmoniously.

There was a small management team, comprising Crosby as Campaign Director, Mark Fullbrook as Deputy Director, Sam Lyon as Media Director and myself as Political Director. Every morning we would meet at 8am for no longer than 15 minutes to discuss the plan for the day. From late February, this meeting would happen at 7.00am. By March, membership of this meeting had expanded to Nick Dines (Opposition watch), Chris Scott (Field Director), Peter Ganney (Operations Director), Eva Barboni (Digital), Bethany Wheatley (Digital), Amy Selman (Policy) and Guy Robinson (or 'Grobbo' as Crosby affectionately termed him. He was officially a 'campaign assistant' but in reality he did far more than that). Ed Lister, Guto Harri and Matthew Pencharz (City Hall political adviser) would also sometimes attend.

As with the 2008 campaign, by mid morning all our teams would be briefed on their priorities for the day. Crosby would convene a meeting of the whole campaign staff at 5pm every day, announced by the same bugle he used in 2008. He would summarise the day's events and what the priorities were, before awarding a pink cardigan to the best campaigner of the day. The cardigan was a truly awful shade of eye piercing pink. I had bought it for Crosby after the 2008 campaign, as a reminder of some of my bright cardigans he used to tease me about. After spending Christmas in Australia, he had found the cardigan and brought it back. Just like Boris, Crosby liked to use humour to break up the stress of the day.

Crosby had also instigated a weekly meeting between the campaign management team, Boris and his City Hall advisers. Usually taking place at our Savile Row HQ, the regular membership of these meetings comprised; Boris, Ed Lister, Crosby, Fullbrook, me, Lyon, Harri and Pencharz. Other Deputy Mayors or members of the campaign staff would join as and when they were needed.

In the first meeting, on 11th January 2012, Boris was fired up. In his Reagan-esque fashion, he outlined the principles and values that he wanted driving the campaign. He was the only candidate who did the right thing for London, no matter what the political consequences. He was the only candidate that had a plan to take Londoners through difficult times and back into prosperity. London's future as a world city was at risk by Ken Livingstone's fraudulent prospectus, and he wanted every Londoner to know it. In tough economic times, it would be madness to go back to the fiscal incontinence of the past.

With this clear direction in mind, Crosby outlined the latest set of internal poll results and what our strategy for the next phase of the campaign should be. The race was still neck and neck, and Ken was still leading on transport and fares. Thus, we needed to move the election onto our strongest issues, most notably the economy. Crosby explained that he understood that not every City Hall initiative would fit perfectly into the themes we needed to push. To mitigate that, he suggested that Boris frame everything around one over-arching theme: investing in London's future. The economy was the main issue for Londoners at this election. At the moment, Ken was the only candidate addressing voters' concerns, but he was doing so from a narrow (if powerful) cost of living angle. Boris was strongly preferred on the question of who was best placed to lead London out of the recession, so he had to demonstrate that everything he was doing was contributing to this goal. He also had to link transport investment with growing London's economy. This would help him neutralise transport by framing it as part of one his stronger issues.

We also had to raise doubts about Ken's fares policy. The media had started to question whether Ken's figures added up, and we had to fuel that curiosity. He had claimed that because the 'surplus' was so big, he could cut fares and maintain current levels of investment. The reality was that he would be taking up to a billion pounds out of the TfL budget which would mean cutting back on investment. It would mean the choice was between Boris, who was investing in London's future and Ken who would cut it back. A key priority would be to present Londoners with a specific list of transport projects that would face the axe if Ken won. We identified two early opportunities to get on the front foot. One was Boris' last budget before the election, where he would be announcing a Council Tax cut and the other was the formation of the new Mayor's Office for Policing and Crime. The latter was a bit of constitutional meddling (as part of the Government's nationwide policy of elected police commissioners) but provided a good opportunity to talk about crime.

Crime and policing was becoming a difficult issue. Londoners still trusted Boris on crime, but constant political rows about crime figures (in particular a recent spike in muggings and knife crime) had eroded our lead on the issue. The result of this was that the public didn't trust our claims that crime was coming down. And there was the looming issue of a gaping hole in the Met police budget that would severely impact police numbers after the Olympics. Ken and Labour were going hard on both and we had to reclaim the issue.

Over the following weeks the meetings continued; the process of changing gear from governing to campaign had begun. Gradually, the really thorny issues were properly masticated. Boris increasingly viewed things from a political standpoint and the debate between City Hall and the campaign about how to deliver what Boris wanted evolved in a considerably more productive fashion.

At virtually each meeting, fares were still the main subject of discussion. As we expected, Ken went hard on the fares issue when people returned to work on 3rd January. Hundreds of Labour activists leafleted tube stations and they made a relatively big splash in the media. Boris was deeply concerned about the issue and he worried that Londoners were being bamboozled into thinking that Ken could actually deliver his economically illiterate pledge. He set Crosby and the team a clear challenge – how could we win the argument and turn the issue to our advantage?

We knew that trust was a big problem for Ken. By launching a sustained attack on Ken's broken promises and lies in the campaign, we could then paint his fares pledge as just another promise waiting to be broken. As Fullbrook explained, it's much easier to convince someone of something they already believe. And there was no doubt that most Londoners didn't trust Ken. Our only chance of blunting the potency of Ken's fares policy was to raise the salience of trust in the election. This meant not only attacking Ken, but also clearly communicating how Boris had delivered the majority of his campaign promises from 2008.

Crosby identified the 'dividing lines' for both campaigns – the clear points of difference that both sides were trying to emphasise. By understanding these, we could make sure that our messaging and activity re-enforced our positive points of difference, not the negative ones Ken was trying to create. For us it was forwards vs. backwards, unifying vs. divisive, optimistic vs. negative, delivery vs. talk (whenever Crosby reminded Boris of these, Boris could never resist chiming in with; "up vs. down, round vs. flat..."). For Ken it was; substance vs. celebrity, Labour vs. Tory, bread vs. circuses.

The campaign had to start framing the choice better. One part of that was to frame our arguments and activity around our positives – pushing transport investment versus transport cuts for example. And an essential part of this was to highlight Ken's negatives as much as possible. The numbers showed that this was a turnout election. Our job was to turn out people already favourable to us and to persuade enough Ken supporters to stay at home. This was not going to be an election solely about swing voters.

In a meeting with Conservative London Assembly members, who wanted more attacks on Ken, Crosby once joked he had never been accused of running a positive campaign, so often has he been criticised by the media for running negative campaigns (who tend to give them disproportionate coverage). However, the truth is more complex than that. There is an assumption among many in politics and the media that you can either run a positive or negative campaign, but not both. Many people, particularly in the Conservative Party, shy away from negative campaigning because they believe it turns voters off. Accusations in the late 1990's that the Conservatives were the 'nasty' party had convinced many of the current generation of leaders that negative campaigns would only prove that the party had not changed. The truth is that a good campaign needs to have a blend of both. Your candidate has to be offering a positive plan for the future. At the end of the day, however, an election is a choice. The winning candidate is the one that defines that choice on his/her terms. And part of defining the choice is highlighting your opponent's negatives in a manner that resonates with people. Voters will often say they don't like negative campaigning – but when they are presented with a campaign that re-enforces the negatives they already felt towards a candidate in a calm and factual way it is incredibly powerful. A blend of 70% positive and 30% negative is about right, and it was the balance we sought to strike on this campaign.

Livingstone breaks clear

After all, Livingstone was campaigning as if this were year zero, and he had no record on which to be judged. The urgency of taking the fight to Ken became clear when, on 19th January, a YouGov poll put Livingstone in front by two points (51% to 49%). It was a five-point swing from the last YouGov poll the previous June, which showed Boris with an 8-point lead. The details of the poll were devastating. By 40% to 30%, people thought that Livingstone had achieved more for London as Mayor. Just 13% thought Boris was in touch with the concerns of ordinary Londoners, compared to 40% who thought that of Ken. To top it all, the Conservatives were 15 points behind Labour in London. Boris's popularity was keeping him in the race, but Livingstone had the edge on the things that mattered. We had a mountain to climb before May 3rd.

The poll confirmed what Boris had feared. Livingstone had made the breakthrough with his fares policy and dogged campaigning over November, December and January. He was appalled that the media had been letting Ken get away with it, and he decided that the only way to get them to see the truth was to become more aggressive on the campaign trail. He was very clear about the message he wanted to convey. In a note to Crosby he wrote; 'KEN IS NOT THE CHEAPER DEAL....At the moment we are being killed because people are shopping around desperately for the best deals. He is trying to get people to believe that he carries a lower price tag than me - and the opposite is true.'

On Monday morning the following week, another poll came out, this time by ComRes. The result again showed Ken in front by 51% to 49%. As I wrote in my diary; 'We're in a race now, that's for sure.' At that morning's strategy meeting, Boris told us that Londoners needed to see that something important was at stake, and that there was a real danger of London tailing off into decline if they voted for Ken; "People want to see a fight, they want to see us slugging it out and grovelling for their vote. They love it."

The next day, Boris was scheduled to appear on LBC Radio's *Breakfast with Nick Ferrari*. Harri had set up the interview, and we had all agreed that Boris would use it as an opportunity to talk about the forthcoming budget and his plan to cut council tax. However, Ferrari had other ideas. Unhelpfully, there were new figures that showed that robbery had increased over the last year. Ferrari put Boris under immediate pressure and he pinned him down on police numbers to magnificent (and for us, disastrous) effect.

Police numbers had been a running sore throughout the entire campaign and Livingstone was getting excellent mileage out of the issue, particularly in outer London. When Boris was first elected in

2008, police numbers stood at 31,398 officers[30]. By the end of the financial year 2009-10, they had increased to 33,260[31]. But by October 2011, numbers had declined back to 31,478[32]. This was due to a combination of a particularly large wave of retirements over 2010-11 and a freeze on recruitment due to the Coalition Government's cuts. Boris had fought hard for extra money to get police numbers back up and had secured an extra £90 million from the Government so that numbers could increase back to around 32,300 and stay there after the Olympics. That was still a thousand more than when Boris was elected. But the brief increase in 2010 to 33,260 meant it was very easy to attack Boris for cutting 1,700 police officers, by comparing it to the October 2011 figure of 31,478 (which was the latest available at the time).

It was the gloopiest, stickiest of wickets. Technically, Boris had 'cut' police if you only took the last two years into account. If you looked at his entire term, he had increased them. Voter perception was that police had been cut and Ken hammered the line that Boris had cut 1,700 police officers. However, his attack hadn't gained much traction in the election thus far. That was, until Boris's interview with Nick Ferrari.

When asked about the rise in robberies, Boris stressed that overall crime had fallen and that police numbers would be increasing. With the speed of a malnourished alligator, Ferrari snapped; "You're down 1,700 in the last two years?" Boris replied evasively; "Numbers go up and down they naturally fluctuate as officers retire." But nothing would loosen the grip of Ferrari's jaw on the bone; "By 1,700?" he intoned with an incredulous breathlessness that would make anyone on the receiving end blush. And then Boris said it. He could have said anything else. What he said afterwards was perfectly on message, but that one word destroyed the entire interview; "Yes, but...."

Crosby was listening to the interview in his office and I was outside in the open plan area. The hail of invective smashed through the glass partition as if it wasn't there and bounced off the walls.

Ken went hard on Boris's admission and for the rest of the campaign he would use it as evidence that Boris had cut police. It worked very effectively and later research would show that it was a critical turning point in perceptions about Boris's record on police. From then on, it became very tough to convince people that Boris had in fact increased police over his term.

The incident demonstrated that the media were starting to come down hard on Boris. He had had an easy ride for three and a half years, and now they felt he needed roughing up.

The next day, Boris fought back. Every year, there is a formal process at City Hall to agree the Mayor's budget for the forthcoming year. This is one of the few areas in which the London Assembly has any power. They debate the budget in several stages, and they have the power to amend (but not block) it if two-thirds of them can agree. In practice, this had never happened because the Mayor's party has always had just enough votes to ensure the budget would pass unchanged. But it still meant participating in the formal proceedings.

Boris had to give a speech to the Assembly presenting the latest draft of the budget. It was a set-piece we had keenly anticipated, launching a 'Back Boris's Budget' campaign with our supporters. It was the perfect opportunity to move the agenda onto tax, highlighting the contrast between Ken's 152% council tax increases and our own record of freezing it every year. The speech Boris gave was the first sign that he had truly woken up. It was terrific and not only energised the Conservatives in the City Hall chamber, but it energised the whole campaign office watching it on TV. For the first time, he properly laid out the choice facing Londoners at the election. He spoke with the passion of someone who was determined to win. He laid into the waste of Ken Livingstone's administration and proudly reeled off his own achievements in office. He outlined the stark consequences of cutting £1 billion from the TfL budget if Livingstone won; "…what will be cut…? The Bank station congestion relief work, or the upgrades on the Piccadilly and Bakerloo lines? Or perhaps the sub-surface lines? Or the congestion relief works at Victoria, Tottenham Court Road and Bond Street stations? Or cutting the Safer Transport Teams and the bus network? Which would it be?"

It was the first time he had spoke in such electorally compelling terms. His conclusion would form the basis of his stump speech from then until polling day:

"We have a choice. We could go for a short-term political swindle that will cut more than a billion from our investments – and which would simply drive fares even higher in the future. Or we can keep going with our programme of driving down crime, investing in transport and growing the London economy. We can go back to the politics of waste and division and posturing. Or we can get on with the work of improving the lives of Londoners. I want to get on with that work and I commend this budget to the Assembly."

Boris was, like a wasp in Spring, slowly stirring from his political hibernation and getting ready to strike.

The following Sunday, Livingstone went hard on fares again, challenging Boris to a live TV debate on the issue. The next day, aware of how much trust had the potential to hurt him, he announced that he would cut fares by 7th October or quit. We refused the invitation to debate, but Boris was pumped up telling Crosby; "we can beat this crap…. and we can cut fares far more than that swindling old desperado". On his return from Davos he sent Crosby a detailed note on how he wanted to run the cost of living argument, drawing a stark contrast between Ken's waste and broken promises and his record of cutting waste and delivering promises.

At the Monday morning meeting on 30th January 2012, fares were again the main topic of discussion. Boris arrived in a determined mood. He said he wanted to able to claim that he would be cheaper than Ken across the board – fares, council tax, everything. Boris said that if he had known the recession would have been this bad, he would not have agreed to a policy of increasing fares by inflation plus 2% every year. He felt it was a political mistake, and now he was being punished in the polls for it. Boris challenged his team; "How do I show I am in touch?" Crosby observed that Livingstone was using fares as a proxy for 'in touch vs. out of touch' and this was driving his vote. Ken was trying to make the election a referendum on his promises versus Boris's record. His promise of a fare cut versus Boris's record of fare increases. What we needed to do was make the election a referendum on Boris's record versus Ken's record, and not give his promises legitimacy. It had to be about Boris's record of cutting waste and delivering on his promises versus Ken's record of high tax, wasteful spending and broken promises. That was the only way to show that Boris was (and would be) cheaper.

Boris agreed, but it clearly didn't satisfy him. He wanted to be able to claim that fares would be lower under him than if Ken won without getting into a bidding war. The problem was his own business plan had already committed him to fare increases of inflation plus 2% for the next few years. To make matters worse, Ken was loudly asserting that Boris was committed to fare increase for '20 years'. Boris's Tory tax cutting instincts kicked in and he demanded to know how he could promise lower fares.

Lister argued that he could plausibly claim lower fares in the 'long-term' as a consequence of automating the tube, and the savings that would result. It was the first time he had articulated what eventually became our formula; by making the system cheaper to run you could, in time, make it cheaper to use. You could only do that by maintaining investment. Cutting investment would simply mean a more expensive system to run, resulting in higher fares in the future.

At one point Boris mused whether he should consider biting the bullet and matching Ken's fare pledge, such was his agitation. Most of the room was against this approach, not least because it was financially irresponsible. When Matthew Pencharz (City Hall political adviser) made a particularly forceful argument against, Boris snapped back at him; "I've lost ten points in the polls on this mate, have you got a better idea?" He was in full, deep sighing, hair ruffling exasperation mode.

Crosby accepted that we had to make a credible commitment to lower fares, without undermining our argument that you had to be responsible with the finances. We needed to make a commitment that only Boris could deliver.

Lister's approach seemed like the perfect way to do that. Only Boris could reform London Underground to lower costs, because Ken would merely pander to the unions that stand in the way of such reform. It wasn't just wordplay. Lister genuinely believed that by properly reforming TfL, you could dramatically reduce fares in a second term. The meeting finished with the issue unresolved.

After the meeting, Crosby and I discussed our concerns. His view had changed and he now believed we needed to move from a strategy of not engaging with fares to treating it more seriously. He said the latest internal poll reflected the negative public polls. I asked him if this was a bigger threat than we feared, and he suggested it was. He said he didn't know what the answer was, but we needed to resolve it quickly.

Crisis point

In each opinion poll, respondents were asked how likely they are to vote in order to get a sense of what the turnout might be. One of the main reasons Ken had taken a small lead in the polls was that our supporters were becoming less likely to vote – particularly in outer London. We had speculated that this was partly to do with complacency and partly to do with the feeling that Boris was out of touch. However the problem was far, far deeper than that. And it plunged the campaign into crisis mode.

Crosby's Australian business partner Mark Textor (Tex) arrived to provide a fresh perspective, having just successfully got a first term incumbent government re-elected in New Zealand. Tex is a veteran of election campaigns the world over, having served his apprenticeship under the legendary Dick Wirthlin, the man who got Ronald Reagan elected twice. Tex had advised on the 2008 campaign, so he was well aware of Boris's strengths and weakness. But he wanted to hear what the voters thought. He immediately convened a fresh round of focus groups to find out what was going on.

I have always found focus groups invaluable. Many media commentators believe they represent a politics that cynically bends to every whim of public opinion and are a poor substitute for real principle and policy. I think that's a complete misunderstanding of their purpose. It is not to find out what is popular or not. It is not to decide what policies you should be pursuing. Rather, it is to dig deeper into the emotional drivers of decision-making. When it comes to voting, we are emotional – not rational – actors. A survey simply shows what box your voter has ticked. Why they ticked it, why they really ticked it is what you need to know. Focus groups, conducted properly, give you a chance to explore those things in depth. This enables you to communicate in a way that motivates your voters.

On 7th February 2012, Tex, Michael Brooks (numbers wizard to Crosby and Tex) and I settled into a plush viewing facility in central London and spent three hours watching our core voters (all from Bromley, all voted Boris last time, all undecided this time) express their disappointment with Boris. It was the most humbling and depressing moment of my time on the campaign.

Going into the session, we needed to know why our core voters had been dropping off at such an alarming rate. After about ten minutes it became clear. Tex – who is an even more abrasive, hard-boiled Australian political strategist than Crosby (and I say that as a compliment to two individuals who are experts in their field) – was quick, precise and damning in his reading of the situation.

Tex is a jovial man, but that joviality sits like a thin film over an intensity that is not to be messed with. When he makes a wise crack, he shoots you a look that almost compels you to laugh (although often with good cause). In this setting, leaning back in his chair observing this group of voters, the wisecracks were gone. In their place was a stream of refined consciousness as he translated, in real time, what the voters were trying to tell us. At a time of great financial hardship, he explained, people had to work harder and longer. They were taking to this challenge with great dignity and responsibility. They were getting on with it. They weren't expecting handouts, and they understood why the country was in a mess. At the same time, they were seeing a political class that was – to paraphrase Tex, who had been to the annual Conservative 'Black and White Ball' the previous night – "fucking around at Westminster parties and not giving a shit." At the heart of it all was a fundamental lack of reciprocity. The punters were working hard and getting on with their lives. Meanwhile, their political leaders were pissing around with political games, pursuing vague concepts like the 'big society', utterly out of touch as a result. They were crying out for the political class to knuckle down and focus on making things better. Instead, politicians were indulging in talking to themselves.

The voters singled Boris out for special attention. They saw a Mayor who was more interested in becoming Prime Minister. Someone only interested in his own career prospects, not London. Only interested in being a celebrity, not delivering for Londoners. Only interested in selling books. The list went on...

Boris out on the campaign trail. He would always draw a crowd, and usually had them eating from the palm of his hand.

Boris celebrating St George's Day outside City Hall in 2009, his first as Mayor.

Boris giving his acceptance speech just before midnight on Friday 2nd May, 2008. He had only written a victory speech in advance.

One of the 'Not Ken Again' posters, displayed at some of the biggest billboard sites in London

Ken Livingstone at the World Economic Forum in Davos during his time as Mayor. He billed the London taxpayer £256.98 for a pair of shoes to use on one of these trips.

Boris at Leadenhall Market celebrating St George's Day in 2009, an event he insisting on celebrating wholeheartedly throughout his first term as Mayor.

Boris watches on as Lynton Crosby, Sam Lyon, Alex Crowley and Guy Robinson digest another opinion poll

Boris and campaign director Lynton Crosby admire the view before the Sky News debate, 19th April 2012

The 9 point plan posters, distributed across London on phone boxes. This was used to demonstrate to voters that Boris had a plan and he was personally committed to it.

My **Greater London plan**

1. Cutting waste a City Hall - freeing up £3.5 billion for services

That is my pledge to you

Investing in London's Future
BackBoris2012.com

Conservatives

My **Greater London plan**

7. Ensuring a true Olympic legacy – 11,000 new homes and 10,000 new jobs

That is my pledge to you

Investing in London's Future
BackBoris2012.com

Conservatives

v

Boris signing the oath of office, 5th May 2012, to confirm his re-election as Mayor after one of the toughest election battles in recent memory

The 9 point plan pledge leaflet used in the run up to polling day.

Campaign director Lynton Crosby addresses the campaign team just before the official election period got under way, 17th March 2012

They were convinced they had got the measure of Boris. They felt that his buffoonish exterior masked a deeper, ruthless ambition. That ambition was to be Prime Minister. They were worried that he wasn't ambitious for London.

For three and a half years, some City Hall advisers had believed that voters would respond well to a Mayor who was an important national figure and who looked like a future Prime Minister. This belief materialized into over-zealous, under-the-counter briefings to the media, inflating the narrative that it was only a matter of time before Boris would become Prime Minister. Westminster journalists, hungry for gossip, would lap these stories up from what was an impeccable (if not always disciplined and loyal) source.

These stories made for good copy, but they did much to put re-election at risk (and continue to cause problems long after re-election was secured). The key voters who would decide whether Boris kept his current job were deeply unimpressed. They didn't have the luxury of changing their job, or moving on to another job because they were bored. They had to stick with what they had or they wouldn't be able to pay the bills. Quite simply, the cumulative effect of this narrative was a feeling amongst voters who would decide the election that if Boris cared so much about being Prime Minister, they would be quite happy to relieve him of his current 'boring' job as Mayor of London on 3rd May. It was a damning indictment of City Hall's approach to communications over the past three and a half years.

It wasn't as if they had fallen in love with Ken again. They just believed that he really wanted the job of making London better. This feeling went to the heart of why people thought Boris was out of touch, and Ken was in touch. It went deeper than anger over fare increases. They were finding it tough and working hard to get out of it. Boris, who was emblematic of the hated political class, wasn't putting in similar effort to help them. Ken looked like he would.

That was how they saw the choice.

Perhaps most damaging and dispiriting was that they could only recall two things about Boris. He was more interested in being Prime Minister, and he was responsible for the bike hire scheme. They didn't know anything else. Nothing on council tax, nothing on crime or police. Nothing. It was soul destroying. The truth was, Boris had achieved great things in his first term; he had secured the long term transport investment pivotal to the city's future success, he was focusing the city's resources on tackling the deep rooted scourge of gang crime for the first time and he had expanded affordable housing at a time when private development had almost ground to a halt. He had much to be proud of and he deserved re-election. But the failure to communicate in a strategic way, that sought to impart a long-term message to the voters, meant that none of the great things were remembered.

As we sat opposite the two way mirror, slumped in our chairs, Tex turned to me and said that in 20 years of polling, this was the clearest example of a group of voters being one step away from saying; "fuck it, you're not worth it". It was, in his view, crisis point. We needed these voters to come out if we were to win. This was critical, because the Conservative vote in London was some 15 points behind Labour. We didn't have much room to play with. If these voters stayed at home, as they were looking likely to, it was game over.

As I heard the litany of negatives I thought back to late 2008/early 2009 at City Hall and the debates about how having a political strategy focused on the concerns of outer London voters was too 'rigid', and how Boris shouldn't be 'repetitive' and 'boring', how we should have 'higher' aspirations. I thought back to Boris's appearance on Eastenders, his photo ops with Barbara Windsor, the excitement about floating pontoons, the Thames Estuary airport, the call for an immigration amnesty and the constant attempts to keep *The Guardian* on side. I thought back to the run of process stories in the summer of 2011 (before the riots) quoting 'sources close the Mayor' about Boris's plan to become leader of the Conservative Party. All of it was now putting Boris' re-election at risk.

Tex convened the senior team first thing the following morning to digest the findings and come up with a plan of action. Tex said City Hall needed to stop the banal, celebrity crap at once. He felt that it would only take one more story about either a trivial issue or Boris's wider ambitions to tip these voters over the edge. We set to work on crafting a new campaign narrative that was a specific plan about what Boris was doing and what he would do if re-elected. The key, Tex explained, was to have something that was ultra specific and relevant and to keep hammering away at this for the remainder of the campaign. Boris had to demonstrate that he was in the middle of a work in progress and it was at risk if Ken Livingstone won.

This would later become the '9-point plan' – drawn up by the team under Boris's instruction as to the issues and priorities he wanted to set. It would form the basis of all our communications from thereon in. We also accelerated our plans for a negative campaign against Livingstone, as we had to raise the salience of the risk of going back to Ken and all that would entail. Tex and Fullbrook spent the rest of the day with blank sheets of paper and marker pens, designing attack posters.

Meanwhile, Crosby had become ill, leaving his mood further soured. He had somehow been persuaded to take a few days off at home. He had still, however, summoned the energy to talk to Boris, who was disappointed that he wasn't getting credit for his achievements and wanting a solution to the problem. Crosby advised that the over-zealous media briefings about Boris's future ambitions should be stopped, and Boris needed to go back to the key themes he first captivated Londoners with in 2008.

The following night, he rang all his key advisers to canvass opinion. He often does that just before he makes a major decision, he likes to weigh up everyone's opinion on the scales right before his eyes and ensure that he has covered all the possible angles.

I was in a restaurant when he rang. We were still in a cold snap, and as I ran outside to be able to speak in private, I realized I hadn't brought my overcoat out and it was freezing. As delicate snow began to fall around me, I had to pace up and down quickly to stop my teeth chattering. Boris must have thought I was more agitated than I was. I told him he faced a dilemma; being right and having delivered was no longer enough. He needed to think like the challenger again. He was in a reflective mood; trying to understanding why his popularity wasn't translating into votes. I felt he had thought too much like a journalist in recent years, always thinking of the new angle for the next day's papers, confident that the big issues were going in the right direction. It was an approach that had undoubtedly raised his media profile, but I argued that his profile didn't need raising. He needed to remind people of what he had achieved, outline what was to come and why it was at risk from Ken.

I asked him how he would feel if he was unable to see through the things he really cared about, like the youth agenda. He replied that it would be a "disaster" and he was determined not to let it happen. As I began to lose the feeling in my face, I bade him goodbye.

The following Monday provided much needed good news. Boris had gone back in front in a YouGov poll, leading Ken by two points. The *Evening Standard* dubbed it the 'Tightest Race Ever'. Ken's momentum appeared to have been checked. The last two bad polls were useful as a means to tackle complacency and motivate Boris. We didn't want a situation to develop where it seemed like Ken was running away with it. Fullbrook speculated that the previous polls could have marked Ken's high point. Did the latest poll show that Ken was like a marathon runner that had put on a sprint too early?

Not Ken Again

The following week we sat down with Boris to finalise the positive and negative poster campaigns that we hoped would give us the momentum as we neared the start of the official campaign period. At the meeting, Boris was a lot more focused and business like. Fullbrook outlined the plan to commission a thousand positive poster sites in the 326 target wards (out of 627) and thirteen negative ones on some of the biggest billboards available. Sites with the highest traffic flows were chosen, to maximize the number of eyeballs seeing giant, backlit reminders of why they disliked Ken Livingstone. The positive posters would be Boris's 9-point plan; his personally signed commitment to tackling the major issues facing Londoners. The negative posters would scream 'Not Ken Again' and warn Londoners that he wanted to come back with council tax rises, broken promises, hypocrisy, waste and Bob Crow (the unpopular leader of the RMT tube union). Indeed, Bob Crow was to feature heavily in all our anti-Ken material, principally because the research showed that he was by far the most unpopular figure in London.

Later in the campaign, Bob Crow – delicate flower that he is – would launch legal action against Boris for apparently defaming his reputation. When the solicitor's letter arrived, we embarked on a genuine process to determine its authenticity; such was the absurdity of it. We eventually realized that this was the first and only time a Tory campaign would be sent a gift from the RMT. An RMT spokesman said (presumably with a straight face, although in print it is hard to be sure) that they believed the poster; "falsely portrays our General Secretary Bob Crow as being part of a culture of political immorality and as having caused serious harm to the interests of people in London.[33]" To have even Bob Crow refusing to be associated with Ken's administration was an insult indeed. In the end, the case was thrown out before it even got to court.

Not Ken Again (NKA) was to be a major campaign in its own right. Right from the start, it was clear that we had to remind voters of what they would be returning to if they voted for Ken. He had many strengths as a candidate, but it would be critical to utilize the fact that he came with so much baggage. NKA started life as a website, chronicling the worst aspects of Ken's regime over the years, from putting up council tax by 152% over 8 years to his cavorting with the tube union bosses who regularly brought London to a standstill. The site pulled no punches – but we made sure that the tone wasn't too over the top and every article was rigorously checked and referenced. There would be no point in simply making up stories about Ken (after all we didn't need to); this would damage the credibility of our attacks. Tone was important too. Ken's team had launched their own attack site called 'Boris Johns-hen', which consisted of videos of a man dressed as a chicken following another man in a blonde wig. It looked like the product of a student's boozy *West Wing* marathon night. They had taken the lazy option, and it had very little impact. I was surprised, given their campaign had been up and running since 2010, you'd have thought they had the time to do a proper attack operation that focused on the detail of Boris's record. We were quite content with cheap shots like this.

However, we were not completely above such stunts either. During the 2008 campaign, Crosby dispatched activists dressed as Fidel Castro to follow Ken around wherever he went. They held banners that read; 'Sorry comrade, like me you've had your day, Fidel' and shouted; "Eight is enough!" It amused our campaign team, but more importantly it annoyed and disrupted Ken's team. It also provided a visual reminder of our message that Ken was more interested in Cuba than London.

This time around, Crosby ordered a dinosaur costume ('Ken-zilla') and a Pinocchio costume ('Ken-occhio') to highlight Ken as a figure of the past and someone who couldn't be trusted (obviously).

However, when the costumes arrived they were so Disney-fied and adorable, we abandoned the plan. Instead, they became motivational tools for the campaign team, with Guy Robinson dressing up as Ken-zilla at one team meeting to howls of laughter.

We also used cheeky attack videos to highlight Ken's negatives. I had experience as a film-maker, so one of my first tasks was to put together a video using newspaper headlines of Ken's antics set to the music of Edith Piaf's 'No regrets'. The video started with an interview in which Ken was asked whether he made any mistakes as Mayor. He answered; "I don't spend my time agonising about the past," which was followed by newspaper headlines such as; 'Murders at a record high' and 'I will be on the picket line next, vows Ken'. These were all genuine headlines from Ken's time in office, the exact copies of which were painstakingly obtained from the British Library newspaper archive.

Perhaps the best one was an animation set to the specially written and composed song 'Not Again Ken'. With images of bendy buses, Ken swimming in taxpayers cash and dancing arm in arm with Bob Crow, Lee Jasper and Lutfur Rahman (the Mayor of Tower Hamlets) it was an amusing video that proved popular. A campaign volunteer performed the song, and the entire campaign team sang the chorus, to the tune of '*In The Navy*' (written by volunteer Robin Knight, following Crosby's initial concept and song choice);

"Not Again Ken
Not your hypocrisy
Not Again Ken
Nor your reckless spending spree
Not Again Ken
When your taxes rise and rise
Not Again Ken
So many porky pies
Not Again Ken

Bad intentions in disguise
Not Again Ken
Breaks a promise every time
Not Again Ken"

We also produced a book called 'The Truth About Ken', which was the first time in Crosby's career that the opposition research brief was actually published in full by a campaign. Copies of the book found their way into every Labour MPs postbag, and campaign volunteers outside Labour's Victoria Street headquarters handed them out to bemused staffers. Alongside this, we also produced a book called 'The Truth About Boris'. We had originally intended this to serve as the pretext for a tube advertising campaign as a way to challenge the rules about political advertising. After all, Ken had his picture all over the tube promoting his autobiography. However, Boris over-ruled us, rightly concluding that he couldn't sanction such a blatant attempt in his role as Mayor and Chair of Transport for London.

The final element was to be the 'Not Ken Again Express', a fully liveried battle bus sent to tour every part of London, with activists distributing leaflets and copies of the 'Truth About Ken' book. Nothing was left to chance. With both candidates polling around 40%, a major part of our plan had to be trying to bring Ken's vote down.

Going over the top

As we approached the end of February the already frenetic pace of the campaign was stepped up. We were reaching the point where you start to feel the waters lapping around your mouth and flicking your nose. We were about to embark on the most exciting part of the campaign – the point at which most normal people start to notice there is an election looming. Having heard the main arguments and issues on auto loop for months, it was hard to believe that there were people who hadn't heard them at all. It gave us all an energy boost. Everything was to play for.

Over the last few months, we had been working flat out to get the material ready that would re-enforce our core narrative and give us something new almost every day for the final 44 days. The political team and I had spent many long nights wading through reams of information on Ken's record on everything from grants and tax rises to personal credit card spending. We had compiled detailed dossiers on Ken and Boris that meant there was nothing we couldn't instantly rebut or counter attack. We were to kick everything off with a 72-page progress report, which listed every one of 2008 manifesto pledges and gave an honest assessment of whether the pledge had been met. We had the 9-point plan ready to launch and a file of Ken attack stories so bulging that, in the end, we didn't have time to use them all. The policy team had taken a blank sheet of paper and filled it with seven manifestos worth of new commitments. Everything was ready.

At the first mayoral debate of the campaign – hosted by Age UK on 21st February – Boris got a taster of how hard Ken would continue to fight to get back into City Hall. Livingstone started the debate by theatrically producing a piece of paper that was his signed pledge not to do more than one job if he was elected. He marched from the lectern to the table at which Boris was sat and whacked it down in front of him, telling the audience he'd left a space for Boris to sign. He spent the rest of the debate savaging Boris on everything from accusing him of being incompetent to his unfortunate comment in 2009 that being paid £250,000 a year to write his *Daily Telegraph* column was "chicken feed". At one point, Ken drooled; "As Mayor I got by on £140,000... if you cannot live on £140,000 you must have a very interesting lifestyle..." Dripping with innuendo and bile. Livingstone had been in top gear for over a year and it showed.

The week ended with a drinks party at Boris's house for the City

Hall and campaign teams. Boris was in jolly form, bounding around the place urging everyone to eat the giant slab of Brie that had been provided for the occasion. It felt like an end of term party, everyone more relaxed than expected thanks to the sheer relief of knowing that the election was almost finally upon us. I surveyed the room at one point and reflected that I could be witnessing history - the last gathering of the Tory administration of London.

Boris gave a rabble rousing speech; almost shouting a series of questions at those gathered. "Do you want to see the return of the bendy bus...?" He was clearly pumped up and when he gets that competitive glint in his eye you know he's up for the fight and determined not to lose. When he gets under pressure, he performs.

A small group of us were left at the end. Boris was, by this stage, very jolly indeed. He leant against the kitchen counter, still pushing Brie on us. We shared jokes about the last campaign, and Boris gave a fine impersonation of Tex, when he had mistakenly given a presentation about how to defeat 'Kevin Livingstone'. It was like the final party before the dawn raid over the top. There was no turning back now.

Meanwhile, Ken Livingstone was about to give us the gift of a lifetime.

CHAPTER SIX

TAX, A BLUE ANCHOR AND THE FINAL 44 DAYS

MARCH 2012 – APRIL 2012

Taxman

In much the same way that lunar cycles affect the behaviour of certain mammals, so with most politicians, once every four years a brief three-month window opens when they suddenly become hypersensitive to the concerns of the electorate and act accordingly. It is an all too fleeting glimpse of what a contented voter/politician relationship looks like. Both sides are listening and responding to each other.

Boris started March a man transformed. He launched his 9-point plan with gusto, giving a rousing speech on 3rd March to the Conservative Spring Forum (a small, annual event for party activists). He warned of the consequences of London falling under the control of "a bunch of newt-fancying, tax-dodging, bank-bashing hypocrites and bendy-bus fetishists". He spoke about how he was a man who had; "….built half a bridge. I can see the other side. I can see what needs to be done." He was so on message, it was like the audience was a particularly complicated lute that he made playing look easy.

The 9-point plan was mocked by some sections of the media who, despite loudly complaining that the election was light on substance, seemed rather fixated on the fact that there wasn't a tenth point. (It just so happened that all the things we wanted to highlight were in 9 points. We didn't start from the premise that he needed a set number of points.)

The 9-point plan was widely talked about. For the first time in this election, Boris was coming across as a man with a plan on the issues that mattered. Even though our key voters didn't necessarily recall every point, they saw that Boris had a clear plan for a second term, and the sum of these parts resonated. After all, we weren't chasing the votes of Pinot Grigio swilling, North London dwelling, pinko members of the media elite – as a certain Australian might put it.

The 9 points reflected the priorities that Boris had set – what he had done and what he was going to do. Each point was couched in terms of a work in progress:

1. Cutting waste at City Hall – freeing up £3.5 billion for services

2. Putting £445 back in your pocket by freezing the Mayoral share of council tax

3. Creating 200,000 new jobs over the next four years

4. Making our streets and homes safer with 1,000 more police on the beat

5. Restoring 300 acres of green space and planting 20,000 street trees

6. Investing £221 million to transform local high streets, supporting small businesses

7. Ensuring a true Olympic legacy – 11,000 new homes and 10,000 new jobs

8. Reducing Tube delays 30% by 2015. Building Crossrail and orbital rail to link our suburbs. Extending the Bike Hire scheme.

9. Securing a better deal for London from No 10

It was my job to make sure the plan was robust and added up. We started from a set of issues that voters cared about, but it would be no use coming up with a vague list of half promises. In order to really convince voters, we needed a plan that not only communicated Boris's achievements, but gave specific detail about his plan for the future.

I embarked on a process of trying to boil down the reams of information on Boris's achievements, and turn them into something concise and easily communicated. I also insisted the figures were closely scrutinised to make sure they would withstand a media onslaught. This would be vital – many a political announcement has fallen apart because the details haven't been subjected to the Stasi treatment before publication. The night before the announcement, I was the last one in the office, personally checking every detail of the 16-page briefing that accompanied the plan and covered every detail the team would need in rebuttals.

It was the first time that Boris's achievements had been presented in this way. For example, with the commitment to create 200,000 new jobs, City Hall had frequently pointed out how many jobs individual schemes would create – 32,000 through the transport upgrades, 10,000 at the Olympic Park etc – but these were never added together into one commitment. Similarly, the money spent on various schemes designed to improve town centres had never been added together, nor had the council tax freezes been expressed as a monetary figure. A seven-page achievements document produced by City Hall had been boiled down into nine pledges that fit on one poster.

Just as Boris was warming up into vote seducing mode, a story broke that would give our campaign a prolonged boost and have profound consequences for the outcome of the election.

On 26th February 2012, *Daily Telegraph* journalist Andrew Gilligan broke a story alleging that Ken Livingstone had been using a perfectly legal loophole to pay less tax than he otherwise would have done. In itself, it would have been a relatively minor story with little follow up. Except that Ken Livingstone was no dyed in the wool capitalist. He was a vociferous campaigner against wealthy tax avoiders. Writing for *The Sun* in 2009 (part of the Murdoch empire he claimed to abhor), Livingstone said; "These rich bastards just don't get it. No one should be allowed to vote in a British election, let alone sit in our parliament, unless they are paying their full share of tax.[34]"

He had also loudly supported the campaign group UK Uncut (who campaign against both legal and illegal tax avoidance) and had attacked Boris as an apologist for the super rich. Indeed, his entire campaign was based on the dividing line that Boris only cared about protecting the interests of the tax avoiding rich, whereas Ken cared about protecting ordinary Londoners' interests. And now he had been caught doing the very thing he, apparently, found so outrageous and immoral. It was a slam-dunk case of eye-popping, breathtaking hypocrisy.

Gilligan established that Livingstone had set up a private company called Silveta Ltd, by obtaining the accounts that had been filed at Companies House. At a first glance it all seemed above board. Ken had gained a lot of lucrative work after losing the mayoralty in 2008, such as hosting a radio show, giving speeches and writing a book. It appeared that the company had been set up to handle these new aspects of his life. All perfectly reasonable, the layman might conclude. Except when you stop to consider why such an arrangement might have been made in the first place. After all, there were only two shareholders – Ken and his wife, Emma Beal. There didn't appear to be any employees. And the amounts going into the company were not trivial. In 2009, the year after he lost City Hall, Silveta Ltd recorded profits of £232,550.[35] In 2010, the company recorded profits of £284,580, with cash in the bank amounting to £319,478.[36] It was speculated that if Livingstone had been paid the money directly, he would have had to pay the then top rate of income tax at 50%. By having the money paid into a company instead, any profits would be taxed at the much lower corporation tax level of 20% or 21%. This would leave him paying less tax than many of the hard working Londoners he claimed to represent, pocketing a lot more cash than they could ever hope to.

There were also further legitimate savings to be made by this arrangement. For example, by paying a portion of his earnings through the company to his wife, the Livingstone household would benefit because she would almost certainly be on a lower personal income tax rate than Ken.

Crucially, the accounts showed that Ken had barely drawn out any of the money from the company. This meant that it could just sit there and be taxed at the much lower corporation tax rate. If he drew it out (as shareholder dividends) then he would have to pay further tax on it. But he didn't. As Livingstone himself had said in response to a story about doing exactly the same thing when he was an MP in 2000 (for which he was censured for not declaring the income[37]): "It is only a tax avoidance option provided you're not drawing the money out.[38]" By his own admission the practice was tax avoidance.

So why did this matter? The issue of wealthy individuals using loopholes to pay much less tax had grown as the recession bit. Stories of millionaires paying less tax than their cleaners had enraged the public. Politicians like Livingstone had gleefully jumped on the bandwagon, condemning those who engaged in such practices. It was an issue of fairness. These practices were not illegal. It was just that most people didn't have the luxury of clever accountants to game the system; they earned their salary directly and paid the rate of tax that was due. It seemed like there was one rule for the elite, and one for everyone else.

The conclusion of many was that Ken had been caught red-handed doing the very thing he criticized others for doing. It was deeply hypocritical to be saying one thing and doing another. However, Ken was adamant that he had done nothing wrong.

As in the 2008 campaign over the Lee Jasper affair, Livingstone again responded with furious denial – completely rejecting the charge of hypocrisy. His natural stubbornness, combined with the fact that it was his long-term nemesis Andrew Gilligan doing the accusing, meant his instant reflex was to label the whole thing a smear. He had spent his entire political career refusing to bow to media witch-hunts, as he might put it, and he wasn't going to start now.

At first, the story gained little traction. Londoners hadn't yet fully switched on to the fact there was an election happening on 3rd May, let alone concentrated on the intricacies of Ken Livingstone's tax affairs. But a slow head of steam was building up and it would explode at the worst possible time.

The story was given the oxygen it needed to reach the voters by the anger of Labour supporters. The tone was set by the *Independent's* Matthew Norman in his diary column on 27th February, where he said: 'The latest of Labour's tax and spend heroes to be outed as a limited company is Ken Livingstone....[This] is, we ritually note, perfectly legal. And so is hypocrisy to have you bent double over the lavatory bringing up breakfast.[39]'

Just over a week later, the then *New Statesman* political editor and prominent Labour supporter Mehdi Hasan penned an article entitled; 'Sorry Ken – own up or face the consequences'. He was damning in his assessment of how Ken had handled the story; 'So what on earth was Team Ken thinking? Why did none of the former mayor's aides raise any objections to his legal yet dodgy tax arrangements? The simple truth is this: you cannot run as the populist, banker bashing candidate, the one who backs higher taxes on "rich bastards", if you're quietly channelling hundreds of thousands of pounds of your own earnings into a company jointly owned with your wife. You just can't.[40]'

Hasan was vocalising what many Labour activists and MPs were saying privately. They weren't surprised that Ken was a hypocrite, but they were astonished that he didn't immediately shut the story down by admitting it was tax avoidance and sending a cheque to the taxman. They could see just how potentially damaging it could be to his election chances, and many feared a re-run of the Lee Jasper story that did so much damage in 2008. As Hasan put it; 'He has to kill this story. And fast.[41]' By this time, well-known political blogger Guido Fawkes had picked up the scent, driving a highly effective campaign against Ken.

For one former Labour parliamentary candidate it was the final straw. In a remarkable open letter on the website *Labour Uncut* he explained, in devastating terms, why he, as a life long Labour supporter could not bring himself to vote for Ken. Jonathan Roberts spoke about how he had walked more miles than he cared to remember for the Labour cause, and stuffed so many envelopes that he had 'single handedly kept my postman in employment.' However, he would not be doing any of these things for Ken. The line-by-line demolition of Ken was so powerful, it is worth quoting at length:

'Your supporters will say I'm disloyal to the Labour Party, but don't seem to mind you campaigning against our candidate in Tower Hamlets.

Your supporters cheered you when you called tax avoiders "rich bastards", but they don't seem to mind the £50,000 you have allegedly avoided yourself.

Your supporters criticise Boris Johnson as a "part time Mayor" for churning out a weekly article for the Telegraph, but they don't seem to mind that you were an MP and a writer for the Independent during substantial parts of your own Mayoral tenure.

Your supporters sing about how you speak the truth, but don't seem to mind how independent fact-checking organisations regularly describe your claims as "fiction".

Your supporters were delighted when you announced you would reintroduce the EMA [Education Maintenance Allowance) for London, giving hope to thousands of kids, but they don't seem to mind that the Mayor has no power to reintroduce EMA at all. Nor do they seem to mind you making a promise you knew full well you would be unlikely to deliver on.

But do you know what Ken? I mind. I do. Your relentless cynicism and negativity is matched only by your hypocrisy. And I mind all three.'

When we saw the article pop up on our screens we could scarcely believe our luck. It chimed perfectly with all the negative feelings the electorate had towards Ken. He had angered his own side so much; they were doing our attack work for us. Indeed, one enthusiastic supporter ensured that every Labour MP received a copy of the letter in their postbags.

For the campaign, the significance of the tax story was not so much that Ken was a tax avoider. It wasn't even that he was a hypocrite. Its real electoral potency was in fuelling the trust issue. That was where the story would do most damage to Ken's vote. Despite Boris's electoral strengths, he still didn't have a compelling 'retail offer' for the voters in an election that Ken had successfully defined as about the cost of living. Livingstone was still enjoying significant cut through with his fares commitment, and every time he got a run on it, we would take a hit. Therefore, we had to try and distract him from his main message by chipping away at stories that highlighted his negative record and the fact he simply couldn't be trusted. We knew we could never match his fares pledge, but we could render it virtually worthless by highlighting the fact that Ken never stuck to his word – on anything. Therefore, once Gilligan had broken the tax story, we set about giving it as much oxygen as possible and framing it squarely in terms of trust. It was to prove a very powerful line of attack.

Labour blogger Dan Hodges very helpfully summed up the impression we wanted to create; 'It's his modus operandi. Say one thing. Do another. Campaign against tax avoidance. Flirt with tax avoidance. Hold more than one job as Mayor. Campaign against people having more than one job as Mayor. Champion gay rights. Embrace a Muslim cleric who advocates the murder of homosexuals. It could be Ken's campaign motto. Do as I say, not as I do.[42]'

It was around this time that we started hearing his team – fearful of what he may do next – had confiscated his Blackberry. We often wished we could overhear the conversations at Labour HQ. We speculated that if Boris had got himself into that situation, our advice would have been to lance the boil immediately, admit wrongdoing and send a cheque to the taxman. Was that was Ken's advisers were urging too? Was he just ignoring them, or did they genuinely believe he could ride it out? Perhaps they had simply underestimated the potential damage the issue could do? Had they learned nothing from the 2008 campaign? Thankfully for us, it appeared that they hadn't.

On Sunday 11th March, Ken Livingstone was interviewed on the *Andrew Marr Show*, the agenda setting political talk show on BBC One. Despite the criticism from his own side, Livingstone stuck to his guns. Looking as if he were a mother being accused of baking an apple pie, he declared; "I'm in exactly the same position as everybody else who has a small business….." Andrew Marr, not betraying the incredulity he must have been feeling as a sane, rational human being, put it to Ken that "the real reason for the company is to avoid paying income tax." Again, Ken artfully swerved; "No, no, everybody who is not directly employed by someone has to have somebody to manage their accounts. You set up a company, the money all comes in, the accountant sorts it out." He refused to accept the premise of the question by arguing that setting up a company to handle your earnings was perfectly normal and he had done nothing wrong. He declined to mention how much income tax he had paid. And then, as Ken so often does when he's backed into a corner, he tried to counter attack with as straightforward a falsehood as has ever been asserted on national television. Looking nervous, Ken claimed: 'But the simple fact is the hypocrisy of all of this is Boris Johnson had exactly the same arrangements to handle his earnings from television,' strongly implying that Boris was using the same methods to avoid tax. It was a neat little trick; tarring Boris with the same brush would re-affirm voter cynicism in all politicians and take the spotlight off Ken.

When he heard the accusation Boris was furious, phoning Crosby straight after the broadcast and ordering him to make clear that Ken was lying. It was true that Boris was a shareholder in a company created to handle his TV work before he was Mayor – but crucially Boris was always paid directly for any work he did, meaning this arrangement was manifestly not for the purpose of avoiding tax. Boris knew that Ken could be outrageous, but such a blatant lie left him apoplectic with rage. It was a rage that wouldn't subside, and would later end up providing a memorable and defining moment of the election. The issue would rumble on right up until polling day.

The day after Ken's interview, the media went to town on him. *The Sun* ran the tax story and in a further bid to humiliate him, ran a photo of the former Mayor standing outside his house wearing only trousers and braces, with no top. Caught unawares by the photographer, he looked like a local crazy, with the sort of faintly hostile look that recommends you cross to the other side of the road. Furthermore, the *Evening Standard* ran a front-page story about how Ken's fare policy would ruin TfL's finances; 'Ken's fare cut damned by the City'. It was damaging to Ken's only policy and exposed its fraudulent nature.

That morning, Crosby marched triumphantly into his office, grinning like a Cheshire cat. He proudly laid out the news clippings on the table and promptly declared; "We're really fucked now!" Ever mindful of complacency, he ruefully observed that you don't get such a good run in the media for free (through an unrelenting campaign communications effort to frame the election about trust).

Crosby's caution was merited. The campaign had scored a good run of tactical victories over Ken throughout early March. We had, throughout the campaign, received regular and numerous leaks from different sources within Labour. In fact, the leaking was of the same magnitude as in the 2000 mayoral campaign, where Ken was standing as an independent and Labour was desperate to stop him winning. Much as No.10 had leaked their private polling to the Steve Norris campaign then, now we got large sections of Ken's 'warbook', including key elements of strategy, major announcements and how many supporters they had in certain areas.

In early March, we had received intelligence that Ken's official slogan was to be 'Better off with Ken'. We cheekily pre-empted it and launched it as 'Better off with Boris'. It had caught them so completely by surprise that they were forced to launch their slogan early and could only circulate a computer image of their campaign bus, emblazoned with the slogan, because the real bus wasn't ready yet. Such game playing was an important part of the psychological war we were waging on our opponents. We wanted to take every opportunity to dent their morale and force them to divert from their plan, wasting valuable time putting out fires we had created.

Yet as satisfying as these individual victories were, the election race was still on a knife-edge major challenges remained.

By mid March internal polling put Ken ahead by 51% to 49%, with turnout in inner London increasing and doubts about Boris's competence depressing turnout in outer London. Crosby felt that even though Boris was improving, it was impossible to win unless we changed this perception. More importantly, Boris still didn't have a clear pledge on the cost of living and it was obvious this was costing him dear. It was an issue that David Cameron had raised directly with Boris in a meeting in mid February, pressing him to say what his 'retail offer' was. Following the meeting, it was reported by *The Times* that the Prime Minister was 'underwhelmed' by Boris's response.

As it happens, Boris was being deliberately cautious. In tough economic circumstances, he felt it would be deeply irresponsible to make a series of uncosted pledges. He only wanted to pledge something if it was right for London, and he knew that the timing of any populist pledge (on council tax, for example) would be critical.

Go too early, and voters may well have forgotten it by election day.

Boris thought long and hard about the cost of living issue. He was frustrated that voters couldn't see that Ken was selling them a dud, but he understood why they were willing to take the risk. He wanted voters to understand that no politician could credibly pledge to cut fares and maintain investment. The money wasn't there to do that. He also felt that Ken (and the Labour Party nationally) had a defeatist argument on the economy. It presumed that the economy was past saving and that the function of Government should instead be to focus resources on protecting the various client groups reliant on the state. It was an approach of battening down the hatches and hoping the storm would pass. By contrast, Boris felt that taking the tough decisions now and being almost pig headed about investing in the things that will pay off long term was a fundamentally optimistic response to the recession. He passionately believed that the function of Government was to be pro-active and to drag the country through the storm, kicking and screaming if necessary. It was a powerful argument, and potent in terms of framing the choice. Boris was optimistic and forward-looking. Ken was pessimistic and had no plan for the future.

However, by relying on this argument alone we were in danger of winning the debate but losing the election. Throughout March, the same internal meeting was had again and again. Each time, no one could come up with a satisfactory answer. It would run something like this; Boris would return from a campaign event demanding that we do something, following a haranguing about the cost of living. We would then debate how much he could cut fares by, before eventually concluding that he would have to cut investment and he wasn't prepared to do that. We would then debate by how much he could cut council tax, before Boris would complain that any cut would be worth less in monetary terms than a fare cut and it would leave him with little money for important second term initiatives.

Each time, it would prove a very difficult dilemma to resolve.

In these meetings, we reminded Boris that he should never accept the premise of Ken's argument. Council tax cuts versus fare cuts should be viewed in honesty terms, not monetary. Ken was effectively offering nothing, because he would never keep his promise. Boris had a record of keeping council tax low and would deliver.

The debate raged on throughout March and eventually Boris took decisive action. He reasoned that the only responsible thing he could do would be to cut council tax. He had a good reputation on the issue, and it was something that affected virtually every Londoner. It particularly affected pensioners, who were a key target group. It also had the added bonus of contrasting with Ken's record of increasing council tax by 152% over eight years. Lister – the man who had delivered the lowest council tax in the country at Wandsworth – would spend the next few weeks trying to find room in the budget for a big enough council tax cut to matter. If anyone could do it, he could.

The final 44 days

On Saturday 17th March, Crosby summoned the entire campaign team into the office for his traditional eve of battle pep talk. On Tuesday 20th March the official election period would begin, we would have full control of Boris' activities and the battle would intensify. Boris would walk into our office as a candidate, not just the mayor. It was the phase of the campaign we had planned meticulously for and looked forward to the most. After this there was no turning back. Many of us couldn't believe it had finally arrived.

Crosby had ordered boxes of bright blue shirts with 'team member' slogans for everyone to wear. Before he began his speech, he pulled on one of the shirts and instructed everyone to do the same.

I looked around and for the first time I noticed just how big the team had become. It seemed like just a few weeks ago that a handful of us had taken possession of this vast office space in Savile Row. Now, the room was overcrowded with two to a desk. One wall was covered with rows and rows of trays, where volunteers deftly sorted postal votes around the clock. In the middle of the room stood an industrial sized shredder – with everyone under orders to shred anything, no matter how insignificant. (Although he could never prove it, Crosby was fairly sure there was a Labour mole somewhere in the office.) Boxes of leaflets occupied every available bit of floor space. It was an impressive, slick operation. It had to be, if we were to beat Ken.

Once everyone had their regulation shirts on, Crosby summed up the state of the race so far. It was going to come down the wire. Boris was almost universally liked, but this didn't necessarily translate into votes. Londoners were finding it tough, and they were extremely receptive to any prospect of relief. Even though they didn't like Ken, many were willing to take a risk on him if it meant a chance of lower fares. It meant that we had to raise the importance of the risk and remind people what they would be returning to if Ken won again. However, he cautioned, we wouldn't win the election just by attacking Ken. Because Boris was liked, people were willing to hear his message. They wanted to hear a specific plan for the future, and a clear sign that he would fix things in the long term. Therefore, we had to constantly talk about the 9-point plan and how we were on a journey. Everything we did and said needed to re-enforce the main campaign narrative;

'This election comes at a critical time. Londoners are going through one of the toughest periods in recent memory. Despite this there are signs of progress which have resulted from a fresh and honest approach at City Hall. But at the Mayoral election on 3rd May this progress is at risk. The

return of Ken Livingstone means a return to waste, high taxes, broken promises and Bob Crow and his cronies back at City Hall.

Don't leave your future to chance. Back the energy and optimism that will truly drive London forward.'

He told us that although these would be the toughest 44 days of our lives, they would also be the some of the most enjoyable. We had to remember that we were part of something important, and that what we did together would influence how our city was run over the next four years. He warned us to always admit mistakes early so they could be corrected with minimal damage, take no notice of the polls or media advice and raise concerns with him not journalists (ultimately there was not a single leak from our campaign). Above all, the most important thing to remember was that we were there to serve Boris. He deserved our unswerving loyalty and dedication for one reason above all else – he was the one with the balls to put his name on the ballot paper to be judged by millions of his peers. That takes guts and bravery. He finished with an appeal for us not to regret anything. Don't wake up the day after the election having lost, and feeling you could have done more.

As I walked home that night, I nursed a quiet confidence. Although the latest internal poll put us behind, I knew we had the material to keep Ken on the defensive every one of the remaining 44 days. We had spent months honing our plan for this moment. Every day was accounted for. We knew what we were going to announce, when and where. We were in much, much better shape than this time four years ago. And we would keep chipping away at the edifice of Ken until it crumbled.

With friends like these....

We didn't have to wait long until the first big test of the election period. We had known for some time that the national budget would be announced on Wednesday 21st March. Negotiations between City Hall and the Government had been fierce, and Boris had pushed hard for as much extra money as possible. Chancellor George Osborne – aware of the political significance of the mayoral election – had made clear to Boris in private that he would do as much as he could. When Osborne stood up to deliver his budget speech to the House of Commons, we already knew that London would get an extra £70 million for economic development. It wasn't a colossal sum by any means, but it re-enforced our argument that only Boris could bring home the bacon.

However, this good news was to be dwarfed by what followed. And it almost sank our entire campaign.

The political debate in the run up to the budget was dominated by tax. As worries about economic growth persisted, Osborne had come under heavy pressure from backbench Conservative MPs to cut taxes in order to relieve the financial burden on people and stimulate demand. In particular, there was a vociferous lobby that demanded the removal of the 50p income tax rate.

Introduced by the previous Labour Government in 2010, it was a measure that meant people paid 50% tax on all earnings over £150,000. It was seen at the time as a populist 'tax on the rich' and a way for the previous Government to show that everyone would have to pay their fair share to help the country get back on its feet. The Conservatives disliked the measure, as they believed it would drive wealthy individuals away from the U.K at a time when our economy needed investors who could create jobs. Boris in particular was a staunch opponent, arguing that London would lose it status as a major financial centre and loudly campaigned for its removal. However, when the Coalition Government was formed, it was

155

decided that cutting the 50p rate was not a priority. No.10 worried about being seen to cut taxes for the richest, whilst cutting back public spending and welfare benefits to the poorest. However, Chancellor George Osborne had always made clear he considered it a temporary rate.

Many Tories believed that the tax would raise much less revenue than Labour had predicted, owing to the fact that wealthy individuals would simply find a loophole in the system to avoid it (much, in fact, as Ken appeared to have done). A review by Her Majesty's Revenue and Customs (HMRC) vindicated their argument; the tax was raising much less money than originally predicted. As the budget approached, it became clear that Osborne was gearing up to cut the 50p rate. The scene was set for an almighty row about the fairness of cutting tax for the richest, the true impact it would have on the economy and what other taxes the Government would increase instead. Liberal Democrat politicians had spent weeks virtually negotiating in public with their Conservative coalition partners, and were demanding a series of trade-offs to ensure the wealthy were contributing in other ways, through a 'mansion tax' for example. At times, it seemed more fractious and complicated than the deal to form the coalition in the first place. And it was to have profound consequences. The negotiating had absorbed so much political energy that little thought was given to the consequences of small but contentious details within the Budget, resulting in weeks of political chaos afterwards that – combined with other difficulties – would see the Conservative poll-rating plummet.

Because so many details in the budget had been leaked, such as taking some of the lowest paid out of tax altogether, there was little positive news to talk about after the announcement. Virtually all that was left for the announcement itself was bad news. The morning after, therefore, the media and the Labour Party went to work.

First up was the so-called 'granny tax'. It was a proposal to phase out the 'age-related allowance', which allowed pensioners to start paying tax at a higher income level than workers. You could tell officials had originated the proposal, because the explanation for it was that it was a "simplification". Ministers didn't seem to be able to provide an understandable rationale for it. Unsurprisingly, most of the papers that morning heavily criticised the Government.

That morning, Boris was extremely worried about the impact of the negative coverage and viewed the 'granny tax' as a direct attack on his electoral base. He had been blindsided like everyone else. And he was right to be worried, if we were to stand a chance of getting back in, we needed older voters to turn out and vote on election day. This was giving them a very good reason not to. He wondered whether attacking the Government would insulate him from the political danger. As he headed out from his home in Islington to his first campaign event of the day in Wimbledon, there was a heated debate about the merits of doing so.

Guto Harri felt strongly that Boris should seize the opportunity and show his voters that he was opposed. He knew that such an attack would dominate the news, and show Boris leading the charge. However, Crosby felt that an intervention would hurt us. He argued that it would merely fan the flames and drag the story out further. We didn't know how big an impact the 'granny tax' would have. We knew it would be unpopular; the last thing we wanted was for it to dominate days (and possibly weeks) of media coverage. A Boris intervention – even though he was opposed – would ensure a prolonged row with potentially fatal consequences for the campaign.

As Boris arrived in Wimbledon, Crosby and Lyon advised that he should say it wasn't his budget and focus instead on how he had delivered the 24-hour Freedom Pass (which entitled pensioners to free travel on the tube and buses). Journalists put him under intense pressure as he met enthusiastic commuters (an oxymoron in any other context). Pippa Crerar from the *Evening Standard* asked him six times about the granny tax, and six times Boris refused to rise to the bait.

That morning demonstrated how stressful a campaign is for the candidate. Such was the tight schedule, Boris ended up doing radio interviews on his phone in the car park of Wimbledon station, simultaneously resisting pressure to attack the Government and smiling to commuters wishing him well. It was a bad day for the Tories, who were becoming more unpopular than ever. And here he was, the Tory candidate for Mayor, being greeted like an old friend by strangers. It was a reaction he got everywhere, no matter what the area or type of person. He is frequently cheered by white van men in particular, honking their horns, leaning out and shouting; "Boris!" as they whizz by.

(Sometimes the attention would get so much that he would frequently duck into second hand bookshops on the campaign trail to clear his head, leaving his aides to carry piles of well-thumbed copies of obscure literature. As the campaign wore on, the pile of books in the office grew steadily taller.)

When Boris returned to the campaign office in mid morning, the issue was still weighing heavily on his mind. He was genuinely unsure about attacking the Government and he could see how damaging a row could become. Although voters hadn't raised the issue with him, plenty of journalists had and he was finding it hard to hold back. He felt that the Government had scored a massive own goal and were threatening his re-election chances. Number 10 was alert to the possibility that Boris would intervene. Almost as soon as Boris had arrived at the campaign office, Cameron was on the phone trying to persuade him to stay out of the row.

Crosby and I waited outside Boris's private office as the two men talked it through. The conversation lasted for some time. Eventually, Boris called us in and he asked us what we thought he should do. Crosby repeated that wading into the row would only inflame the situation and alert more voters to the issue. Boris replied that Cameron had urged him not intervene, making much the same point as Crosby. Boris accepted it was just too risky to escalate. Whereas in the past he would have got into a big political row that would have been interpreted as yet more positioning for the leadership, this time Boris focused on his own message and distanced himself from the Government by staying out of the story. It was a symbol of how the campaign had taken control of the communications strategy, and staying out of rows with the Government would continue right up until polling day.

The incident demonstrated how the relationship between Cameron, Boris and Osborne really works. The media would have you believe that they are in a constant state of war, flicking barbs up and down the Thames from their respective riverside strongholds. Behind the scenes, however, they are always talking via a constant stream of text messages and phone calls. A professional respect exists between them. Indeed, they have been well co-ordinated ever since they entered Parliament together in 2001, sharing many of the same views and understanding, in a realpolitik way, that they each have considerable strengths. Each man knows where he stands. It is as close to a genuine triumvirate, in the Roman sense, as you are likely to find in a modern political party.

Over the following weeks, the media picked apart the budget like ravenous hawks, generating political rows about a 'pasty tax', 'caravan tax' and a tax on charitable giving. The Government's approval rating plummeted and the Conservatives' hard won reputation for economic competence vanished almost over night. It was widely judged as the Government's worst few weeks since it came to power. Boris and the campaign team observed the whole spectacle with ever growing frustration and disbelief. There was a giant blue anchor, and it was firmly tethered to our ankle.

Ken Livingstone wasted no time in going on the offensive. After a difficult few weeks, this was a golden opportunity to link Boris with the unpopular measures by virtue of his support for the abolition of the 50p rate. It was widely perceived that things like the 'granny tax' were linked with the scrapping of the 50p rate. People believed that the Government was trying to fill the gap with new 'stealth' taxes. It gave Labour the perfect line; the Tories were cutting taxes for millionaires and increasing them for pensioners/pasty eaters/caravan owners etc.

A week after the budget, Livingstone's campaign leaked an 'internal memo' that signalled a switch in strategy (a classic tactic – faking a supposedly secret memo for a media hungry for stories about process). Ken's field director Patrick Heneghan wrote;

'....after a difficult period, last week's budget has given us a golden opportunity that we must take. The budget and more specifically, the "granny tax" have the ability to make the election campaign change tack.....[it] shows that the Tories are out of touch; it is funding the 50p rate cut that Boris campaigned so hard for. If we can get our campaign right in the next few days then we have a real chance to move the main narrative of this election away from Ken's taxes and onto what Boris and his Tories [sic] friends have done to older people.'

Our own research confirmed their analysis. In focus groups a week after the Budget, although Boris's 9-point plan was getting through and was well received, there was anger at the 'granny tax' proposals that threatened to swamp our positive message. The reaction confirmed that if Labour could tie Boris in with the Government, we would be in real trouble and Ken would be back in the game. Thankfully, the voters weren't blaming Boris. Yet. But the mess the Government had got themselves into would prove to be an almost irresistible drag on Boris's vote. If Ken were to succeed in making the election a referendum on the Government, we would be at great risk of losing control of the terms of the campaign.

And then they stepped into a lift...

It had seemed like Chancellor George Osborne may as well have presented the budget to Ken Livingstone wrapped in a pretty bow with a box of chocolates and a troupe of dancing girls. However, the budget held significant dangers for Ken too. It put tax at the forefront of the political debate. More specifically, it re-charged the debate about wealthy tax avoiders at the very same time that Ken's name was linked with the issue. At precisely the moment when Ken should have been hammering us on the Government's unpopular taxes, he was once again dragged back down by a problem entirely of his own making. He was about to hand us an even bigger gift, with a prettier bow and a man-sized box of chocolates.

The first live broadcast debate of the campaign was scheduled to take place on LBC radio on 3rd April, moderated by Nick Ferrari. At first, we had been reluctant to agree to debates because we were determined to involve real voters as much as possible in more 'town hall style' debates instead of the stage-managed affairs that usually occurred. The LBC debate – with ordinary Londoners phoning in – presented this type of opportunity.

In the run up to the debate, Crosby scheduled intensive preparation time to put Boris at ease. We put Boris through his paces, firing tough questions at him, interrupting him with the kind of barbs that Ken Livingstone would throw at him. Although he hated debates, he showed in these sessions that he had considerably improved over the four years. He was confident in the detail. In fact, he knew so much, that he often had trouble being concise and would often veer off on interesting but irrelevant tangents. His planet-sized brain could not be boiled down to the killer sentence that he would need in a debate. As he put it himself in one of these sessions; "I never know when to stop."

The challenge was different from four years ago. Then, he needed to show that he could match Livingstone for the detail and come across as a credible alternative. Now he was the incumbent, he had to defend his record as well as attack Ken. There had already been two meetings between Boris and Ken. Neither was televised and we knew from both that our biggest challenge was getting Boris to keep his cool in the face of Ken's provocative attacks.

At one of the previous debates there was a foretaste of what was to come, when Ken had again accused Boris of setting up a private company to avoid paying the full rate of tax. After the debate, Boris pulled Ken aside and calmly told him that it wasn't true and asked him not to use it again. Like the gentleman he is, he believed that would be the end of the matter.

In the final prep session, we ran through what Boris would say for his opening statement, which would be strictly capped at one minute. We decided to go straight in for the kill and define the election in terms of trust. Boris's opening line captured the essence of his message and decanted it into a dainty little bottle: "This election is about trust. It's about who you trust to be honest about where the money is coming from and how is it going to be spent." He was relaxed and confident. And he was motivated. When Crosby asked him why he was running again, Boris – in an attempt to relieve the tension – replied: "because I can't stand Ken."

The Sunday before the debate, we had ensured that Ken would be on the back foot. The campaign research team and I had spent months digging through obscure City Hall documents to establish the true extent of Ken's spending on his City Hall credit card while he was Mayor. Boris had refused to use a corporate credit card, rightly judging that it was still Londoners' money, and had sacked former Deputy Mayor Ian Clement for abusing one. We felt it would be a very nice contrast. After a Conservative Assembly member had asked the right questions of the officials – who kept the data – we were handed a treasure trove. We had, in full glorious Technicolor, an itemised breakdown of everything Ken spent public money on over his eight years in charge. For a political team with the explicit objective of dumping as large a bucket of manure over Ken's head as possible, this was nothing other than divine revelation. It wasn't so much the total amount of spending that looked bad, it was the relatively inexpensive individual items he felt the London taxpayer should fund. He spent £256.98 on a pair of shoes for a trip to the exclusive Swiss resort of Davos, £135.94 on a desk lamp, £41.25 on a shirt and £1.89 on a cup of coffee. He wasn't a poor man, so why did he feel the need to bill the London taxpayer for such small items?

The story had clearly riled Ken, because during the LBC debate the following Tuesday he spoke with the combativeness of a man who had just been stung by a wasp on his buttocks. The debate was fractious from the start. LBC had invited Ken, Boris, the Liberal Democrat candidate Brian Paddick and the Green candidate Jenny Jones. Despite Nick Ferrari's best efforts at playing peacemaker, the debate very quickly descended into four spleens being simultaneously vented. Like a geeky version of a food fight, statistics were hurled across the studio until they became indistinguishable; truth emulsified with lies, dripping down the walls into a soggy mess on the floor.

The debate lasted a full hour with nothing particularly revelatory. Just towards the end, however, a caller named Steph from Sutton lit a small fuse and placed it in the middle of the studio; "Ken, in a recession, where we're all feeling the pinch, what makes you think that London wants a mayor candidate who avoids paying his taxes?" The campaign office cheered at this point relieved that Ken's taxes had made it into the debate. Livingstone stuck to his dogged defence, insisting that he paid income tax on everything he earned (artfully leaving aside the issue of how much he had paid) and dismissing the evidence as nothing more than smears. Nick Ferrari gently pointed out that it wasn't a smear to say Livingstone had used a private company for his media work; "It's not a smear, it's the truth." Ken replied; "Yes, but to say it's a tax avoidance thing isn't." He then went on the offensive, accusing Boris of having personally benefitted from the Chancellor's decision to cut the top rate of income tax. Boris hit back hard, calling Ken's tactic "reprehensible".

And then, with a well-rehearsed turn of the screw, Livingstone again accused Boris of effectively doing the same thing. The exchange was one of the most bad tempered of the campaign, and no transcript can truly convey the ill feeling. Set against the backdrop of the other two candidates trying to interrupt, Ken masterfully turned the screw tighter and tighter, ignoring Boris's pleas to stick to the truth. Boris was left in the breathless rage of a man who had just been told that day was in fact night, and up and was in fact down:

Ken Livingstone: *The simple fact here is that Boris and myself are in the exact same position-*

Boris Johnson: *No I'm sorry that's a complete lie. The man's a liar!*

Ken Livingstone: *We both had media earnings, we both put them through a company-*

Boris Johnson: *No! That's not true, I'm sorry. The guy's a liar. The guy's a bare faced liar! He really can't be allowed...*

When the debate finished, Boris was in a fury. Boris could accept Ken misrepresenting his policies. What he couldn't accept was Ken repeating something that he had been told, categorically, was not true. All four candidates followed a staff member from LBC into the lift to the top floor for a photo-call. They crowded into the enclosed space and the doors closed.

When the doors opened again on the top floor, the four candidates walked out as if nothing was amiss. They posed for the photo-call, the strained smiles no different from the usual expression of rival politicians forced to pretend they are friends. After the photo, as they gravitated to their entourages, Brian Paddick approached Sam Lyon and warned that Boris was "shaken" and that he had had an argument with Ken in the lift. Lyon pulled Boris aside and Boris told him that he was angry. After they left the building, Boris explained to Lyon what had happened.

In the campaign office, a few moments later, Lynton Crosby pulled me aside. Apparently, as soon as the lift doors had closed, Boris squared up to Ken and called him a "fucking liar" three times in quick succession. Ken was so stunned, he couldn't reply. Boris would later say that Ken looked sheepish in response. Like the bully he was, Ken didn't like it when confronted.

For months afterwards, the LBC studio had a sign on the wall that said 'no fighting in the lift'.

When Boris returned to the campaign office he was in a calmer mood. He regretted losing his temper, but was unapologetic about the language he used. To him, it was a clear-cut case of Ken over stepping the mark. Ken was saying something he knew not to be true. That could not be allowed to stand. In another age, the matter would have been settled with a duel on Hampstead Heath.

The story soon exploded. The *Evening Standard, BBC London* and *ITV London* all went big on it. We were relatively relaxed about how it would play with the voters. On the one hand, it was further fuel for the media narrative that the election was just a battle of two big egos. We knew from our research that voters certainly felt this way, and many were getting sick of the Boris and Ken show. On the other, this was another day where the story was about Ken's tax arrangements and his duplicity. It wasn't about fares. And it showed that Boris was a man who wouldn't allow someone to get away with murder. More importantly, it put the issue of trust at the forefront of the election, precisely where we wanted it.

The tax returns

A week later, the four candidates gathered at the BBC Television Studios in White City for the re-match. The stage was the *Newsnight* debate with Jeremy Paxman. It was the debate that changed everything.

There was no re-run of the battle in the lift, or 'liftgate' as the media had dubbed it. Instead, Boris was calm, on message and on top of the detail. By contrast, Ken was more grouchy than usual. He was unsettled by Brian Paddick's highly effective attacks on the tax issue, and wholly unused to having to defend himself against a Liberal Democrat, with whom he usually ganged up against the Tories. The attacks were clearly getting to him. Before the debate, the campaign launched 'Ken-go'; bingo cards with his false claims that supporters were encouraged to fill in during the debate. Whoever got the most 'Ken-gos' would win. In his closing statement, Ken inexplicably urged Boris to sack Crosby as his campaign manager because he was running a negative campaign. Paxman looked at him in disbelief.

After the debate, Livingstone approached Crosby and said it was nothing personal. With a smile, Crosby introduced him to Ed Lister; "the man you called the Mladic of local government." Before he had time to answer, Ken's people whisked him away, presumably for fear of what he might say next (this would become a familiar pattern at each debate; Ken's minders almost never allowed him to stay and have a drink with his rivals.) Evidently, Crosby's name check in the debate had impressed one candidate – Jenny Jones (Green) approached him afterwards and asked if he would consider working for the Green Party, apparently in all seriousness.

Jones had provided the debate's defining moment, when she challenged all the candidates to disclose their tax returns in order to settle the row about tax once and for all. Of course, everyone immediately agreed – not wanting to be the odd one out. Livingstone was particularly gung-ho, trying to make it seem like Boris was reluctant to reveal his earnings;

Boris Johnson: *Whatever is necessary to publish I'll publish*

Ken Livingstone: *Was that a yes or a no Boris? I'm happy to publish details of everything I've earned in the last four years. Are you going to do the same?*

Boris Johnson: *Of course I will.*

Ken Livingstone: *Good that's easy.*

As the *Newsnight* credits rolled, we debated the merits of being the first to publish. It was an unprecedented situation. The publishing of tax returns was not common practice in British elections, and no politician had ever voluntarily published theirs. Where would it lead?

At 6am the following morning, Sam Lyon received a message from the *Evening Standard* saying they would hold all the candidates to their word. At the 7am strategy meeting, the debate continued as we poured over the transcript of what was said and what was actually committed to. Boris immediately concluded that he would have to publish and Crosby concurred. Both he and Fullbrook saw the opportunity. They knew that the more open we were, the more open Ken would have to be. And we were in no doubt that Ken would come out looking worse. We felt that this time, we really had Ken in a corner.

Crosby got the necessary information from Boris's accountant. Jenny Jones and Brian Paddick were first out of the blocks, publishing full details of their earnings and tax before 10am. When Boris's figures came through it was as we expected. He had earned a lot over the last four years, but he had also paid a lot of tax. Just over half a million pounds in fact. Crucially, he hadn't diverted money through a private company. It was entirely above board.

When he was shown the figures, Boris was surprised that he had paid so much tax. We joked that he was too honest for his own good and that he needed better financial advice (perhaps Ken's accountant, it was suggested). Amid the gentle mocking, he seemed relatively calm, saying with a certain amount of dignity; "well, that's how this country works." The comment reflected the values that drove his administration and his campaign. He felt it fair game that those who earn more pay more in tax.

At 11am, we published the figures, which left Ken as the last man standing, despite his bravado the night before. As silence wafted over from the Livingstone camp, we sat around and waited for Ken to come clean. As we waited, we speculated as to the options available to him. Surely he couldn't wriggle out of this one? His commitment the night before had been crystal clear. If he wavered even slightly, his campaign would be sunk.

Coming under increasing pressure, Ken initially tried to stall, getting his campaign director to issue a pompous letter saying he would only disclose his details once all the candidates had revealed their spouses earnings. They tried to argue that this was relevant because the tax row had involved Ken's wife. It was a smokescreen and the delaying tactic did nothing to reduce the pressure.

Just before 2pm, Ken finally relented and published. As we scrutinised the figures, we realised that, unbelievably, Ken was trying to wriggle out of his commitment. He had promised to publish details of "everything I've earned in the last four years." But the rather amateur looking spreadsheet we were looking at only contained a fraction of the true picture. He had only given details of the money he earned from his private company Silveta Ltd. However, we knew from Companies House records that Ken had significant earnings that went into Silveta Ltd and had stayed there as part of a cash pile of around a quarter of a million pounds. He had already admitted to Andrew Gilligan that his clients paid the company, not him personally[43]. The figures we were looking at clearly didn't include these earnings.

As with all these things, Nick Dines (opposition research) had made a point of checking the document closely. Leaving nothing to chance, he checked the document properties to see if the author was named (as is usually recorded in the electronic file). Ken's team had been sloppy and left the original author's name on the file. It was Mark Watts, one of Ken's former City Hall staffers and certainly not a registered accountant. It purported to show that Ken had paid an average tax rate of around 36% - lower than his rivals. But given it left out the money going into Silveta Ltd, and was authored by a crony, it was neither reliable nor credible.

As Gilligan put it; 'We can't in fact say exactly what tax rate Ken has paid – he hasn't given us enough information – but what we can say is that since losing the mayoralty he has paid a substantially lower rate than any of his rivals, and a substantially lower rate than the vast majority of ordinary Londoners whose votes he's seeking.[44]'

This was a 'Lee Jasper moment' all over again. Just like the 2008 campaign, instead of shutting the story down, he was trying to divert attention with half-truths and misinformation. It just meant that there were still more questions to answer, when what he should have been doing was moving on.

The media coverage of the disclosures was more balanced than we would have liked. The Right went to town on Ken's hypocrisy. The Left focused on how much Boris earned. As ever, the BBC went with the Left's angle. Commentators on Left and Right condemned Ken. Many Labour people on sites like *Labour Uncut* saw straight through Ken's duplicity and were similarity damning. The whole episode had a big impact on morale within Labour. The story would drag on right up until polling day.

We were delighted, in so far as this was another lost opportunity for Ken. It meant another few days where he couldn't talk about fares. It would give us the ammunition to keep pushing the story hard – but at arms length. As soon as Ken published, Crosby insisted that Boris move straight on to talking about his policy agenda, because there were risks for us too.

The media reaction over the following weekend confirmed that the election was seen as nothing more than a personal grudge match between Boris and Ken. It meant that the media were no longer interested in the policy announcements from either side. Just as Ken was prevented from talking about his positive issues, so were we. A personal spat would do nothing to convince our wavering voters that they should vote for Boris. For many, this incident would be the first time they were even aware an election was approaching. We felt that voters needed more than confirmation of Ken's hypocrisy. Our primary focus needed to be Boris's positive agenda for London. And in the background, we would hammer Ken on tax for all it was worth.

That weekend, with three weeks to go, I reflected on where we stood. We had pulverised Ken of late, constantly putting him on the back foot and preventing him from talking about his most effective issues. Labour morale was low and many of his own supporters were writing off his chances. However, it was equally clear we had not sealed the deal. And while Ken was being written off in the press, he was quietly organising his heartlands, getting those postal votes filled out, distributing scaremongering literature and hammering the line that this election was a referendum on the Tories. He had given us a lifeline, but we were under no illusions – there was much to do and nothing was in the bag.

The final weeks

On Monday 10th April a poll by ComRes put Boris four points ahead. The media claimed it was a reaction to 'lift gate', and it was certainly true that the survey took place at the time it happened. Anecdotal evidence suggested that people were more likely to view Boris favourably after the incident; it said something positive about his character and re-enforced the view that Ken was deceptive. Crucially, the *Standard* went on what we thought the key finding was – 48% were now less likely to trust Ken as a result of his tax affairs (and his credit card spending as Mayor). We had succeeded in framing the tax row about trust, and it was hurting Ken on his signature policy.

Ken's behaviour was becoming ever more erratic. At his manifesto launch the following week he made a very theatrical show of crying at his own campaign video. The video purported to be of ordinary Londoners saying why they were voting for Ken. The crescendo to the video was each person saying; "Come on Ken, you can do it!" When asked why he had cried at the video he gave a cringe worthy response about the "huge responsibility" of running London. The picture of his tear stained face made the front page of the *Evening Standard*. At the debate that evening hosted by the paper, Ken came under more pressure about his tax affairs. Paddick went on the offensive, and the largely left-wing audience booed Ken's lacklustre response. Yet again, the headline from the debate was Ken's tax.

The following day, a story emerged that some of the so-called ordinary Londoners in Ken's campaign video were not entirely speaking from the heart. After being accused of using actors in the video, Ken's campaign team were forced to admit that the participants had actually been hired by an ad agency, paid expenses and were scripted[45]. What's more, Ken knew this before the launch.

As if that weren't enough, more diligence on our part had established that Ken's team had tried to quietly amend the financial return he had released after the *Newsnight* debate. When his original return was published, Nick Dines had made a point of taking a screen grab of Ken's website, to make sure that we would be able to spot any changes. It was exactly this kind of thorough approach that gave us the edge in these tactical battles. Sure enough, carrying out a regular check of Ken's website, Dines spotted they had changed the amount he had earned in 2008/09 from £21,645 to £63,390. It would later transpire that he did this because they had forgotten to include his pay off from City Hall when he lost the election. We pushed the story hard through third parties. Another day, another run of stories undermining trust in Ken.

By now, Boris was firmly in his stride. He was focused and determined. In debate prep sessions he needed very little practice or advice. Seeing Boris at the very top of his game is perhaps one of the most thrilling and rewarding sights in British politics. He's simply electric. He becomes a political Dyson, elegantly and efficiently hoovering up every last voter. He was so on message that the media became increasingly exasperated with him. This was amply demonstrated when Rod Liddle, cigarette in hand, interviewed him for the *Sunday Times* website after a campaign event and was reduced to pleading with him to give a funny answer about Ken crying. Boris resolutely refused.

The final issue we needed to resolve in order to seal the deal was Boris's 'retail offer'. By 15th April Ed Lister had finished squeezing the bureaucracy and made a 10% council tax cut over four years stack up financially. Crucially, the big trade off had been averted. He could find the money without hurting the police budget, which comprises a large part of the mayoral budget. It meant making more aggressive savings in a second term, but Boris judged the electoral impact to be worth it. We would finally have something to match Ken's offer.

10 days to go

On Monday 23rd April, YouGov released a poll that put Boris narrowly ahead of Ken, by 51% to 49%. It also showed that the Conservatives were now 19 points adrift from Labour in London. Even though Ken's personal ratings hadn't improved, it was clear Labour voters were returning to him. Our ship was in remarkably good shape, but the blue anchor dragging it down looked to have continuing momentum.

Boris and the team were in despair. We had fought hard to put Ken on the back foot and take maximum advantage of his mistakes. We had a strong message and a positive agenda for London's future. Yet it could all count for nothing, thanks to the Government's standing. Ever since the botched budget, Boris and Crosby had been receiving almost daily messages from No.10 apologising and asking what they could do to help. In response, more than one member of the campaign team remarked; "They could shut up".

As we discussed the latest poll, Boris gave a wry smile in response to our ranting. He put forward the theory that deep down Cameron and Osborne would be disappointed if he lost, but not for the reasons we thought. The real reason, he explained, was because they preferred him "boring on in City Hall" and out of their hair. This was particularly true of Osborne, he pointedly reflected. It was the briefest flicker of a hint of his wider political ambitions – even more striking because he would rarely raise the subject. Often, Crosby and Harri would tease him about it in briefing sessions, to which he would allow nothing more than a coy, slightly embarrassed smile. His analysis certainly had a point; it would be difficult for Boris to return to Parliament before the completion of a second term as Mayor. The triumvirate may have open channels of communication, but at the end of the day they're still rivals.

We resolved that all we could do was keep hammering our positive themes on the one hand and make sure Ken's taxes were still being talked about on the other.

Although we were nervous during these final days, if Boris was he didn't show it. As we waited in the green room before the final live TV debate of the election on *ITV*, Boris stood outside gathering his thoughts. The other candidates seemed to ease off too. Ken Livingstone held court amongst the assortment of other candidates and advisors; loudly bemoaning the loss of a political drinking culture and how it had made politics a duller affair. He jovially explained that he could drink a bottle of wine and the only person that would notice any difference would be his wife.

After the debate, Boris and those of us with him decamped to a nearby steakhouse and had dinner. He was feeling confident and relaxed. It was one of the rare times that we had all switched off for a moment and just enjoyed each other's company. Boris opened up quite a bit, expressing his admiration for Ken as the most resilient left wing politician of his era. Although he disliked him, he respected his opponent.

Boris also spoke very openly about what he wanted to achieve in a second term. He spoke as if the prize was in touching distance. Not complacent, but secure in the knowledge that the hard work was paying off. At one point, he spoke passionately about using the mayoralty to intervene more in education and about how the riots were a direct result of an attitude that accepted too many underperforming schools, particularly in poorer areas. He was excited about what he could achieve. All he needed was for Londoners to vote for him.

With a week to go, the opinion polls gave us breathing space for the first time. ComRes put us 8 points in front, although we kept telling ourselves that it would be much closer because the polls had consistently over-estimated turnout (this one suggested 57%). Crosby put it into perspective; "Mate, this is coming down to hand to hand combat in the muddy trenches." The Conservatives had fallen to 20 points behind Labour in London. It was probably accurate to say we were hanging on by our fingertips. Early postal vote turn out suggested we were holding up reasonably well, but turnout was down in some very important areas. Boris's final public debate with Ken was at the London Citizen's 'Accountability Assembly'. It was a hostile audience (like last time) but Boris came out unscathed. After the debate, I asked Boris what he thought of it. He replied that he thought the reaction to Ken was "valedictory", with his trademark cheeky grin.

With only days remaining, we were delighted that *The Sun* had given the tax story one final push. They had gone to an independent accountant to estimate how much tax Ken would have saved, based on the all figures that had been made public. They estimated he had saved up to £220,000.

The penultimate poll of the campaign (by YouGov) put us four points clear. The *Evening Standard* finally gave Boris their endorsement, running the editorial on the front page and giving him a generous double page spread outlining his policies. Over the final weekend, the sight of senior Labour figures attacking Ken, including Lord Sugar who wrote a scathing piece in *The Sun*, greatly heartened us. He had tweeted to his 1.2 million followers earlier in the campaign 'I seriously suggest NO ONE votes for Livingstone in the Mayoral elections[46].'

We were feeling de-mob happy. The office had rapidly emptied, as all available manpower was deployed to the target areas. The mountains of leaflets had gradually disappeared, as Crosby ordered everything out and into voters' hands. Aware of the closeness of the race Crosby and Fullbrook followed the instructions they had given and headed out to leaflet commuters on their way home at Fulham Broadway tube station with a final appeal.

Like heartburn, we were trying to ignore the rising feeling of confidence that it would be all right. Yet there was still evidence on the ground of Labour pushing hard. They distributed four costly personalised pieces literature over the weekend before polling day, whereas we had volunteers out delivering in the rain. The end of term feeling had crept back into the team, but were we about to be hit by a nasty shock on Thursday 3rd May? That was the nagging doubt within. And the frustrating thing was our destiny was not in our own hands. All policies announced, all attack stories done. The big unknown was just how far had the Government's unpopularity dragged us down? Labour had, by this stage, expurgated Ken's name from their material. Their message was clear; on 3rd May send a message to David Cameron and the Tories.

In a final push, Labour had got the BBC to try one last time to disrupt Boris. Tim Donovan (BBC London political editor) had run a spurious story about how Boris had lobbied News International to sponsor the bike hire scheme during the Metropolitan Police investigation into allegations that their journalists had hacked the mobiles of public figures and ordinary people. Inferring a conflict of interest that was entirely baseless, it was in my view transparently partisan story and typical behaviour from the supposedly neutral BBC.

Thankfully it disappeared into the general noise of an election campaign that was fast approaching a thrilling conclusion.

CHAPTER SEVEN

JUDGEMENT

3rd - 4th MAY 2012

Getting out the vote

The beauty (or perhaps curse) of democracy is that there is only so much a political campaign can do. We expend a huge amount of energy in order to maintain at least the appearance that we can control our destiny. Ultimately we submit our fate to the voters who, like the Roman emperors casting judgement on the gladiators, will either turn their thumbs up or down. We have no idea, really, which way they will go. And that's what makes an election campaign so addictive and so gut wrenchingly ghastly in equal measure.

In the final days the campaign office, once so bustling and buzzing, quickly shed its identity. The boxes of leaflets had all been cleared out. The posters and war room maps were gone. The giant shredder was puffing away on overtime as mountains of paper were fed into it. The only people left in the office were Crosby, Fullbrook, Lyon, the digital team and I. Everyone else was ordered onto the campaign battle bus, on a tour of the target areas in outer London. During the last 48 hours, Boris virtually lived on the battle bus, working hard to get every last vote out.

Ours was the HQ that no longer had a purpose. We had traveled that familiar curve; from powerless to powerful and back to powerless again. It was now in the hands of the voters to decide our fate.

The day before polling day, I shredded all my remaining papers, packed up my things and headed home for a rare early night.

For many others, and me Thursday 3rd May 2012 started with a dawn raid. I was up at 3.15am and even though I had gone to bed at a very sensible 9.30pm my sleep was light and restless. It was a bit like that fitful sleep you have as a child the night before the big summer holiday, where you steal glances at the alarm clock, willing it to wail at some ungodly hour so you can begin that middle of the night trek to the airport.

Even though we had all worked our fingers to the bone over the last 6 months, the work we were about to embark on was what really mattered. If the voters in our good areas did not come out, we would lose the election – no matter how good a campaign we ran, the leads in opinion polls, Ken's gaffes or media support. None of it would matter unless our vote came out.

I arrived in Bromley at 5am and was greeted by an eclectic mix of local activists handing out bundles of leaflets and maps. Each person was given a particular street to cover. Our aim was to deliver all the leaflets before people would start leaving for work.

The purpose of the dawn raid is to make sure a powerful leaflet is waiting on your voter's doormats when they leave for work in the morning. It is the leaflet that delivers your final message to them before they go and vote. It must convey the thought you want them to have in their mind as they walk up to the polling booth, pick up the pencil and decide where to drop its tip. Ours was very simple. On the right hand side was a picture of Boris with a blue background under the heading 'future'; on the left hand side was a picture of Ken with a red background under the heading 'past'. The text at the bottom read; 'Your vote on Thursday 3rd May will make the difference.' On the reverse was Boris's 9-point plan. The leaflet reflected our message in the final days. The election was about London's future and a straight choice between Boris, who would take London forward and Ken, who would be a return to the past.

The atmosphere in Bromley at 5am was strangely beautiful. The streets were deserted and the air was full of birdsong. A light mist of drizzle fell, making the pavements shiny under the streetlights. We quietly went about our delivery, creeping up crunchy gravel driveways and gently slipping leaflets through heavy letterboxes – praying not to wake anyone up.

As the light came, it became clear this was going to be a grey day. Our worst fears had come true. The light was dim and the drizzle persisted. On rainy miserable days, voters have yet another excuse not to go and vote. When you're trying to convince wavering supporters to come out and vote, rain is the last thing you need. It was quite a contrast with the bright sunshine of four years ago. We marched down long roads with large houses and substantial driveways, wondering what on earth we could do to coax the Tory vote out.

About 8am we ran out of leaflets, so we found a small café on the high street and had a wonderful fry up. Hot tea and mounds of toast fortified us, and we headed back out determined not to let the rain get us down. As we ate, the final *Evening Standard* poll came through – it had us winning by 6 points. I wasn't pleased though. It was yet another signal to our core supporters that the election was in the bag, and they had no need to come out.

For the rest of the day, we knocked on our supporters' doors to remind people to vote. The response was mixed. Quite a few said they had already voted. But many others said that although they liked Boris, they were angry with David Cameron and the Government. They didn't know if they were going to vote at all. Gradually it dawned on us that, even in this relatively small sample, we might be in trouble. This was Tory country. If they weren't enthusiastic here, what chance did we have elsewhere?

We pushed on until early evening, grabbing snacks and cups of tea whenever we could. Pure adrenaline overpowering fatigue. I spoke to Crosby and Lyon throughout the day to get a feel for what other areas were doing. All the reports seemed to be the same – the Government's unpopularity was keeping many of our voters at home. The news spurred us to overcome our tired legs. We pounded the streets for hours. We were cold and tired. But we were driven and determined to get as many people out to vote as possible.

At about 7pm, after doing one last leaflet run at Beckenham Junction station (a dispiriting affair, we were largely ignored by tunnel vision commuters), the team I was with called it a day. I had timed it so I could get back to my polling station in time to vote in person. I got there about 8.30pm and it was very busy. Bermondsey has a strong Labour vote, and that worried me even further.

I returned home exhausted. I showered, changed and headed back out to our post close of poll drinks party. When I arrived, everyone was in a good mood – relieved that the campaign was finally over. The overwhelming mood was one of happiness. Everyone felt they had given their all. We shared anecdotes of campaigning, and interrogated each other on what had happened with turnout. Some tales were good, others bad. The truth was, no one really knew.

Boris gave a short speech, in which he thanked everyone for their hard work – giving a particularly warm thank you to Crosby, who looked uncharacteristically emotional. He said the Tories would be bonkers not to get Crosby to run their 2015 General Election campaign, at which Crosby exaggeratedly shook his head. Boris then observed how we had survived the Budget, rain, BBC London and – cheekily – David Cameron's endorsement to get this far. We all roared with laughter. Then, he jumped down to the dance floor and started a rather strange boogie that involved all manner of facial contortions. I resigned myself to the fact that, this time, he had earned the right to embarrass himself as much as he liked.

I thanked my team, sank a glass of red wine and headed out – just as the younger volunteers were getting into full swing. I was full of exhaustion and elation in equal measure. I had been awake for around 22 hours and was desperate to crawl into bed. But I was anxious. The votes wouldn't be counted until the next morning, so we would have to wait at least another 24 hours to find out if our efforts had paid off. Had we truly bucked the national trend? Had we got our people out? Or had Ken pulled off a famous victory?

The results

The process for working out who has won the mayoral election is needlessly complicated and drawn out. This adds a layer of tension and uncertainty that is simply unbearable, as the media attempt to work out what is happening and then explain it to people in a way that isn't Swahili.

The votes are taken from each local polling station and collated at three regional vote-counting centers across London. The votes are then counted by scanning machines. As the ballot papers stream through these contraptions, large TV screens at City Hall (and the *London Elects* website) show the overall progress that is being made, as well as an indication of which candidate is ahead – represented by colour coded bar charts. Frustratingly, they don't tell you the actual numbers until the results in each of the 14 GLA 'super constituencies' are declared. This means you only have a rough idea of how you're doing, nothing more than that.

Once every constituency is declared, they count the first preference votes for each mayoral candidate. If no candidate has more than 50% of the vote, the top two candidates go into a second round. This involves counting how many 2nd preference votes each one has been given by people who voted for another candidate as their first preference. So, for example, if you voted for Jenny Jones (Green) as your first preference and Ken Livingstone as your second preference, the latter vote would be counted as part of Ken's second preferences. If you voted Boris first and Ken second, this wouldn't count. The 'legal' second preferences are then added to the first preferences to find out who of the top two candidates has the most votes. This person is then declared the winner.

I knew from the 2008 election that the results would take a long time to filter through. I took the opportunity for my first lie-in in months. When I woke up I was calm, but on the inside my head was thumping with an anxiety-induced headache. The fat lady was perched on my cranium, and the pressure wouldn't relent until she sang.

I knew we had done everything we could to ensure victory. We had kept Ken's campaign on the back foot throughout the final weeks. Boris had been excellent as polling day approached; his mountain-sized intellect had been concentrated into a high intensity beam that was pointed directly at the electorate. His final media appearances had left journalists exasperated, as he answered virtually every question – no matter how mischievous – with "I have a 9 point plan…" The whole team had worked their socks off, and virtually no mistakes had been made. Every recent opinion poll bar one had put us in the lead. And yet, there was a nagging feeling echoing out from the pit of my stomach.

At around 3pm I left the house and walked over to City Hall. It's only a 15-minute walk from where I live, but it seemed to take forever, each step taking me closer to the grand finale.

When I arrived at the Hilton hotel opposite City Hall (where we were to be based), I met Crosby, his wife Dawn, Ed Lister, Mark Fullbrook and Sam Lyon. There was a high state of nervous tension and very little was said.

We all went upstairs to the suite where Boris and his family were. As I entered the room, I felt the tension rise suddenly. There must have been about ten people in the room. And although it was quite spacious, it felt claustrophobic with so many people. There was only so much space for each individual to pace up and down without colliding with someone. We were like a tank of sharks, seemingly on collision course, only to gracefully divert at the last second – all without expression. Boris sat on the sofa, his eyes glued to the TV screen, quietly taking it all in.

At that stage in the afternoon, all we had to go on was a bar chart on the *London Elects* website, which merely showed who was ahead and how many votes had been processed. It showed that Boris was comfortably ahead of Ken and it was being reported that Ken's team had all but conceded defeat. The media had concluded that Boris had won comfortably and it was only a matter of time before the official numbers confirmed this.

Although obviously nervous, Boris was in relatively good spirits. He took a good luck phone call from David Cameron, who seemed to be trying to find out what Boris would say in his victory speech. I overheard Boris trying to re-assure him that he wouldn't dump on the party and that of course, the Prime Minister (not that he ever calls him that) would be invited to the victory party.

Boris started canvassing for ideas for his victory speech. He joked that he would praise Ken, and say that they should have that drink he promised four years ago on the condition he never runs again. He also joked about taking him to the nearest lift. This helped eased the tension a little. Everyone in the room was also calmed by a collective belief that – surely – we had pulled it off.

The jollity didn't last long. A very worrying narrowing of the gap on the *London Elects* bar chart started to appear. Although we were still in the lead, it was beginning to look very close with the majority of votes still to be counted. It was looking like we were about to be overtaken. To add to the tension, we got calls from Conservative Party officials at the counting centers saying at least two Tory London Assembly members were in danger of losing their seats. Did this mean our vote had collapsed in those areas as well? The BBC then went from saying that Boris was sure to win, to describing the race as too close to call. This concentrated everyone's minds.

Crosby was particularly nervous. I don't think I've ever seen him so uncertain. He was tearing up the carpet as he paced up and down the room, briefly returning to his laptop to check the bar charts, before leaping back up again.

In between these bouts of pacing and checking, he mused about the awesome power of democracy and it's ability to leave us political hacks weak, powerless and frustrated. Exactly, I suppose, what voters feel like in between elections.

Boris observed how beautifully destructive the whole thing was, and I think he felt a bit in awe of the system – even though it could ruin him. It's at times like this I thought to myself that you really have to respect anyone standing for elected office. Whatever we may think of politicians, whatever japes they get up to, you have to admire the sheer bloody bravery of putting themselves through the ultimate judgement like this. We all obsess about what people think of us; imagine putting that question to millions of voters? And imagine if our jobs relied on a positive answer? I could never do it, and I can't even begin to imagine how he really felt as we waited for the result.

We knew that we needed at least a million votes to be sure of re-election, which meant our focus was on the total number votes we received in each of the 14 GLA constituencies and how this number compared to 2008. It didn't matter whether we had 'won' or 'lost' each constituency, as the final result did not depend on which candidate has won the most constituencies. We were solely focused on getting to our million-vote target.

Data analyst Eric Sukumaran had set up a counting system based on comparing our vote in each constituency with our score from 2008. We would be able to calculate the exact margins we would need as each result came in and the situation evolved. It was our final attempt at convincing ourselves we had some control over our destiny.

The first concrete numbers from the GLA 'super constituencies' started to trickle in around 4pm. The first one to declare was Merton and Wandsworth – an area we expected to do well in. Thankfully, Boris's vote had held up well compared to 2008, falling just 183 votes short of the total he got in that area in 2008 and comfortably beating Ken. This was despite a decline in turnout of 7%. By contrast, Ken was about 9,000 votes down on what he got in 2008. The machine that Ed Lister had built up in Wandsworth over the years had served us well.

This was followed in quick succession by Bexley and Bromley – our safest area and one where we had to pile up as many votes as we could. Although Boris comfortably beat Ken, turnout was down by 11% and we had shed 17,000 votes as a result. However, Ken had also fallen back by about 3,000 votes. This greatly sobered the room. Such a big fall in turnout in such a crucial area for us was not good news. It meant we were relying on Ken's good areas to suffer similar falls in turnout, something that couldn't be guaranteed. It seemed the disillusionment I had experienced on the doorstep in Bromley was making itself felt in the results.

The result was such a concern that Crosby said with all seriousness that he thought we could lose. Even Fullbrook, who was usually the most optimistic man in the room, was looking a little pale at this point. Boris was staring hard at the figures in silence.

Then, my phone bleeped and we had another set of results. Everyone crowded around the computer as I read out the figures for Croydon and Sutton. It was another must-pile-'em-high area. Again, we were seeing the air seep out of the balloon. Turnout was down 14%, and we had shed around 7,000 votes on last time. Ken had held his own, adding a few hundred to his 2008 score.

We reminded ourselves that although these results were disappointing, we were still some 120,000 first preference votes ahead of Ken. But a pattern of Tories staying at home was beginning to emerge and it was making us very nervous indeed. We were in the lead, but Ken's good areas were still to come in. He could overturn our lead. Boris's head was spinning with numbers, and he kept asking us what it all meant. It's hard to tell your candidate that his lead could turn into a deficit at any moment.

Then came Greenwich and Lewisham, the first of the Ken

strongholds where he needed to pile up the votes. This would be our first indication of whether Ken's turnout was similarly dented. It was, but not by as much as ours. Alarmingly, although turnout was down 6%, Ken's vote held up, growing by a few hundred on last time. By contrast, we had fallen back by around 7,000 votes.

We comforted ourselves with the fact that Ken needed to do a lot better than add a few hundred votes in his good areas if he was to overturn our lead, which now stood at around 101,000.

This initial flurry was completed by Havering and Redbridge, another vital part of outer London we had to turnout in large numbers. Yet again, like everywhere else, people were staying at home. Turnout dropped by 9% on last time, and our vote declined by around 13,000 votes. Ken had added a few thousand votes to his 2008 total in this area despite the fall in turnout, which further darkened our mood. Although looking back, it shouldn't have done, given our lead had gone back up to around 120,000 votes.

It was at this point that Boris, Crosby and Lyon headed over to City Hall to prepare for the final declaration. There was a rumour going round that the declaration would happen imminently. Election nights are often fuelled by rumour, and I still felt we were a long way from the result. They headed off and Fullbrook, Dawn Crosby, Sukumaran and I stayed behind to crunch the numbers. I would feed our analysis back to Crosby as the numbers came in.

The BBC started claiming that Ken was in with a chance of winning, even though his spokespeople were conceding defeat. I stood with eyes glued to my phone, waiting for the next email from Chris Scott, the field director who was at City Hall getting the raw numbers before the media.

An agonising half an hour dragged by until another bleep jolted us from our pacing. We all rushed over to the table where my phone showed the results for Lambeth and Southwark – another Ken stronghold. Please, please let the turnout be low, I said to myself.

A glimmer of light – turnout was down by 5% and Ken had received 1,000 fewer votes in this constituency since 2008. We were up by 100. This was encouraging – if Ken couldn't rack up the votes in a place like Lambeth and Southwark, then there was no way he was going to claw back the difference. That said our lead had fallen back to around 95,000 votes.

This was quickly followed by West Central, one of our bastions, which includes Kensington & Chelsea, possibly the most Tory area in the country. This time the fall in turnout saw both Boris and Ken lose votes on last time. Yet again, it was another case of a Tory stronghold failing to deliver. Although our lead had crept up to around 140,000 votes, had we delivered enough in our strongholds to offset the big gains Ken would make in his? We still had City and East to come, which included Tower Hamlets. This was the constituency where we expected Ken to receive over 100,000 votes alone.

In Ealing and Hillingdon it was a similar picture; turnout down, our vote down and Ken's vote up. The sad news had also filtered through that Richard Barnes, the Tory Assembly member for the constituency and one of Boris's Deputy Mayors had lost his seat – a victim of national Conservative unpopularity. Crucially, Ken was failing to make up the ground he needed, our lead went up to around 150,000 votes.

Then came the result we feared – City and East. As expected, this delivered a shed load of votes for Ken. His vote in the constituency was up by around 11,000 on 2008, giving him a life saving 106,000 odd votes to add to his overall total. To make matters worse, our vote in this area was down by around 7,000 votes. Our overall lead had narrowed to 91,000 votes.

The story was unfolding in a way that looked very ominous. Tory turnout down, Labour turnout up. The only question was whether it was up by enough to overturn the lead we had established.

Nine constituencies had declared, which meant there were five still to come. Of those five, one could be considered a Ken stronghold (North East, which includes Hackney and Islington) and one a Boris stronghold (South West, which includes Richmond). The remaining three were too close to call.

By about 6pm, I was getting very negative messages from Crosby who was by now ensconced in Boris's office in City Hall. The mood had apparently darkened after the City and East numbers came in. Boris was fearing the worst and reports emerged that some advisors had started packing up their belongings. Crosby shared their pessimism. We all knew that our slender lead was under threat, given that most of our supposedly good areas had already been declared. It was entirely possible that Ken could overturn the lead and sneak in by the narrowest of margins. We braced ourselves for the worst.

Boris's wife Marina and their kids had popped over to the hotel suite briefly, and she was anxiously looking at the numbers on our screen. She asked me what I thought. I gave her my honest assessment; no one expected Ken to be so competitive at this stage, but we had to remain optimistic because he had only one more good area to come in (North East) and we still had one more good area to come (South West). If we could get a good turnout in South West, we would safeguard our lead. I told her I felt it was too early to throw in the towel, and that Ken still had a long way to climb.

When we got the South West result at around 6.30pm, it was a Godsend. There was a fall in turnout, but it was much less than other areas and we received over 90,000 precious votes. We had increased our vote in the area by around 2,000 votes, whilst Ken had fallen by around 6,000 votes. This was a fantastic result. The South West constituency has always gone the way of the winner in each of the four mayoral elections there have been. It always used to be a Ken stronghold because many people in that area tended to support the Lib Dems and voted tactically against the Conservatives. Right from the start, we were very nervous about what the collapse of the Lib Dem vote since the coalition would do in this area. It wasn't unreasonable to assume that many disillusioned Lib Dem voters would go back to Ken.

Crucially, this hadn't happened. Our lead was back up to around 130,000 votes. It was the safety margin we desperately needed.

The drama continued with the news that the automatic counting machines had started eating ballot papers at one of the counting centers, meaning officials had to stop the process and start counting them by hand. A polling station in Brent and Harrow had also briefly mislaid some ballot boxes. We were told not to expect the result from this constituency until at least 9pm and in the event it didn't emerge until much later. We settled ourselves in for a long night.

Next up, at around 7.30pm was Barnet and Camden, a split constituency with Barnet normally favouring Boris and Camden normally favouring Ken. Despite the sitting Conservative Assembly member losing his seat, Boris had bucked the party trend and added a thousand votes to his 2008 score. Ken had fallen back by around 5,000. We were starting to gain ground again, and our lead was up to around 150,000 votes

With 11 of 14 constituencies declared, it was now down to North East, which included the Labour strongholds of Hackney, Waltham Forest and Islington. Ken needed to win, and win big if he was going to claw back the lead we had built up.

My phone buzzed at 8pm with the North East results. It was another huge win for Ken, giving him 106,000 votes – 6,000 more than last time. We had fallen back by 3,000 votes. The nerves were back, as our lead was pulled back to 107,000. With just two constituencies left to declare, did Ken have enough left in the tank to catch us?

At this point Crosby was feeling more optimistic. The mood in City Hall seemed to have improved, so much so that pizza was ordered and Boris had set-up an impromptu 'whiff-whaff' game, using books as a net. Crosby confided to me that he thought we would just about make it.

Half an hour later we got Enfield and Haringey, 13 of 14. Again, Ken performed better than expected in what is another split constituency, adding around 2,000 votes to his 2008 score as we slipped back by around 8,000 votes. Our lead narrowed to 90,000.

This was at 8.30pm. We had one more constituency left to declare, Brent and Harrow. An unscheduled sprinkler test had blown the electrics at one of the counting centers, meaning we wouldn't get this result until 11.30pm. All we could do now was wait.

So we waited and stared at the numbers we did have, speculating as to what would happen. There were two main factors at play. First, we knew that we were ahead on first preferences and that in all likelihood we would still be ahead after Brent and Harrow. It was another split constituency, meaning it was extremely unlikely that Ken would beat us there by 90,000 votes or more. Fullbrook estimated that we would still be ahead by at least 60,000 votes, based on what happened in that constituency in 2008. Second, we were very unsure about what would happen with second preferences. This was important. Ken couldn't overtake us on first preferences, but he might just nick it on second preferences.

As each result was declared, they also revealed the total number of second preference votes the candidates received. On the raw numbers, we maintained a small lead on second preferences too. However the raw numbers we had weren't necessarily going to be the final ones that counted, which added to the uncertainty. This is because many second preference votes get knocked out in the 2nd round. For example, if you voted Boris first and Ken second, your second vote for Ken would get knocked out and vice versa. Also, a surprisingly large number of people vote for the same candidate twice.

We knew that the knock out rate was about 50%, based on the results from last time. On that basis, we were pretty confident we would win – but it would be agonisingly close. And no one felt confident enough to assert our victory.

The wait was horrible. We ate, ordered wine and paced up and down. The empty punditry on TV grew tiresome, as political reporters exhausted the ways to say they had no idea when a result was expected or what would happen.

Every so often I would field a call from either Crosby, Lyon, or someone back at the win/lose party in Millbank. Same question, same answer. I didn't know.

We were waiting for the one result that would confirm once and for all if we had scraped over the line, or if Ken had managed to catch up. It would all come down to Brent and Harrow. It was stomach churning. In a situation like that, the pressure feels like a sumo wrestler with deep fried Mars bar issues pinning you down. I looked out of our 12th floor suite into the night. Outside London was getting on with its Friday night, oblivious to the little drama happening beside the Thames. The second hand on my watch was dragging itself in slow motion.

Finally, at around 11.30pm, my phone bleeped. I was immediately jolted out of my tiredness. The all-important result from Brent and Harrow was in. I slowly and carefully read out the numbers to Sukumaran, who entered them into his computer. We crowded around him. Turnout was down, Ken's vote was marginally up and ours was marginally down. Most importantly, our first preference lead was still a healthy 82,000 votes – more than Fullbrook had estimated. Now we had all the numbers and frantic calculations began on what would happen with second preferences. Did Ken have enough to pip us at the post?

The raw numbers were heart stopping. They showed that if there was no drop off in second preferences, we had a total lead of just

324 votes. Everyone in the room gasped when we did the calculation.

We then used the 50% drop out rate that happened last time to calculate a lead of around 55,000 votes. Either way, it looked like we had won – just. I called Crosby and told him that it was good news, but the majority would be anywhere between 324 and 55,000 votes. He relayed the information to Boris. However, we weren't celebrating yet. We still couldn't be sure until the officials had done their own calculations. If we really had won by only 324 votes, that wouldn't be the end of the story. Ken would surely call a re-count on anything less than a lead of around a thousand votes.

Then, about 15 minutes later, the candidates were called to the Chamber in City Hall. In the hotel suite, we gathered around the TV, only half in expectation – we had had a lot of false dawns throughout the night. Just before the candidates went out onto the stage, Crosby sent me a message confirming we had won. But he only had the raw numbers showing a lead of just 324 votes. We still didn't know how close it would really be.

As the candidates walked out, Boris had the faintest hint of a smile lurking beneath a stern exterior. Ken was grinning like a Cheshire cat, which produced a momentary zap of displeasure in the pit of my stomach. The other candidates shuffled by, but such was my focus on Ken and Boris, I didn't even notice them.

The returning officer began speaking. Behind him, Ken's eyes started to glisten. The first preference totals were read out, and they matched our numbers. Then the all important second preference totals came. We concentrated hard;

"Boris Johnson received 82,880… this gives him a total of 1,054,811"

"Ken Livingstone received 102,355… this gives him a total of 992,273"[47]

As soon as the returning office began saying the words 'nine hundred' I let out a bloody great big roar, as did everyone else. There were only five of us in the room, but we sounded like twenty. In that split second, all the pressure melted away. All the tiredness and the stress just vanished. It was like these things were never there in the first place. After the most closely and bitterly fought election of recent times, we had won.

We had achieved our million-vote target and we had beaten Ken Livingstone – the great survivor of British politics – by 62,538 votes. We had done this at a time of deep unpopularity for the Conservatives and with a candidate who, just six months previously, was teetering on the edge of defeat. We had run a campaign based on leaving nothing to chance and extracting the tiniest of margins from everything we did. That work had paid off. Most importantly, Boris would have a second term to see through his work and London was spared Ken Livingstone.

Looking back, my reaction surprised me. It was the thing I most wanted at that moment. It was the thing we had been fighting for day and night, the thing that pre-occupied my every thought and dream. And yet at that moment, I wasn't ecstatic or overcome with emotion. I'd like to say that a wave of euphoria swept over me and I was totally lost in the moment. But I wasn't. The overwhelming feeling I had was one of relief and a deep sense of satisfaction. I had spent many sporting occasions, involving people I didn't care about, getting overwhelmed with emotion. At this moment, where I was intimately involved and much was at stake, I was calm. Quite simply, everything was as it should be. Finally, I was able to release that tiny little feeling I kept locked away in the pit of my stomach for all this time; the feeling that we were going to win. It was a feeling I had worked hard to suppress, to ignore and prove wrong. And now, it was free, fully justified and made real.

Just before midnight, Boris was declared the Mayor of London – again.

Boris delivered his acceptance speech, which was a version of his stump mixed in with some gracious observations about Ken (Boris even invited him to have a drink afterwards) and those Conservative London Assembly members who had lost their seats. Ken's concession speech struck me as being typically graceless and undignified – blaming his defeat on media 'smears'. He claimed this was his last election, but quite frankly I didn't believe him. As we had found out only too well in the reams of research we conducted during the campaign, Ken has made a career of saying one thing and doing another (indeed, just weeks later he was elected to Labour's National Executive Committee).

Nevertheless, his speech was a shame. If this really was his last election, he should have gone out with the dignity of a statesman, not a bitter man.

We jumped into a cab and made our way to what we could now officially call the victory party in Millbank Tower, which overlooked the glittering lights of the city. The city we had re-captured. When we arrived, the atmosphere was strange. It was if we had arrived at a pub just after last orders had been called. People had been at the party since around 6pm and they were mostly very drunk and tired. Many had already gone home. By contrast, we were stone cold sober.

Boris arrived a few minutes later to a rapturous reception. I began the chant of "four more years", which everyone picked up straight away. He waded his way through the admirers and up to the stage. The microphone didn't work very well, so he had to shout to be heard – although by this stage his voice was hoarse. He did a re-hash of his speech the night before, and repeated his line about surviving the Budget and David Cameron's endorsement. It got the same thundering laughter.

I shook his hand afterwards and he gave me a bear hug. I congratulated him on a job well done, and then he was swallowed back up into the crowd.

It was approaching 2am and the bar had shut. I said goodbye to Crosby and the remaining members of the campaign team and stepped into a cab with my wife Robyn and set off for home and a long, much needed sleep. A sleep safe in the knowledge that my job was done, and Ken Livingstone was never to return – at least for now.

CHAPTER EIGHT

EPILOGUE

How the election was won and lessons for the future

The day after results night, Boris attended his second swearing in ceremony as Mayor of London. Unlike 2008 this was a calm, orderly affair. Boris looked more humble this time, relieved that the campaign was over and understanding of the reality that it was a close run thing. His speech was short and business like. His brush with political death had injected him with a sense of focus. There was important work to be done.

Many political pundits were surprised at how close the final result was. All the polls leading up to 3rd May had indicated that Boris would win comfortably. No one expected Ken to perform as well as he did. The immediate judgement was that on a bad night for the Conservatives nationally (other local elections were held on the same day outside London) Boris had bucked the trend and got in on the strength of his personal appeal. By contrast, Ken Livingstone had failed to take advantage of the Labour Party's strong performance, principally because he had alienated many natural Labour supporters over his tax affairs, among other things. Did the evidence bear these conclusions out?

Despite his flaws Ken was still a formidable figure and a ruthless campaigner. Boris had delivered 91% of his promises and had an impressive record as Mayor. In tough economic times, he had delivered for Londoners and had a clear plan for the future. Yet he couldn't quite shake Ken loose and he really had to fight for the victory. General disillusionment with the Government made it tougher to turn key voters out when it mattered.

The overall fall in turnout, from 45% in 2008 to 38% in 2012, disproportionately affected Boris. Turnout fell most in our strongest areas costing us more votes than it did Ken. Our research during the campaign suggested that this was because our supporters were disillusioned with the Government or politicians in general and felt that – in any case – Boris was going to win. Complacency mixed with disillusionment is a powerful sedative when it comes to turnout.

For example, in Bexley and Bromley (our best area in 2008) turnout fell by 11%. As a result, we received 17,000 fewer votes than in 2008. It was a similar story in Havering and Redbridge. Turnout fell 9% and we received 13,000 fewer votes. The biggest fall in turnout was in Croydon and Sutton, where it declined by 14% denying us 7,000 votes. In total, Boris received 72,000 fewer votes compared to his 2008 score. Much of this can be attributed to the decline in turnout in usually rock solid parts of outer London.

Nevertheless, to have overcome the challenge in the way that he did was an extraordinary personal achievement. Boris's instinct right at the start – that delivery on his commitments would ultimately be rewarded – turned out to be correct. Londoners saw that he had done a good job in difficult circumstances, and felt that he had a plan to take the city forward.

Boris was – and has always been – more appealing than his party. The evidence in 2012 demonstrates this. A useful comparator is the London Assembly 'top-up' list vote. This is where voters were asked to choose a party, not a candidate, to determine how many extra London Assembly members each party got. These results showed that the Conservatives received 32% of the vote, whereas Boris received 44% on first preferences and 51% after second preferences. The individual results for each of the 14 GLA constituencies also showed a 'Boris bounce'. He consistently outperformed the Conservative candidates standing for the London Assembly in the same area, sometimes by a ratio of 2:1.

If Boris being more appealing than his party was a major factor in his win, was the reverse true of Livingstone's defeat?

The fall in turnout hurt Ken much less. His 2008 vote had only gone down by around 4,000 votes. His bigger gains came in rock solid Labour areas. For example, his vote increased by 11,000 in

City and East – his traditionally best performing area. This latter result showed that Ken had no problem motivating the Labour base. His second best area, North East, saw him add 6,000 votes to his 2008 score. He had also made gains in some parts of outer London, such as Enfield, Ealing, Hillingdon and Harrow that mirrored Labour's success in the 2010 local elections. So why, in the immediate aftermath, were many saying that a different Labour candidate would have done better?

On the face of it, this was an absurd suggestion. Not only had Ken outperformed his own vote in the 2000 and 2004 mayoral elections (with similar turnouts), he had virtually matched the Labour London Assembly vote (Ken got 40%, Labour got 41%) on first preferences and outperformed it on second preferences (by 48% to 41%). Furthermore, we knew from our own research that he was the most popular candidate Labour could have selected. The only person more popular was Boris. The bottom line was that only Boris could have successfully defied a tomb stoning Conservative vote. Would any Labour candidate have been able to beat that?

Delve a little deeper into the results and you find that although Ken did well, his negatives still cost him votes from Labour supporters. In such a close election, this was critical to his defeat. In virtually every GLA constituency, the Labour candidate for the London Assembly (whether they won the seat or not) got more votes than Ken Livingstone. If you add up the votes each Labour candidate got and compare it Ken's first preference votes, you find that Ken missed out on 43,480 votes that, by rights, he should have had in the bag. These were votes that people were willing to give to a local Labour candidate most of them had never heard of, but not to Ken. To put that into perspective, if all those people had voted for Ken, he would have been just 19,058 votes behind Boris after second preferences. Not enough to win, but a heck of a lot closer.

Ken's tax hypocrisy was a hugely significant factor on his

performance. Right from the moment the story broke in late February, the anger was most keenly felt among Labour supporters. His stubborn refusal to accept he had made a mistake only alienated them further. When combined with his myriad other offensive gaffes, it amounted to a significant proportion of Labour supporters splitting their votes. This was anecdotally the case – most Labour supporters I know refused to vote for Livingstone.

The tax scandal checked Ken's momentum and he never recovered. By digging his heels in, Ken allowed us to ensure that the pressure in the final two months of the campaign was on him. He needlessly lost two months on the defensive where he could have been hammering us on fares and the cost of living. We saw in November through to January how effective Ken was when he was free to go on the offensive. I look now at what the margin could have been had Labour supporters not split their votes and seriously question whether we could have maintained our lead – despite Boris's record and impressive display on the stump. My honest conclusion is were it not for the steps we took to keep the story alive in the media (ably assisted by Ken), we may well have lost.

The truth is that Ken was popular enough to win, in that sense Labour had selected the right candidate. But they had selected someone with a stubbornness that ended up plucking defeat from the jaws of victory. He not only lost Labour votes, but such a colossal tactical error gave us the space to convince wavering voters to pick Boris. To put Ken's failure into context, Boris ended up winning an election on the implicit promise to increase fares indefinitely as Londoners struggled to make ends meet. He could only do this because the tax story eroded trust in Livingstone, making his enticing election promises worthless in the eyes of wavering voters.

It is also worth pointing out that although Ken's signature pledge was highly effective, he had undeniably launched it far too early. It got him back in the race at the time, but he gave us six months to pick it apart. If he had launched it in March, it is doubtful whether we would have had the time to undermine it as successfully as we did.

In one sense at least, Ken was unlucky. He would have beaten any other Conservative candidate easily.

The closeness of the result clearly shows that the steps our campaign took were vital in securing victory. The result can be summed up thus: in a bad year for the Conservatives, Boris was the only candidate who could have won for the party, but he couldn't have won without our campaign.

The wildly successful British Olympic cycling team has a dedicated 'marginal gains' unit, whose sole purpose is to find tiny gains in everything from the weight of the bikes to how much time is lost because of sweaty shorts. In doing so, they can look back and pinpoint which individual actions or events add up to a winning margin. If I were to perform the same analysis on our campaign, the list of our marginal gains would look something like this:

1. Boris. *Boris is a creative and effective politician who has a strong record as Mayor, and worked hard to convince Londoners he deserved another term. He is popular, but he knew that in itself wasn't a guarantee of votes. He was determined to show that he was the best candidate to take London forwards in what is a critical time for the city. When Boris used his exceptional skills to communicate the 9-point plan, reminding people of his record and future plans, voters responded well. In the final weeks of the campaign he was electric, delivering a meaningful message with clarity and passion. He showed what a class political performer he can be and it was a delight to see him in action.*

2. The postal vote machine. *Postal votes are now one of the main battlegrounds in British elections and can mean the difference between victory and defeat. With turnout in general*

decline, postal votes buck the trend. If you can get a known supporter to sign up for a postal vote, there is a very strong chance that they will use it. Mark Fullbrook made postal votes the focus of the 'get out the vote' machine; after a similar operation had helped his wife, Lorraine Fullbrook, win her seat of South Ribble in the General Election of 2010. Paul Bolton from Conservative HQ set up a postal vote machine that was purring within weeks, with armies of volunteers collecting the forms we had sent out, organising them and submitting them to town halls in every Borough for approval within the tight legal deadline. It was logistics the army would be proud of. Using data provided by our expert in house analyst Eric Sukumaran, we targeted our meagre resources to register at least 50,000 more supporters for postal votes as the surest way of increasing our turnout. The final results show we exceeded our target, with Boris gaining 76,434 more postal votes than in 2008. In an election where the winning margin was 62,538 votes, the success of the postal vote operation was critical. It was also significant when you consider that turnout declined across the board, but our postal vote turnout increased in every part of London.

3. The attack/rebuttal operation. *Crosby and I had experienced just how ruthless a street fighter Ken Livingstone was in the 2008 election campaign. We knew this time he would throw the kitchen sink at us, so Crosby tasked me with putting together a political unit that would be equal to the task. The substantial body of work we put together enabled us to continually put Ken under pressure and blunt his attacks against us. It meant we won most of the day-to-day tactical battles and were able to gradually define the election on our terms.*

4. The positive/negative balance. T*he election campaign, as a whole, was perceived as a dirty fight between two big*

personalities – partly because the media much preferred negative stories to positive ones. However, we contributed our fair share towards this perception, with an aggressive 'Not Ken Again' campaign. But Crosby was insistent from the start that overall our campaign needed to be positive. We aimed for a balance of 70% positive 30% negative. Boris's message was about his positive plan for London's future. The vast majority of literature was positive. Rarely did Crosby recommend a direct attack from Boris on Ken (the incident in the lift was all Boris and a rare exception). When we did go on the offensive, it was with a measured tone and backed up by the facts. Any successful campaign must have that balance and ours did. A wholly negative campaign wouldn't have worked.

5. Lynton Crosby and Mark Fullbrook. *Above all, we had one major advantage. We had a driven, united team that was led by two of the best practitioners in the business. Crosby and Fullbrook assembled and motivated a talented team that became a slick fighting unit. Election campaigns are stressful affairs, populated by strong-minded people who are prone to falling out with out with each other. Candidates often lose elections when their teams are poorly led and divided. Boris could rely on Crosby and Fullbrook to make sure that didn't happen. As a result, everyone performed to the best of their ability and we rarely put a foot wrong. When we did, the mistake was corrected calmly and quickly. The atmosphere was open and collegiate, but there was clear leadership. Everyone knew who was in charge. Everyone who stepped through the front door was given the opportunity to show what they could do, regardless of whether they were senior political figures or first time volunteers. This created a real sense of camaraderie and togetherness that saw us through. Such high quality leadership and professionalism is all too rare in*

politics and its impact on the result of the election cannot be
overstated. It was a privilege to be led by such men.

It is sobering to reflect that the 2008 and 2012 mayoral campaigns
are the only two major elections a Conservative has won outright
since the 1992 General Election. When David Cameron was elected
Conservative leader in 2005 he made it his aim to change that. The
party's analysis was that they had to present a radically different face
to the British public if they were to be trusted with Government
again. It needed to be a more cuddly face, more in tune with issues
such as climate change and poverty at home and abroad. The party's
big pitch at the 2010 General Election was how they were going to
create the 'big society'. Astonishingly, this pitch was never tested
with voters before the decision was made to make it the central
theme of the campaign. Unsurprisingly, it didn't re-assure voters
uncertain about the future and struggling to pay their mortgages.
Against Gordon Brown, the most unpopular Labour leader in a
generation, the party failed to win a majority. It is unclear whether
the party has learned the lessons from this failure. One thing is
certain; the mayoral campaign of 2012 provides important insights
for how the Conservatives should view election campaigns in the
future.

First, as turnout declines and voter disillusionment hardens; the
potential pool of active voters is shrinking. Much punditry is based
on the premise that everyone who is eligible to vote will actually do
so. From this is derived the argument that parties are better to focus
most of their energies on a relatively small group of 'floating voters'
who aren't loyal to any single party. This view has led the
Conservative Party to heavily skew activity towards chasing a group
of voters that not many people can agree how to define and who are
increasingly less inclined to vote at all. The result has been – whether
deliberate or not – a confused message that chops and changes
according to the perceived priorities of an ill-defined group of voters.

This had led to the very abandonment of authenticity that alienates most voters – whoever they usually support. It has also neglected the party's natural supporters. It is true that you cannot win an election with your base alone – you need to add waverers to the mix. But neither can you win if your base stays at home. The sense of alienation felt by voters towards politicians shows no signs of abating, particularly when times are tough. It is hard to see turnout increasing in these circumstances. Therefore, elections are increasingly about which party can successfully turn out their natural supporters.

Second, a focused message is hard to achieve but absolutely essential to success, particularly for an incumbent. Voters do not expect their politicians to have easy answers. But they do expect them to have a clear plan and to focus on the issues that matter. Too often, politicians on both sides have made heroic assumptions about what the average voter thinks is important or what is popular. They have also tended to focus on what the media thinks is important. As a result they chase peripheral issues, further undermining their electoral support. This is the true driver of the 'out of touch' sentiment. Voters can stomach a politician who went to Eton and Oxford. They can't stomach one that bangs on about climate change in a recession, for example. As we found with Boris, what he thought were popular issues or initiatives (such as the cable car across the Thames) actually made voters less likely to support him. In a recession, voters don't expect tax cuts or immigration crackdowns – that is too easy a conclusion to draw. Rather, they expect focus and discipline from their leaders on thé things that matter. When the money has run dry, incumbent governments need to worry less about the next day's headlines and more about consistently articulating what their plan is to fix the economy in the long term.

Third, as participation in politics further declines, parties need to find new ways to build a machine that can win. As long as there are limits on how much parties can spend on election campaigns, they will have to continue to rely on volunteers. This problem is particularly acute for the Conservatives, who do not have access to the vast resources of the trade unions as the Labour Party does. As we found in London, the state of activism on the ground in some parts is dire. When time is limited, it requires innovation in order to get the most out of meagre resources. We built a sophisticated targeting database in two months, where it took the Conservative Party years. In the longer term, parties need to find a new way of engaging supporters and enlisting their help. Simply asking them for money in return for a floppy membership card and little say over anything in the party that matters will no longer cut it. (How this could be reformed could easily be the subject of another book.)

Fourth and perhaps most important of all, none of this matters if you don't have good enough candidates. Our campaign was successful because Boris is a great candidate and has been a fantastic Mayor of London. There is, however, only one Boris. Politics is a famously closed shop that is becoming ever more inward looking. If the parties do not find new ways for different people to become involved, the gene pool of future leaders will shrink to the point where we will never get anything other than machine pressed suited automatons with no true convictions or useful life experience.

No one could accuse Boris of being an automaton. As he embarks on his hard earned second term, the future looks bright. He is a double election winner in a city resistant to Conservative charms. Although he has weaknesses (which of us doesn't?) his strengths are phenomenal. For that reason alone, it would be very unwise to say this is the end of his ascent.

1 BBC News website, 16th July 2007

2 Extract from BBC News, hosted via Adam Bienkov on YouTube

3 Ken Livingstone, Transcript of Mayor's Question Time, p.11, 18th July 2007

4 News article, The *Daily Telegraph*, 29th July 2007

5 News article, *Daily Telegraph*, 2nd September 2007

6 News article, politics.co.uk, 21st August 2007

7 Boris Johnson, *Daily Telegraph*, 10th January 2002

8 Ken Livingstone, transcript of Mayor's Question Time, p.19, 12th September 2007

9 Boris Johnson, internal note to campaign directors, 'Why I want to be Mayor', 30th December 2007

10 Peter Oborne, *Daily Mail*, 14th December 2007

11 *Evening Standard*, editorial comment, 5th December 2007

12 News article, *Evening Standard*, 28th March 2008

13 Internal note to campaign directors, Why I Want To Be Mayor, Boris Johnson, 30th December 2007

14 Annual London Survey, Greater London Authority, 2009

15 *Evening Standard*, 24th February 2009

16 Boris Johnson, as cited on Conservatives.com

As cited in the article for Labour Uncut; 'Lions were led by donkeys in Labour's London mayoral election campaign', Atul Hatwal, Labour Uncut, 5th May 2012

17 As cited in the blogpost; 'Why Ed must call an inquest into Ken's selection', Joe Murphy, *Evening Standard*, 3rd May 2012

As cited in the article for Labour Uncut; 'The status quo in London is not an option', Rob Marchant, Labour Uncut, 16th May 2012

18 As cited in the blogpost; 'Why Ed must call an inquest into Ken's selection', Joe Murphy, *Evening Standard*, 3rd May 2012

19 As reported in *The Guardian*, 17th May 2010

20 Extracts from Boris Johnson's speech to the Conservative Home rally, *Daily Telegraph* website, 4th October 2010

21 At the time of writing, the inquest into what happened had not yet been held.

22 *Evening Standard*, 4 November 2011

23 Your Local Guardian, 2 June 2011, link. General Ratko Mladic was the Bosnian Serb army chief throughout the Bosnian war - and the man many hold responsible for the worst atrocities in that bloody conflict and he has been indicted by the UN war crimes tribunal on charges of genocide and other crimes: BBC News Online, 27 May 2011

24 The *Daily Telegraph*, 17 November 2011

25 Internal TfL note, 'Balancing TfL's business plan', 23rd September 2009

26 Mayor's Questions, 20 June 2007

27 Mayor's Question Time, 25 January 2006

28 Metropolitan Police Authority, Annual Accounts, 2008-09, p.31, numbers at end of 2007-08 financial year

29 Metropolitan Police Authority, Annual Accounts, 2009-10, p.35, numbers at end of 2009-10 financial year

30 Metropolitan Police Authority, rolling monthly police officer numbers as at October 2011

31 BBC News website, 23rd April 2012

32 As cited in a *Daily Telegraph* article, Andrew Gilligan, 26th February 2012.

33 Abbreviated balance sheet, Silveta Ltd, 30th June 2009, obtained via Companies House

34 Abbreviated balance sheet, Silveta Ltd, 30th June 2010, obtained via Companies House

35 S&P Select Committee, Seventh Report Appendix, 8 March 2000

36 Sunday Times, 23 January 2000 as cited by Andrew Gilligan, *Daily Telegraph*, 26th February 2012

37 Matthew Norman, *The Independent*, 27th February 2012

38 Mehdi Hasan, *New Statesman*, 8th March 2012

39 ibid.

40 Dan Hodges, *Daily Telegraph*, 9th March 2012

41 Transcript of phone conversation between Ken Livingstone and Andrew Gilligan, published on Gilligan's blog on 26th February 2012, *Daily Telegraph*

42 Andrew Gilligan, *Daily Telegraph*, 6th April 2012

43 As reported in the *Daily Mail*, 13th April 2012

44 As cited on the BBC News website, 20th April 2012

45 Mayoral declaration speech, 4th May 2012, Greater London Authority

APPENDICES

Appendix 1
Progress Report

The Boris 2012 campaign kicked off in February with the publication of the "Progress Report to Londoners on the 2008 Manifesto". The aim of this document was to show that Boris had delivered on the many promises that he had made when first elected as Mayor of London in 2008. That earlier manifesto had been both detailed and sweeping in its scope. If Boris's new manifesto for the 2012 election was to be taken seriously and his promises believed, it was essential that he and his campaign team were able to show convincingly that he had delivered on his 2008 manifesto. This document was produced as a glossy leaflet and widely distributed in London, and to political journalists and bloggers. In fact a careful reading of the document showed that some promises made in 2008 - though admittedly not many - had not been delivered. In those instances the document explained why the promise had not been delivered and - wherever possible - sought to pin the blame on somebody other than Boris. We reproduce this document here in its entirety as it was the bedrock of the Boris campaign from day one.

My Progress Report to Londoners on the 2008 Manifesto

Mayor Boris Johnson

Letter from Mayor Boris Johnson

Dear Londoner

In the coming weeks I will be setting out my manifesto commitments for taking this great city forwards in the right direction over the next four years.

I will be making those commitments with utter seriousness and determination.

And I want my promises to be judged by the determination and success with which I have fulfilled the promises I made to Londoners in 2008.

I am proud of our record of delivery, and I hope you will take the time to read this Progress Report to London.

- I said we would make London safer
- I said we would improve our transport network
- I said we would cut the cost of City Hall for hard-pressed Londoners
- I promised to improve the quality of life for Londoners and build a record number of homes

I also promised to run the most open and transparent administration in Britain, and that is why I am determined in this Progress Report to level with Londoners. If we have not achieved a goal - or not yet - then I am determined that we should be honest about the reason.

But with a 91 per cent success rate, I believe that overall it is a record of very substantial achievement.

We have ended the culture of waste at City Hall, and the high-handed misuse of taxpayers' money. In tough times, we have put scarce resources to work where they will deliver the maximum benefit for Londoners.

We have put 1000 more police on the street, and found the funding that will keep police numbers high - and as a result we have cut crime by more than 10 per cent. The murder rate is down by a quarter and crime on buses is more than a third. We have stepped up investment in our creaking transport infrastructure, and cut tube delays by 40 per cent.

We have done simple things to improve the lives of Londoners.

We have introduced - and will guarantee - a 24 hour Freedom Pass.

We have put the Oystercard on the overground rail.

We have brought in the best bike hire scheme in the world.

For just over the cost of one year's fare evasion on the bendy buses, we have developed and designed a new Routemaster-style bus for London.

After eight years of eye-watering rises under the previous Mayor, we have cut the council tax and saved Londoners £445 for an average household.

And yet there is so much more that we want to do. We want to continue to modernise and automate the Tube - investing in the new technology that will allow us to keep fares low, in a way that is honest and sustainable.

We want to get on with the work of generating 200,000 jobs that will flow, in the next four years, from our investments in transport and housing.

We want to keep boosting London's high streets and shopping centres, and to expand our growing programme of opportunities for young people. We have helped create 54,000 apprenticeships. We want to reach 100,000 by the end of the year.

We want to tackle the continuing scandal of illiteracy in this city, and much else besides.

To judge the strength of our intentions for the next four years, please look at what we have done.

It is easy to make promises. It is hard work to keep them.

It is because I am so proud of our work, and because we have kept our promises to London, that I believe we can achieve even more over the next four years.

Mayor Boris Johnson

Making London's Mayor Accountable

Manifesto
2008

Mayor Boris Johnson

My Progress Report to Londoners on the 2008 Manifesto

3

Giving Londoners their say

Pledge	What has been achieved so far

Communicate in plain English and listen to the results of consultations (Boris Johnson, *Making London's Mayor Accountable*, 2008, p.4).

Promise delivered.

I pledged that I would listen to Londoners and I have done just that.

You may remember that after a consultation, I scrapped the Western Extension of the Congestion Charge Zone (WEZ) in line with the wishes of residents, businesses and other organisations. The last day of charging was 24 December 2010. (Mayor of London, Press Release, *48 hours until the end of the Western Extension Zone*, 22 December 2010).

In addition, I have taken action to 'communicate in plain English' and simplify GLA Group publications. For example the London Underground house manual is being reduced from 1200 to just 400 pages (HMT, *National Infrastructure Plan 2011*, p.11).

This is in stark contrast to my predecessor who imposed the WEZ despite 603 per cent of businesses opposing the scheme (Daily Mail, *Ken gives go-ahead for congestion charge extension*, 30 September 2005).

Hold more Public Question Times, where Londoners will be able to directly question the Mayor (Boris Johnson, *Making London's Mayor Accountable*, 2008, p.4).

Promise delivered.

I have been delighted to hold more public meetings, as well as meet thousands of Londoners whilst out and about.

Between November 2008 and November 2011 I held 7 People's Question Times (GLA Website, People's Question Time).

In addition, other platforms have been created to work alongside People's Question Times, such as the 3 Talk London events and the 9 Mayor's Consultation meetings on specific issues important to Londoners held so far. As Mayor therefore I have held 24 meetings inviting my constituents to question me. (Talk London Website, GLA Website, Mayor's consultation meetings).

This is more in 4 years than the 16 which Ken Livingstone held in his two terms in office (GLA Website).

Chair the Metropolitan Police Authority, so Londoners can hold me to account over what happens with the police (Boris Johnson, *Making London's Mayor Accountable*, 2008, p.4).

Promise delivered.

I became the Chairman of the Metropolitan Police Authority shortly after my election in May 2008.

Once the direction of London policing had been set I stood down from this role in January 2010 and promoted my Deputy, elected Assembly member, Kit Malthouse, preserving democratic accountability (BBC News Online, *Boris Johnson steps down from police authority*, 27 January 2010).

A Revised Approach

The MPA has since been replaced by the Mayor's Office for Policing and Crime (MOPC) which is headed by my Deputy Mayor for Policing and Crime. This change means that as Mayor and Deputy Mayor we will be even more accountable to Londoners for police performance, setting local priorities and allocating resources (GLA Website, About MOPC).

When we appointed the new Met Commissioner, I made it clear that this would be someone who has a clear strategy for tackling gang violence and youth crime and restoring pride in our great city. (BBC News Online, *Bernard Hogan-Howe new Metropolitan Police commissioner*, 27 September 2011)

As a result of my personal lead, crime has fallen in London by 10.6 per cent, robberies are down 16.7 per cent and murders have decreased by 24.4 per cent (MPS statistics, Comparing 44 months of Ken Livingstone September 2004 - April 2008 with 44 months of Boris Johnson May 2008 - December 2011).

Ensure local police chiefs hold monthly open public meetings (Boris Johnson, *Making London's Mayor Accountable*, 2008, p.4).

Making progress.

Although monthly public meetings with the Police Borough Commander are not held in every borough, many boroughs hold some sort of regular public meetings. These allow residents to question their local police.

My introduction of crime mapping has opened up local policing to residents, transforming the accountability of the Met (Metropolitan Police Service, MPS, *Police Crime Map*).

Hold regular meetings with business leaders, so businesses large and small can have direct, personal contact with the Mayor (Boris Johnson, *Making London's Mayor Accountable*, 2008, p.4).

Promise delivered.

I pledged to hold meetings with businesses at least every six months. I have far exceeded this by holding 106 meetings on business issues, including 8 meetings with the London Business Advisory Council alongside many meetings with individuals (Mayor of London, *Mayor's Report to the Assembly*, May 2008 – November 2011).

This has enabled me to listen and respond to the concerns of small businesses, leading to the creation of the £50 million Outer London Fund (GLA Website, *Outer London Fund*).

I have also therefore been able to negotiate good deals for Londoners, such as securing private sponsorship for the cycle hire scheme and cycle superhighways saving taxpayers money whilst delivering services (Mayor of London, Press Release, *Barclays saddle up to sponsor London Cycle Hire Scheme*, 28 May 2010).

Work closely and co-operate with locally-elected Councillors instead of bullying and berating them (Boris Johnson, *Making London's Mayor Accountable*, 2008, p.4).

Promise delivered.

I meet with the leaders of London boroughs twice a year at the London Congress (GLA Press Release, *Mayor's vision for better focused GLA with more say and more power on key London issues*, 15 June 2010, London Councils website, *Congress of Leaders*).

At the April 29th 2009 meeting at the London Congress, I agreed with London's Borough Leaders the London City Charter, a ground-breaking new agreement that sets out how the GLA, the boroughs and their delivery partners will work together to ensure that London's public services continue to improve and to be delivered as efficiently as possible. (London Councils website, *Congress of Leaders*).

I have a strong relationship with local councils, of all political colours, which has enabled me to achieve more for London, such as the redevelopment of Stratford and East London (Mayor of London, *The revised London Housing Strategy*, December 2011).

Ending the culture of cronyism at City Hall

Pledge   *What has been achieved so far*

Create a Cabinet for London, to run London in a more business-like and efficient manner (Boris Johnson, *Making London's Mayor Accountable*, 2008, p.10).

Promised Delivered.

I have run London in a more business-like and efficient way, which has resulted in cutting £2bn of waste, freeing up taxpayer's money (GLA, *Final Draft Consolidated Budget 2012-2013: Explaining of Proposals*, 1 February 2012, p. 117).

To ensure my governance is as open as possible, Mayoral decisions are placed online at the earliest opportunity once they are formally agreed (GLA Website, *Mayoral Decisions*).

I have also ensured transparency in decision making, all GLA expenditure over £500 and decisions relating to expenditure over £50,000 are accessible to the public (GLA Website, *Making decision making*, August 2011; GLA Website, *Making expenditure clear*).

A Revised Approach

On reflection it became clear the Mayoralty was not best suited to a Cabinet system of government. This is what distinguishes it from other forms of local and regional government and ultimately makes it more effective. What I have done is open City Hall and my team up to the same level of scrutiny that a Cabinet would have (Mayor of London, *Mayor's Questions*, 15 July 2009, 2143/2009).

Strengthen the accountability of Mayoral advisers by putting a separate register of interests online, and requiring them to appear before the London Assembly on a regular basis (Boris Johnson, *Making London's Mayor Accountable*, 2008, p.11).

Promise delivered.

For the first time, the GLA website now has a section on the appointments to my Mayoral team.

Each member also has their expenses, interests, gifts and hospitality published. (GLA Website, *Mayoral Team*).

The GLA website also contains the ways that members of the public can get involved, meet me or contact the GLA (GLA Website, *Contact us*).

Stand for only two terms (Boris Johnson, *Making London's Mayor Accountable*, 2008, p.11).

Promise delivered.

I am currently standing for my second term as Mayor.

By contrast Ken Livingstone said in the past that he would only stand for one term but has served two terms and is contesting his 4th Mayoral election this year (Ken Livingstone, *Manifesto for a Mayor and London Assembly*, 1998).

Restoring trust in how City Hall spends your money

Pledge

What has been achieved so far

Launch an immediate review of City Hall and its finances within the first 100 days (Boris Johnson, *Making London's Mayor Accountable*, 2008, p.13).

Promise delivered.

In the first week, after I was elected as Mayor of London I announced the formation of the Forensic Audit Panel which reported in July 2008 (Legacy London Website, *Report of the Mayor's Forensic Audit Panel*).

The report concluded that Ken Livingstone's LDA 'misspent' money 'on a massive scale, say tens of millions (GLA, *Report of the Mayor's Forensic Audit Panel*, 15 July 2008).

Launch an immediate independent review of the London Development Agency and all grants given by that body (Boris Johnson, *Making London's Mayor Accountable*, 2008, p.13).

Promise delivered.

The review of the LDA was conducted by the Forensic Audit Panel which reported in July 2008.

The report concluded that Ken Livingstone's LDA 'misspent' money 'on a massive scale, say tens of millions".

It also found that there were failings in the LDA's leadership, governance and basic controls which led to the conclusion that the former LDA board was ineffective (GLA, *Report of the Mayor's Forensic Audit Panel*, 15 July 2008).

Enable Londoners to view all GLA expenditure over £1,000 with a comprehensive search engine on the Mayor's website (Boris Johnson, *Making London's Mayor Accountable*, 2008, p.13, transparency by that body).

Promise delivered.

I have been determined to make my City Hall as transparent as possible. Now for the first time we have published all significant GLA expenditure.

Since 2008 all GLA expenditure over £1,000 has been published online. In 2010 the reporting threshold was reduced to £500. I have also enabled detailed scrutiny of all GLA expenditure via the London Datastore (GLA Website, *Expenditure*, London Datastore Website).

I believe that Londoners now have the transparent City Hall they deserve, and that they can see my commitment to streamlining City Hall finances.

This never happened under Ken Livingstone.

Review the process of making appointments to all the functional bodies to ensure maximum transparency (Boris Johnson, *Making London's Mayor Accountable*, 2008, p.13).

Promise delivered.

The GLA Act was amended by the Government in 2011, to include confirmation hearings for chairs of functional bodies (GLA Website, *Proposed amendments to the GLA's Standing Orders Appendix 1*, 2011).

I have been determined to be as transparent as possible, such as when one of the Mayor's two direct appointments to the London Fire and Emergency Planning Authority became vacant and an open and transparent recruitment process was established to fill the place (GLA Website, *Mayoral Decisions - MD914*).

Ensure Londoners pay no more than 38p per week for the Olympics (Boris Johnson, *Making London's Mayor Accountable*, 2008, p.13).

Promise delivered.

I have frozen Council Tax for three consecutive years and cut it this year. This includes the £20 precept for a band D property that is levied for the Olympic Games. This equates to 38 pence a week for the average London home (GLA, *Consolidated Budget and Component Budget 2011-12*, February 2011, p.15).

This is a contrast to the approach under Ken Livingstone which saw the GLA precept of council tax increase by 152 per cent in just eight years, costing the average household £364 (Annual Figures can be found at GLA Website, *Budget* archive).

Making London Safer

Manifesto 2008

Mayor Boris Johnson

Providing strong leadership

Pledge

What has been achieved so far

I will chair the Metropolitan Police Authority (Boris Johnson, *Making London Safer*, 2008, p. 9).

Promise delivered.

I became the Chairman of the Metropolitan Police Authority shortly after my election in May 2008.

Once the direction of London policing had been set it stood down from this role in January 2010 and promoted my Deputy, elected Assembly member, Kit Malthouse, preserving democratic accountability (BBC News Online, *Boris Johnson steps down from police authority*, 27 January 2010).

A Revised Approach

The MPA has since been replaced by the Mayor's Office for Policing and Crime (MOPC) which is headed by my Deputy Mayor for Policing and Crime. This change means that both the Mayor and the Deputy Mayor will be even more accountable to Londoners for police performance, setting local priorities and allocating resources (GLA Website, *About MOPC*).

When we appointed the new Met Commissioner, I made it clear that this would be someone who has a clear strategy for tackling gang violence and youth crime and restoring pride in our great city. (BBC News Online, *Bernard Hogan-Howe new Metropolitan Police commissioner*, 27 September 2011)

As a result of my personal lead, crime has fallen in London by 10.6 per cent, robberies are down 16.7 per cent and murders have decreased by 24.4 per cent (MPS statistics, Comparing 44 months of Ken Livingstone September 2004 – April 2008 with 44 months of Boris Johnson May 2008 - December 2011).

I will stand up against excessive form-filling, and support the scrapping of the stop and account form, lobbying the government hard for its removal (Boris Johnson, *Making London Safer*, 2008, p. 9).

Promise delivered.

I have been focused on getting police officers out from behind their desks onto the street. In the two years from May 2008 to May 2010 the Met took 209 forms out of use (Mayor of London, *Mayor's Questions*, 19 May 2010).

In March 2011 the Government gave police forces the option to scrap the stop and account form (Home Office Website, *Stop and search*). The Met has however decided to continue using the stop and account form either as an MPA consultation found robust support for recording "stop and account" to make sure the process was transparent and accountable (The Guardian, *Met police will retain recording of "stop and account" street encounters*, 23 September 2011).

From January 2009 a shorter revised stop and search was launched, with the time it takes to complete reduced from 8-10 minutes to 3-5 minutes. (MPA, *A Practical Guide to stop and search community monitoring groups*, August 2009).

I will expect PCSOs to take some of the administrative burden from police officers, so more can get out on the streets (Boris Johnson, Making London Safer, 2008, p. 9).

Promised delivered.

In 2009 I introduced Operation Herald, a scheme focused on cutting administrative tasks and paperwork for London's police officers (Mayor of London, Mayor's Questions, 14 July 2010).

A revised approach.

The scheme found that many of the administrative tasks could be cut altogether or done by civilian staff, rather than PCSOs, thus enabling more police presence on the streets.

Operation Herald moved clerical duties away from trained police officers to general staff, put more police on the front line and achieved efficiencies of 451 positions (Mayor of London, Mayor's Questions, 14 July 2010).

We continue to work to get more officers out on the streets. There will be 1,000 more police officers than in 2008 by May 2012 (GLA, The Mayor's Consultation Budget, 22 December 2011, p 1).

There are now 630 Safer Neighbourhood Teams, 1 for each of London's 624 neighbourhood wards, plus 5 more for the city of Westminster and 1 more for Crystal Palace where three boroughs meet. These are made up of at least 2 Police Constables and 3 PCSOs. There are over 4,100 police officers dedicated to neighbourhood policing (MPS Website, Safer Neighbourhoods).

Making trains, buses and stations safer

Pledge — *What has been achieved so far*

Pledge

I will require under 18s who have had their free bus travel withdrawn for anti-social behaviour to earn it back through voluntary and community work (TfL Press Release, Under 18s free travel rules begin, 1 June 2008).

Double the strength of Safer Transport teams, by raising funding for PCSOs to patrol the buses and 50 more fully-warranted British Transport Police officers to patrol the worst suburban stations.

Promise delivered.

Launched in August 2009, Payback London scheme requires under 18s who have free bus travel withdrawn to earn it back through community service (Boris Johnson, Making London Safer, 2008, p. 13).

I am pleased that we have used this scheme to show to young people the importance of caring for their city - clearing graffiti, picking up litter, and helping community schemes.

10,088 individuals have had their passes withdrawn since 2009 (Mayor of London, Mayor's Questions, 14 December 2011).

Promise delivered.

I prioritised safety on London's public transport. An extra 440 uniformed officers were recruited to the Safer Transport Teams (Mayor of London, Mayor's Questions, 16 July 2008).

There are now an extra 50 Transport Police on the Overground and particularly outer London stations (Mayor of London, Mayor's Questions, 21 May 2009).

Pledge

I will make buses safer by running a trial of live CCTV (Boris Johnson, Making London Safer, 2008, p. 13).

Promise delivered.

I launched a trial of live CCTV on 21 buses in October 2008.

The trial found that live CCTV provided no additional benefit and there are no plans to roll it out (BBC News Online, Live CCTV on buses to be tested, 20 October 2008, Mayor of London, Mayor's Questions, 17 March 2010).

In 2008, I also banned alcohol on the Tube (TfL, Press Release, Alcohol ban comes into force on the Tube, trains and buses from this Sunday, 1 June, 30 May 2008).

Bus crime has decreased by 30 per cent during my term (MOPC, Monthly Report: Police and Crime Committee, 8 March 2012. Comparing 45 months of Ken Livingstone (August 2004 – April 2008) with 45 months of Boris Johnson (May 2008 – January 2012).

I will focus on reducing fare evasion by directing the MPA and TfL to investigate giving Revenue Protection Inspectors more powers (Boris Johnson, Making London Safer, 2008, p. 13).

Promise delivered.

A trial giving a team of Revenue Protection Inspectors additional powers started in March 2010 (Mayor of London, *Mayor's Questions*, 19 May 2010).

Subsequently we launched the Community Safety Accreditation Scheme (CSAS) to assist these Revenue Protection Inspectors in dealing with a range of anti-social behaviour on the bus network. The CSAS powers mean that Inspectors can collect information and issue Fixed Penalty Notices (TfL Board, *Commissioner's Report*, 29 June 2011).

TfL have now enhanced 50 Revenue Protection staff on London's bus network with additional powers, granted by the MPS under the CSAS scheme (Mayor of London, *Mayor's Questions*, 6 November 2011).

Since May 2011, there have been 38 CSAS specific intelligence led deployments resulting in 640 penalty fares, 470 prosecutions, 45 CSAS related offences and 2 Penalty Notices for Disorder. (GLA website, *Keeping crime low on our transport system*)

There has been a significant reduction in fare evasion rates on the buses and Tube from their highest levels under Ken Livingstone in 2007 and 2004, which was 3.5% and 3.8% respectively. The current rate of fare evasion across the network is stable at 2.2 per cent (GLA, *Mayor answers to London*, 18 August 2011).

I consulted on increasing penalties for fare evasion, and as a result, TfL have this year increased fines from £50 to £80 (TfL Press Release, 16 February 2012).

My removal of the bendy buses will save around £7 million a year in reduced fare evasion (GLA Press Release, 9 December 2011).

Tackling knife and gun crimes

Pledge

I will make it a policing priority to tackle knife and gun crime and not accept defeat. I will drive out the culture of political targets that distort priorities (Boris Johnson, *Making London Safer*, 2008, p. 21).

What has been achieved so far

Promise delivered.

It is a priority of the new MOPC to tackle knife and gun crime (MOPC Website). At my direction, the Met introduced an intensified stop and search regime called Operation Blunt 2, and over 11,000 knives have been taken off the street since then (Mayor of London, *Mayor of London's Annual Report 2010-2011*, May 2011).

When we appointed the new Met Commissioner last year, I made it clear that this would be someone who has a clear strategy for tackling gang violence and youth crime and restoring pride in our great city. (BBC News Online, *Bernard Hogan-Howe new Metropolitan Police commissioner*, 27 September 2011)

I will provide funding for handheld scanners and knife arches to use at Tube and rail stations, and other large-scale public events (Boris Johnson, *Making London Safer*, 2008, p. 21).

Promise delivered.

I have provided funding for handheld scanners and knife arches to be used more, with £3.8m allocated to support the additional costs of Operation Blunt 2 for 2008/09 (Mayor of London, *Mayor's Questions*, 19 May 2010, Mayor of London, *Mayor's Questions*, 15 October 2008, Mayor of London, *Mayor's Questions*, 12 November 2008).

This has led to over 11,000 knives being taken off the street (Mayor of London, *Mayor of London's Annual Report 2010-2011*, May 2011).

We have also focused on large-scale public events. In 2011, police officers manned knife arches throughout the Notting Hill Carnival day at various underground stations across London, particularly those in and around the carnival procession route. (Metro, *Notting Hill Carnival's 'peaceful' start belies knife arches and 6,500 police*, 28 August 2011).

Londoners are noticing the benefits. Responses to surveys about the deployment of knife arches and screening equipment showed a figure of 79 per cent of pupils feeling more reassured through the use of knife arches at key locations on routes to schools. (Mayor of London, *Mayor's Questions*, 12 November 2008)

I will direct the LDA to fund youth community groups that provide mentoring schemes (Boris Johnson, *Making London Safer*, 2008, p. 21).

Promise delivered.

The Mayor's Mentoring Programme will provide appropriately trained adult volunteer mentors for a minimum of 1,000 black boys aged 10-16 who may be at risk of offending in seven target boroughs in London (GLA Website, Mentoring).

To date £1.3million has been committed in the form of grant funding and the associated administrative costs of the small grants fund (Mayor of London, Mayor's Questions, 23 March 2011).

I have also launched Team London which provides a conduit for volunteers and London's disadvantaged (Team London Website).

I will ring-fence part of the LDA budget specifically for community sports projects (Boris Johnson, *Making London Safer*, 2008, p. 21).

Promise delivered.

The Mayor's Sports Legacy Fund provides £15.5 million worth of funding, which have ring-fenced for community sports projects (Mayor of London, Mayor's Questions, 15 September 2010, Mayor of London Press Release, 23 November 2011).

Mayor gives community sports facilities a boost with £1m cash injection.

I will make designing out crime a key priority in Mayor's Housing strategy to prevent creating poor-quality housing where crime flourishes (Boris Johnson, *Making London Safer*, 2008, p. 21).

Promise delivered.

The London Plan sets out my designing out crime policy, which calls on boroughs and others to create safe, secure and appropriately accessible environments where crime and disorder, and the fear of crime do not undermine quality of life or community cohesion (GLA, *The London Plan, July 2011).

Our Housing Strategy also sets out that new homes and developments should be built to principles that design out crime risks (GLA, *Revised Housing Strategy*, December 2011).

Help the ignored victims of sexual violence

What has been achieved so far

Pledge

I will provide stable, long-term funding to set up new Rape Crisis Centres in London (Boris Johnson, *Making London Safer*, 2008, p. 27).

Promise delivered.

As part of my long term plan, three new Rape Crisis Centres opened in London in 2010, making four in total based in North, South, East and West London. (Mayor of London, Press Release, 8 March 2010).

15,882 victims of sexual abuse were helped with support, counselling and therapies at these four rape crisis centres in 2010- 2011 alone, (Mayor of London Press Release, *Mayor's Rape Crisis centres helping over 15,000 women*, 25 November 2011).

I have committed to continue to provide funding for the three new centres and the existing Croydon centre if re-elected (Mayor of London, Mayor's Questions, 15 December 2010).

Getting Londoners Moving
Manifesto 2008

Mayor Boris Johnson

Demanding a police service accountable to you

Pledge

I will provide local neighbourhoods with New York-style crime maps, to enable residents to hold local police to account (Boris Johnson, *Making London Safer*, 2008, p. 30).

I will direct the MPA to ensure Borough Commanders hold public meetings open monthly, (Boris Johnson, *Making London Safer*, 2008, p. 30).

I will ask for regular meetings with the Home Secretary to ensure that Whitehall is listening to Londoners' concerns (Boris Johnson, *Making London Safer*, 2008, p. 12).

What has been achieved so far

Promise delivered.

My introduction of crime mapping has opened up local policing to residents, transforming the accountability of the Met (Metropolitan Police Service Website, *Crime Mapping*).

The Government launched a UK wide crime map website in early 2011 (Police UK Website).

Making progress.

Although monthly public meetings with the Police Borough Commander are not held in every borough, many boroughs hold some sort of public meeting, even if they are not monthly.

The most frequent and consistent of these are the quarterly consultative group meetings (Community and Police Engagement Group) where members of the public have the opportunity to question the Borough Commander (Mayor of London, Mayor's Questions, 14 December 2011).

Promise delivered.

I regularly meet with the Home Secretary and Home Office ministers. My strong relationship with the Government has resulted in extra financial support for the Met, including £90 million to keep officer numbers high (Mayor of London, Mayor's Reports 2008-2012; GLA, Mayor's Final Budget 2011-12, February 2012; Evening Standard, Met getting £90m to keep police numbers up on capital's streets, 30 January 2012).

221

Putting commuters first

Pledge

What has been achieved so far

I will re-phase traffic lights to get traffic flowing more smoothly (Boris Johnson, *Getting Londoners Moving*, 2008, p. 10).

Promise delivered.

We have taken concrete steps to improve congestion in London. 2,000 traffic light signals have been reviewed since 2008 and a further 1,000 signals are being reviewed in 2011/12 (TfL Website, *Smoothing traffic flow*).

Changes made to over 1,000 traffic light signals in 2010 delivered a six per cent reduction in unnecessary delays at traffic signals. (TfL Website, *Smoothing traffic flow*).

A list of 145 signals which could be removed was also published in June 2010 and a further 26 were added to the list in November 2011.

Out of the 204 suggested removals, 22 have already been removed with removal agreed for another 15 and 80 under discussion with boroughs. It has been agreed between TfL and the boroughs that the remaining 87 signals will be maintained (TfL Website, *Suggested signal removal list*, Feb 2012; TfL Website, *Smoothing traffic flow*).

I will campaign for the Mayor to at last be given the power to fine utility companies who cause delays through badly planned roadworks (Boris Johnson, *Getting Londoners Moving*, 2008, p. 10).

Promise delivered.

I have strongly lobbied the Government for this power, resulting in new legislation. The London Permit Scheme, submitted by TfL, was launched in 2010 and resulted in a 17 per cent cut in the number of road works by utility companies (London Councils, *London Permit Scheme: First Year Evaluation Report*, 27 May 2011, Mayor of London, Mayor's Questions, 9 September 2009).

At my urging, legislation to give Fixed Penalty Notices to companies who cause delays under the Scheme has now been tabled by DfT.

TfL's Lane Rental scheme would come into effect from Spring 2012, subject to new regulations and approval from Department for Transport, expecting lane rental to reduce serious and severe disruption from roadworks by 40 per cent by 2015. (Mayor of London, Mayor's Questions, 12 October 2011; Department for Transport Statement, Street works: lane rental, 26 January 2012).

I will not introduce Ken Livingstone's £25 Congestion Charge and I will make the Congestion Change fairer and more effective by reforming it when the current contracts expire (Boris Johnson, *Getting Londoners Moving*, 2008, p. 10).

The Western Extension of the Congestion Charge Zone (WEZ) was removed following a consultation in December 2010 (TfL, Press Release, *Mayor confirms removal of Congestion Charge Western Extension Zone by Christmas and introduction of CC Auto Pay in New Year*, 20 October 2010).

Following the removal of the WEZ there was a lower than expected increase in traffic driving into and within the former zone and no discernable impact on air quality were reported (TfL, Press Release, TfL announce initial results following removal of the Western Extension of the Congestion Charging Zone, 3 June 2011).

I will not introduced the £25 Congestion Charge. We also now have a flexible Congestion pricing. It has been made easier through the introduction of an online account system to register now for Congestion Charge Auto Pay accounts, 24 November 2010).

Promise delivered.

I will hold a new consultation on the Western extension and abide by the result (Boris Johnson, *Getting Londoners Moving*, 2008, p. 10).

Promise delivered.

I held a consultation on the future of the Western Extension of the Congestion Charging zone in 2008 (GLA, Press Release, C charge overhaul, 15 October 2009).

On 27 November 2008 I announced that, based on the results of the public consultation, I would begin the legal process required to remove the Western Extension in line with the wishes of residents, businesses and other organisations (Mayor of London, Press Release, Western extension: Londoners have spoken and the Mayor has listened, 27 November 2008).

The final day of the Western Extension Zone was 24 December 2010 (TfL, Press Release, Mayor confirms removal of Congestion Charge Western Extension Zone by Christmas and introduction of CC Auto Pay in New Year, 20 October 2010).

222

I will seek to re-instate tidal flow at the Blackwall tunnel, to ease congestion in South East London (Boris Johnson, *Getting Londoners Moving*, 2008, p. 10).

Not met - a revised approach.

After a detailed analysis, I listened to experts and decided to adopt a revised approach to improving South East London congestion.

This was not delivered because a TfL review found that returning to the tidal flow at the Blackwall Tunnel would not improve traffic management (Mayor of London, *Mayor's Questions*, 17 March 2010).

In addition, there are issues around fire risks associated with introducing two way traffic flows in a tunnel with a high proportion of HGVs with no separate means of escape, as shown by the 2009 incident when a truck catching fire caused a blaze inside the tunnel which closed it for days (Evening Standard, *Blackwall Tunnel shut by fire for days*, 30 November 2009).

Furthermore, in a tunnel with two way flow there would be no choice but to pass fire smoke and/or toxic fumes over one or other queue of traffic, whereas with one way traffic the system ventilates in the direction of traffic flow thus protecting the queue of vehicles behind the fire.

The principal causes of serious and severe disruption in the Blackwall tunnel are vehicle breakdowns, accidents and HGVs exceeding the northbound height restrictions (Mayor of London, *Mayor's Questions*, 3 March 2011).

TfL have introduced a number of measures to reduce these unnecessary tunnel closures, including an additional lane for HGV vehicles on the northbound Blackwall Tunnel approach. This will enable all over-height vehicles to be diverted away from the tunnel before they reach the entrance, reducing unnecessary delays (Mayor of London, *Mayor's Questions*, 3 March 2011).

I will, on behalf of Londoners, oppose Government plans to increase charges at the Dartford crossing, and lobby for residents in the London boroughs affected to have the same discounts as those proposed for residents in Dartford and Thurrock (Boris Johnson, *Getting Londoners Moving*, 2008, p. 10).

Promise delivered.

I called for the Government to delay planned toll increases at the Dartford crossing (Kent News, *Boris Johnson calls for delay on Dartford toll hikes*, 15 October 2011).

I also wrote to then Secretary of State for Transport asking that the discount given to residents in Dartford and Thurrock be extended to those living in Bexley and Havering (Mayor of London, *Mayor's Questions*, 19 May 2010).

My request was acknowledged by the Parliamentary Under Secretary of State, Mike Penning MP, on 17 October 2011. In light of the responses to the consultation, the Minister announced on 24 November that he would delay the implementation of the proposed charge rises at the Dartford crossing. The Government is considering when any changes will now be made, and TfL will continue its discussions with the DfT to ensure the smooth operation of the Olympic Route Network (Mayor of London, *Mayor's Questions*, 22 December 2011).

I will allow motorcycles in bus lanes (Boris Johnson, *Getting Londoners Moving*, 2008, p. 10).

Promise delivered.

Following the completion of two trials, motorcycles have been given permanent access in bus lanes from 23 January 2012 (TfL Website, *Motorcycles in bus lanes*).

I will trial orbital express buses for outer London, to encourage modal shift in these areas (Boris Johnson, *Getting Londoners Moving*, 2008, p. 10).

Promise delivered.

I conducted a thorough trial, which showed that although the buses were used, they were not very cost effective (TfL, *Surface Transport Panel Report*, November 2009).

However, the East London Transit bus is now running services from Ilford to Dagenham Dock via Barking town centre. The second phase will run from Barking town centre to the Barking Riverside development (TfL Website, *East London Transit*, 22 February 2010).

I will order TfL to look again at air conditioning on the Tube (Boris Johnson, *Getting Londoners Moving*, 2008, p. 10).

Promise delivered.

Despite the difficult economic circumstances, we have made great progress on this. After I asked TfL to look into again, air conditioned trains have now been introduced on the Metropolitan Line. They will start to be introduced on the Hammersmith & City and Circle lines in late 2012 and on the District Line from 2013. The roll-out of this new fleet of trains will be complete by 2016 addition. The number of ventilation shafts on the Victoria line is set to double to 26 when work is completed later this year. (TfL Website, *Taking the heat out of your journey*, 29 June 2011).

I want to see the Tube open one hour later on Friday and Saturday nights (Boris Johnson, *Getting Londoners Moving*, 2008, p. 10).

Not met.

Unfortunately it was not possible to keep the Tube open later due to exorbitant demands made by trade union bosses at a time of strained economic circumstances (Mayor of London, *Mayor's Questions*, 17 March 2010).

I will seek to negotiate, in good faith, no strike deals with the Tube unions to end the disruption caused by unnecessary strikes (Boris Johnson, *Getting Londoners Moving*, 2008, p. 10).

Not met.

Via London Underground's management, I have offered the Tube trade union bosses several opportunities to enter into negotiations on this point, but they refused. Their behaviour has sadly shown they have absolutely no interest in a no strike deal (Mayor of London, *Mayor's Questions*, 3 March 2011).

My Progress Report to Londoners on the 2008 Manifesto • Getting Londoners moving
223
24
My Progress Report to Londoners on the 2008 Manifesto • Getting Londoners moving

223

Promise delivered.

I will focus on upgrading the track and signals on the Tube to get a faster, more reliable service (Boris Johnson, Getting Londoners Moving, 2008, p. 10).

200km of track have been replaced so far (TfL Website, What's the plan).

The whole of the Victoria Line has already seen its track renewed and new signalling installed (TfL, Upgrade Plan, February 2011).

Work to install a new signalling system on the Jubilee Line is now also complete (TfL Website, What's the plan).

We have focused on upgrading the Tube. Overall, I have secured £4.6 billion in the next four years alone for Tube upgrades (TfL, Business Plan – GLA Budget Update 2011/12- 2014/15, p.10).

I will fight for rail commuters, and call an emergency summit with Train Operating Companies to demand longer trains, more frequent services, and lower fares (Boris Johnson, Getting Londoners Moving, 2008, p. 10).

Promise delivered.

I have now held three annual Train Operating Summits with train companies (Association of Train Operating Companies, Mayor brings London's rail industry together to get set for the Games, 27 February 2012).

This resulted in agreements on key areas including improving customer information, improving and station standards, increasing the frequency of services, simplifying the fares structure for London Underground and National Rail, and planning for future growth (Mayor of London, Mayor's Questions, 24 February 2010).

In addition, I completed a deal with the Government on Oyster Pay As You Go, making the commute easier for Londoners (Mayor of London, Mayor's Questions, 17 June 2009).

Platform wait time fell by 67 per cent between 2007/08 and 2011/12. Customer satisfaction with customer information and cleanliness increased, respectively from 79 to 82 and from 72 to 76, between 2007/08 and 2010/11 (TfL, Performance Data Almanac, 9 December 2011).

Making trains, buses and stations safer

Pledge   What has been achieved so far

I will require under-18s who have had their free bus travel withdrawn for anti-social behaviour to earn it back through voluntary and community service (Boris Johnson, Getting Londoners Moving, 2008, p. 24).

Promise delivered.

Launched in August 2009, Payback London scheme requires under 18s who have their free bus travel withdrawn to earn it back through community work (TfL, Press Release, Under 18s free travel rules begin, 1 June 2008).

I am pleased that we have used this scheme to show to young people the importance of caring for their city – clearing graffiti, picking up litter, and helping community schemes.

10,068 individuals have had their passes withdrawn since 2009 (Mayor of London, Mayor's Questions, 14 December 2011).

I will double the strength of Safer Transport Teams, by releasing funding for approximately 440 extra PCSOs to patrol the buses and 50 more fully warranted British Transport Police officers to patrol the worst suburban stations (Boris Johnson, Getting Londoners Moving, 2008, p. 24).

Promise delivered.

I prioritised safety on London's public transport. An extra 440 uniformed officers were recruited to the Safer Transport Teams (Mayor of London, Mayor's Questions, 16 July 2009).

There are now an extra 50 Transport Police on the Overground and particularly outer London stations (Mayor of London, Mayor's Questions, 21 May 2009).

In 2008, I also banned alcohol on the Tube (TfL, Press Release, Alcohol ban comes into force on the Tube, trams and buses from this Sunday, 1 June 30, May 2008).

Bus crime has decreased by 30 per cent during my term (MOPC, Monthly Report: Police and Crime Committee, 8 March 2012. Comparing 45 months of Ken Livingstone (August 2004 – April 2008) with 45 months of Boris Johnson (May 2008 – January 2012).

I will make buses safer by running a trial of live CCTV (Boris Johnson, Getting Londoners Moving, 2008, p. 24).

Promise delivered.

I launched a trial of live CCTV on 21 buses in October 2008.

The trial found that live CCTV provided no additional benefit and there are no plans to roll it out (BBC News Online, 20 October 2008, Mayor of London, Mayor's Questions, 17 March 2010).

However, under my Mayoralty bus crime has reduced by 30 per cent within 45 months (May 2008 – January 2012) (MOPC, Monthly Report: Police and Crime Committee, 8 March 2012. Comparing 45 months of Ken Livingstone (August 2004 – April 2008).

I also banned alcohol on London's public transport in 2008 (TfL, Press Release, Alcohol ban comes into force on the Tube, trams and buses from this Sunday, 1 June, 30 May 2008).

I will focus on reducing fare evasion by directing the MPA and TfL to investigate giving Revenue Protection Inspectors more powers (Boris Johnson, *Getting Londoners Moving*, 2008, p. 24).

Promise delivered.

A trial giving a team of Revenue Control Inspectors additional powers started in March 2010.

Subsequently we launched the Community Safety Accreditation Scheme (CSAS) to assist these Revenue Protection Inspectors in dealing with a range of anti-social behaviour on the bus network. Since May 2011, there have been 38 CSAS specific deployments resulting in 640 penalty fares, 470 prosecutions, 45 CSAS related offences and 2 Penalty Notices for Disorder (GLA website, *Keeping crime low on our transport system*).

I have also saved £7 million in lost fares from scrapping the unpopular bendy buses (Mayor of London, Press Release, *Final bendy buses banished from the streets of London*, 9 December 2011).

I will crack down on illegal minicabs by doubling the strength of the Cab Enforcement Unit, from 34 officers to 68 (Boris Johnson, *Getting Londoners Moving*, 2008, p. 24).

Promise delivered.

I am a strong supporter of London's cabbies. We have doubled the police team dedicated to tackling illegal minicabs, with 34 extra police officers in addition to the original 34 officers in 2008 (TfL, Website, *Cab enforcement*, Mayor of London, *Mayor's Questions*, 25 January 2012).

I have also introduced tougher penalties for any licensed driver convicted of tax touting to send out a clear message that this will not be tolerated. Since August 2008 licensed drivers convicted of tax touting now lose their licence for a minimum of one year. Over 600 private hire licenses have been revoked (Mayor of London, *Mayor's Questions*, 25 February 2009; TfL, Website, *Cab enforcement*.

Fresh perspectives on transport

Pledge

What has been achieved so far

I will end the era of the bendy bus by scrapping them (Boris Johnson, *Getting Londoners Moving*, 2008, p. 31).

Promise delivered.

I was elated when the last bendy bus went out of service on 9 December 2011, saving £7 million in lost fare revenue (Mayor of London Press Release, *Final bendy buses banished from the streets of London*, 9 December 2011).

I will launch a competition to produce a new, iconic London bus, a 21st century Routemaster with conductors, of which Londoners can be proud (Boris Johnson, *Getting Londoners Moving*, 2008, p. 31).

Promise delivered.

Following a competition to design a new London bus, the first new Routemaster bus, complete with conductors, entered service on 27 February 2012. I am proud that it is British designed and built and one of the greenest buses in Europe. (Mayor of London, Press Release, *Mayor unveils iconic final design for London's new bus*, 17 May 2010, TfL, Press Release, *First passengers jump aboard the new bus for London*, 27 February 2012).

I will make London a genuinely cycle-friendly city by introducing a central London cycle hire scheme and increasing the number of cycle parks (Boris Johnson, *Getting Londoners Moving*, 2008, p. 31).

Promise delivered.

As a dedicated cyclist, I notice everyday just how genuinely cycle-friendly London now is. I am proud of the fresh thinking, innovative approach that we have taken towards cycling.

The Barclays Cycle Hire scheme was rolled out across central London in mid 2010. (*The Guardian*, 30 July 2010, Mayor of London, Press Release, *Mayor's flagship cycling scheme - Barclays Cycle Hire - opens for business*, 30 July 2010).

Four Cycle Superhighway routes have also been opened and four more routes will open in 2013 (TfL, Website, *Cycle Superhighways*).

Between 1 April 2008 and 31 March 2010, over 40,000 cycle parking spaces were delivered across London (Mayor of London, *Mayor's Questions*, 26 January 2011).

We are also working hard to make cycling in London safer by improving junctions on Cycle Superhighways and have recently launched a major review of other junctions (Mayor of London, *Mayor's Questions*, 16 November 2011; TfL, *Press Release*, 7 February 2012).

I will use my influence as Chair of the MPA to ensure the police take cycle theft more seriously (Boris Johnson, Getting Londoners Moving, 2008, p. 31).

Promise delivered.

I have ensured that cycle theft is treated more seriously. The Cycle Security Plan produced by TfL, British Transport Police, City of London Police and Metropolitan Police Service was launched in July 2010 sets out what we have done, and plan to do, to prevent and deter cycle theft and criminal damage (TfL, Cycle Security Plan, 7 June 2010).

One of the Plan's proposed initiatives was the dedicated MPS Cycle Task Force, which was launched in July 2010. In its first year of operation alone, the Task Force made 175 arrests for crimes related to cycle theft and security marked over 12,000 bicycles. In 2010 cycle theft fell by 3 per cent (Mayor of London, Mayor's Questions, 14 September 2011).

I will encourage better integration of river services (Boris Johnson, Getting Londoners Moving, 2008, p. 31).

Promise delivered.

My team and I worked hard to improve integration for commuters who travel by riverboat. In 2009 we formed the River Concordat to bring boat operators, borough councils, pier owners, and others together to improve services. From November 2009 Riverboat services are now Oysterised (GLA Report, By the river, April 2009).

I will protect London's cab trade (Boris Johnson, Getting Londoners Moving, 2008, p. 31).

Promise delivered.

As a strong supporter of London's cabbies, I ensured that Black cab drivers to have formal representation on the TfL Board (TfL, Website, Board Member).

We have also reduced the bureaucracy they faced, scrapping half yearly taxi inspections by the Public Carriage (TfL, Press Release, Transport for London to abolish mid-year inspections of taxis, 6 November 2008).

We have doubled the police team dedicated to tackling illegal minicabs, with 34 extra police officers in addition to the original 34 officers in 2008 (TfL, Website, Cab enforcement, Mayor of London, Mayor's Questions, 25 January 2012).

I have also introduced tougher penalties for any licensed driver convicted of taxi touting to send out a clear message that this will not be tolerated. Since August 2008 licensed drivers convicted of taxi touting now lose their licence for a minimum of one year. Over 600 private hire licenses have been revoked (Mayor of London, Mayor's Questions, 25 February 2009; TfL, Website, Cab enforcement, 23 February 2009).

Making transport more convenient

Pledge   What has been achieved so far

I will provide Londoners with new LiveBus technology, so that every Londoner will be able to see in real time, online, where their bus is as they journey (Boris Johnson, Getting Londoners Moving, 2008, p. 37).

Promise delivered.

Londoners are now able to plan their journeys in real-time. This LiveBus technology was launched in 2011, allowing Londoners to check live arrival times online (TfL, Website, Live Bus).

Having already launched live bus arrival information for all 19,000 bus stops across London via the web and text messaging, our current focus is TfL's rollout of 2,500 new on-street signs at key bus stops (Mayor of London, Mayor's Questions, 25 January 2012).

I will stop the proposed Tube ticket office closures in outer London (Boris Johnson, Getting Londoners Moving, 2008, p. 37).

Promise delivered.

All stations including those in outer London which had a ticket office when I became Mayor have retained their ticket offices.

London Underground has changed the opening hours of ticket offices so that all stations with a ticket office have retained that facility, which is now open at times that reflect demand. This has also enabled a more efficient deployment of staff, who are often now freed from their position behind a glass screen to locations such as gate lines and platforms where they can be of most help to passengers. (Mayor of London, Mayor's Questions, 23 February 2011; Mayor of London, Mayor's Questions, 20 June 2007).

We intend to ensure that the number of Oyster outlets continues to increase in outer London (Boris Johnson, Getting Londoners Moving, 2008, p. 37).

Promise delivered.

The total number of Oyster Tickets Stops in London has increased from 2,578 in May 2008 to 3,823 in May 2011. Approximately 3,663 stops of the May 2011 provision are located in outer London (Mayor of London, Mayor's Questions, 14 December 2011).

I will allow Londoners to set up a direct debit to renew their travelcards (Boris Johnson, Getting Londoners Moving, 2008, p. 37).

Not met - a revised approach.

This has not been delivered, but Londoners can now pay their Congestion Charge by direct debit. Londoners can use direct debit to renew their oyster card on any journey. (TfL, Press Release, Auto Pay hits the mark, 16 September 2011)

226

Appreciating Our Seniors

Manifesto 2008

Mayor Boris Johnson

Making London safer

Pledge

Chair the Metropolitan Police Authority to make our streets safer (Boris Johnson, *Appreciating our Seniors*, 2008, p. 4).

What has been achieved so far

Promise delivered.

I became the Chairman of the Metropolitan Police Authority shortly after my election in May 2008.

Once the direction of London policing had been set I stood down from this role in January 2010 and promoted my Deputy, elected Assembly member, Kit Malthouse, preserving democratic accountability (BBC News Online, *Boris Johnson steps down from police authority*, 27 January 2010).

A Revised Approach

The MPA has since been replaced by the Mayor's Office for Policing and Crime (MOPC) which is headed by my Deputy Mayor for Policing and Crime. This change means that as Mayor and Deputy Mayor we will be even more accountable to Londoners for police performance, setting local priorities and allocating resources (GLA Website, *About MOPC*).

When we appointed the new Met Commissioner, I made it clear that this would be someone who has a clear strategy for tackling gang violence and youth crime and restoring pride in our great city. (BBC News Online, *Bernard Hogan-Howe new Metropolitan Police commissioner*, 27 September 2011)

As a result of my personal lead, crime has fallen in London by 10.6 per cent, robberies are down 16.7 per cent and murders have decreased by 24.4 per cent (MPS statistics. Comparing 44 months of Ken Livingstone September 2004 – April 2008 with 44 months of Boris Johnson May 2008 - December 2011).

Stand up against excessive police form-filling and support the scrapping of the stop and account form, lobbying the Government hard for its removal (Boris Johnson, *Appreciating our Seniors*, 2008, p. 4).

Promise delivered.

I have been focused on getting police officers out from behind their desks onto the street. In the two years from May 2008 to May 2010 the Met took 209 forms out of use (Mayor of London, *Mayor's Questions*, 19 May 2010).

In March 2011 the Government gave police forces the option to scrap the stop and account form (Home Office Website, 'Stop and search'). The Met has however decided to continuing using the stop and account form after an MPA consultation found robust support for recording "stop and account" to make sure the process was both transparent and accountable (The Guardian, *Met police will retain recording of "stop and account" street encounters*, 23 September 2011).

From January 2009 a shorter revised stop and search was launched, with the time it takes to complete reduced from 8-10 minutes to 3-5 minutes. (MPA, *A Practical Guide to stop and search community monitoring groups*, August 2009.)

22

My Progress Report to Londoners on the 2008 Manifesto – Appreciating our seniors

227

Promised delivered.

In 2008 I introduced Operation Herald, a scheme focused on cutting administrative tasks and paperwork for London's police officers (Mayor of London, Mayor's Questions, 14 July 2010).

A revised approach.

The scheme found that many of the administrative tasks could be cut altogether or done by civilian staff, rather than PCSOs, thus enabling more police presence on the streets.

Operation Herald moved clerical duties away from trained police officers to general staff, put more police on the front line and achieved efficiencies of 451 positions (Mayor of London, Mayor's Questions, 14 July 2010).

We continue to work to get more police out on the streets. There will be 1,000 more police officers than in 2008 by May 2012 (GLA, The Mayors Consultation Budget, 22 December 2011, p.1).

There are now 630 Safer Neighbourhood Teams, 1 for each of London's 624 neighbourhood wards, plus 5 more for the city of Westminster and 1 more for Crystal Palace where three borough meet. These are made up of at least 2 Police Constables and 3 PCSOs. There are over 4,100 police officers dedicated to neighbourhood policing (MPS Website, Safer Neighbourhoods).

Making progress.

As Mayor of London, I immediately delivered a ban on the alcohol on the Tube, bus, Docklands Light Railway, and tram services and stations across the capital (Mayor of London Press Release, Mayor unveils plans to ban alcohol on the transport network, May 2008).

The London Health Inequalities Strategy 2009 commits to enable Londoners to take action to reduce alcohol related harm. City Hall has been working with London Councils and other partners to improve the management of the night time economy and to reduce under-age sales. I also supported the work of the Greater London Alcohol and Drug Alliance (GLADA). I hosted the first Health leadership summit on 1 November 2010 (GLA, Health Inequalities Strategy one year on report, June 2011).

Alcohol abuse was one of the early priorities of the London Health Improvement Board, which was set up in 2011. Proposals include more support for alcohol abusers, working with licensing authorities to ensure alcohol is supplied responsibly, and developing an area scheme to highlight best practice in town centre management and bars and off-licences which sell alcohol responsibly (Mayor of London, Mayor's Questions, 15 June 2010, GLA, Press Release, Health priorities for London set by new board, 16 January 2012).

In addition, in February 2012 I announced that criminals convicted of serious drink-related offences will be fitted with 'sobriety bracelets' under a new pilot scheme in London. Anyone continuing to drink will be arrested and brought before a judge who has the option of sending them back to prison (Mayor of London, Press Release, Mayor welcomes new approach to alcohol related crime in London but says more is needed, 10 Feb 2012, PA News, Bracelet scheme for drink offenders, 11 February 2012).

Expect Police Community Support Officers to take some of the administrative burden from police officers, so they can spend more time out on the streets (Boris Johnson, Appreciating our Seniors, 2008, p. 4).

Crack down on binge-drinking and 'name and shame' councils that fail to use their powers to tackle the problem (Boris Johnson, Appreciating our Seniors, 2008, p. 4).

Helping older people get around safely

Pledge

What has been achieved so far

Protect and extend the

I moved quickly to ensure the Freedom Pass is now valid 24 hours a day. The pre 9.00am validity is paid for in full from the Mayor's Budget (Mayor of London, Mayor's Questions, 17 December 2008, Mayor of London, Mayor's Questions, 9 November 2011).

Increase safety on buses

I prioritised safety on London's public transport. An extra 440 unformed officers were recruited on the Safer Transport Teams (GLA Website, Mayor of London, Mayor's Questions, 16 July 2008).

There are now an extra 50 Transport Police on the Overground and particularly outer London stations (Mayor of London, Mayor's Questions, 21 May 2009).

In 2008, I also banned alcohol on the Tube (TfL, Press Release, Alcohol ban comes into force on the Tube, trams and buses from this Sunday, 1 June 30 May 2008).

Bus crime has decreased by 30 per cent during my term (MOPC, Monthly Report, Police and Crime Committee, 8 March 2012. Comparing 45 months of Ken Livingstone (August 2004 – April 2008) with 45 months of

Crack down on the young

Launched in August 2009, Payback London scheme requires under 18s who have their free bus travel withdrawn to earn it back through community work (TfL Free travel rules begin, 1 June 2008).

I am pleased that we have used this scheme to show to young people the importance of caring for their city – picking up litter, and helping once community schemes. 10,068 individuals have had their free passes withdrawn since 2009 (Mayor of London, Mayor's Questions, 14 December 2011).

Pledge

Protect and extend the Freedom Pass by working with the local councils (who fund it) to make it valid 24 hours a day (Boris Johnson, Appreciating our Seniors, 2008, p. 8).

Increase safety on buses by doubling the amount of police officers on patrol, adding 440 extra officers, and fund 50 extra fully-warranted British Transport Police Officers to patrol the worst railway stations in outer London (Boris Johnson, Appreciating our Seniors, 2008, p. 8).

Crack down on the young people who create trouble on the buses through the Payback London scheme, which will withdraw their right to free bus travel and allow them to earn it back (Boris Johnson, Appreciating our Seniors, 2008, p. 8).

Work with the Government and train operators to make more Overground stations step-free (Boris Johnson, *Appreciating our Seniors*, 2008, p. 8).

Promise delivered.

Despite tough financial times 15 Tube stations have been made step-free during my term in office, including Green Park, now a key step-free gateway to the West End, and Hainault Station in Redbridge (TfL Press Release, *Hainault Tube Station is now step-free with three new lift*, 3 March 2010).

At one of London's busiest Overground stations, Clapham Junction, I opened a new entrance and nine new lifts in 2011 (South West Trains, *Station upgrade gives Clapham Junction a big lift*, 20 May 2011).

A further two interchange stations (Blackfriars and Farringdon) will be made step-free in early 2012. Another five major Tube stations will be made step-free within the current Business Plan period, to 2014/18. At my instruction, TfL is also continuing to look at opportunities for developer-funded schemes at stations like South Kensington.

The Department for Transport announced last year that six London Overground stations will be made step-free, more than anticipated, and accessibility improvements will be made at Stratford DLR (Mayor of London, Mayor's Questions, 14 December 2011).

Making London age friendly

Pledge   What has been achieved so far

Encourage developers to design safer walkways, better paving, and greener spaces in new developments, including in the Thames Gateway (Boris Johnson, *Appreciating our Seniors*, 2008, p. 11).

Promise delivered.

The New London Plan includes a commitment to ensure that the design of all new housing developments and social infrastructure should be accessible to and take particular account of the needs of older people (GLA, *The London Plan*, July 2011).

Preserve the existence of small, independent shops through better protection in planning legislation (Boris Johnson, *Appreciating our Seniors*, 2008, p. 11).

Promise delivered.

My London Plan sets out a new policy to provide and support affordable shop units (GLA, *The London Plan*, July 2011).

I vocally supported the Evening Standard 'Save our Shops!' campaign, a new £4 million High Street Fund to offer supports to small business (London Evening Standard '*Big business boosts £3m fund to get London's high street working again*': 24 August 2011; Mayor of London, Mayor's Questions, 14 September 2011).

My Outer London Fund is a £50million three-year initiative launched in 2011, which will strengthen the vibrancy and growth of London's high streets and local areas. (London Assembly, *Mayor's Question Time*, 9 February 2012).

Improve open spaces in London, and work with local councils to improve street cleanliness (Boris Johnson, *Appreciating our Seniors*, 2008, p. 11).

Promise delivered.

Under the Help a London Park scheme, 11 parks have been awarded £6 million (GLA Website, Help a London Park).

The 'Love Clean London' application was launched in March 2011 to engage citizens and reduce litter and associated costs. (Mayor of London, Press Release, *Mayor launches assault on 'grime-crime' ahead of Olympic year*, March 2011).

I have been a vocal supporter of the Capital Clean-Up campaign, to make London cleaner and greener for the Olympics 2012 by co-ordinating events from litter-picks to litter enforcement and education activities across the capital. Around 1,700 volunteers took part in nearly 150 events across 22 boroughs during the summer 2011 campaign (Mayor of London, Mayor's Questions, 14 September 2011).

Safeguard domestic gardens by preventing developments on them (Boris Johnson, *Appreciating our Seniors*, 2008, p. 11).

Promise delivered.

In 2010 the Government changed the definition of brownfield sites so that domestic gardens are not included and no local authority is obliged to build on gardens if it does not want to (DCLG, Press Release, *Clark - new powers to prevent unwanted 'garden grabbing'*, 9 June 2010).

These changes were reflected in my new 2011 London Plan, under which private residential gardens are no longer classed as previously developed land and boroughs are allowed to introduce a presumption against development on back gardens or other private residential gardens in their Local Development Frameworks (GLA, *The London Plan*, July 2011).

As part of the Capital Growth project to encourage volunteering in London, 1032 food gardens have been unveiled with a target of 2000 spaces by the end of 2012. Grants from City Hall for the gardens range from £200 to £1000 (GLA, *Mayor announces 1000 + community food gardens tended by 35,000 Londoners*, June 2011).

Improve respect for older people by encouraging organisations to recruit older people as volunteers, including for the Olympics (Boris Johnson, *Appreciating our Seniors*, 2008, p. 11).

Promise delivered.

My team and I are working across all policy areas to improve respect for older Londoners. The GLA now encourages older people to volunteer (GLA Website, *Helping yourself and helping the community by volunteering*).

As part of a drive to improve respect for older people, through Team London, my £4m volunteering programme, young people will teach older people IT. Additionally to help vulnerable and elderly Londoners, eighty 'Contact the Elderly' groups have established across capital supported by 1,200 volunteers. (GLA Press Release, *Mayor of London supports London's isolated and older residents through Team London*, 15 December 2011).

Fighting for essential services

Pledge   *What has been achieved so far*

Making progress.

Support local health services by campaigning against closures and fighting to save local GP services (Boris Johnson, *Appreciating our Seniors*, 2008, p. 17).

I have persistently and vocally stood up to Government of London's local health services, including meeting with Andrew Lansley, Secretary of State for Health, to discuss health service in London and the Health and Inequality Strategy.

Two important facilities I have joined you in campaigning to save include the children's heart surgery unit at the Royal Brompton Hospital and the Urgent Care Centre at Queen Mary's Hospital in Bexley. (Evening Standard, *Boris joins fight to save children's heart centre*, 15 September 2011, Bexley Times, *Campaigners furious that the A&E and maternity closure at Sidcup are going ahead before review*, September 2010).

Campaign to protect Post Offices (Boris Johnson, *Appreciating our Seniors*, 2008, p. 17).

Promise delivered.

As soon as I took office I began lobbying the Government to protect London's post offices from closure (Mayor of London, Press Release, *Boris Johnson calls on Government to save London's Post Offices*, 28 June 2008).

However the then Labour Government failed to take action to reform the Post Office network. Currently there are no plans for a closure programme for the network of 11,500 branches and the Government has announced that the Post Office will receive 1.3 billion over the next four years to reform the network (BBC Online, *Post office to offer new services*, 9 November 2010).

Encourage awareness and take-up of entitlements by older people, especially Council Tax, through a 'Your Rights' information campaign (Boris Johnson, *Appreciating our Seniors*, 2008, p. 17).

Promise delivered.

I launched the 'Know your rights campaign' in partnership with Age UK, Citizens Advice Bureau and benefit and debt advice agencies in October 2011. The campaign aims to raise awareness of the support available to vulnerable Londoners to help them meet their homes and pay their energy bills this winter (London older people strategies group, *Mayor know your rights campaign*, 2011, Mayor of London, *Mayor's Questions*, 14 December 2011).

Backing London Business
Manifesto 2008

Mayor Boris Johnson

Introduce an automatic one-off Council Tax rebate to encourage home insulation, making homes warmer and more environmentally friendly (Boris Johnson, *Appreciating our Seniors*, 2008, p. 17).

Not met - a revised approach

Instead of a introducing a council tax rebate scheme, more effective initiatives have been introduced to increase the energy efficiency of London's homes:

I have committed £7.8 million to RE:NEW – an area-based homes energy efficiency programme which is installing free 'easy' energy efficiency and water efficiency measures such as showerheads and radiator panels in 55,000 London homes by March 2012, as well as referring homes for further insulation and heating measures. This means that every household in a RE:NEW area can receive free energy efficiency measures, no matter what type of home they live in or their income. This is particularly helpful for the nearly 60 per cent of homes in London with solid walls. (LDA website, *RE:NEW – Homes Energy Efficiency for Tomorrow*, accessed on 8 March 2012)

I have also frozen my council tax precept for the last three years to ensure that Londoners are protected from tax rises while maintaining London's public services and investing for the future (Mayor of London, Mayor's Questions, 15 June 2011).

231

Working with London's businesses

Pledge | What has been achieved so far

Hold biannual summits with representatives from across London's business communities (Boris Johnson, Backing London Business, p.5).

Promise delivered.

I have held quarterly meetings of the London Business Advisory Council (GLA Website).

As part of my 24 public meetings with Londoners I have held 5 Business Question Times. (GLA Website).

I have also therefore been able to negotiate good deals for Londoners, such as securing private sponsorship for the cycle hire scheme and cycle superhighways saving taxpayers money whilst delivering services (Mayor of London, Press Release, Barclays saddle up to sponsor London Cycle Hire Scheme, 28 May 2010).

Listen to the results of consultations (Boris Johnson, Backing London Business, p.5).

Promise delivered.

I pledged that I would listen to Londoners and I have done just that.

A key example is the re-opening of the Western Extension Zone consultation on 4 January 2011 (TfL, Consultation Results).

Listening to Londoners, Boris subsequently scrapped the scheme at 62 per cent of those who responded to the consultation wanted (TfL, Press Release, Mayor confirms removal of Congestion Charge Western Extension Zone by Christmas and introduction of CC Auto Pay in New Year, 20 October 2010).

Transport for London undertook a consultation on a traffic signal site in Croydon. Based on the feedback by Londoners, the decision has been made on 24th February to remove these signals. (TfL, Traffic Signal Removal Programme, 24th February).

In contrast, Ken Livingstone imposed the WEZ.

Review the LDA's enterprise activity to ensure that London's businesses and communities are getting the support they need (Boris Johnson, Backing London Business, p.5).

Promise delivered.

As Mayor I have delivered targeted investment through regular dialogue with business. At the very beginning of the recession we formed an Economic Recovery Action Plan. This has helped London's businesses in dealing with the impact of long term economic problems and short term events such as the riots. I have focused on the long term economic well being of local borough centres and high streets.

In my first week as Mayor I formed a Forensic Audit Panel to examine the activities of the LDA and suggest reform of the body (GLA, Report of the Mayor's Forensic Audit Panel, 15 July 2008, p.9). This led to changes at the top and efficiencies being made to tune of £445,000 a year (Communities and Local Government Department, Location Bill Impact Assessment, Jan 2011, All Business Website).

As a result of this scrutiny, I decided to abolish the wasteful LDA in order to cut bureaucracy and its functions will be brought into the Mayor's office, leading to greater accountability (BBC News Website, Mayor Boris Johnson proposes more powers for office, 15 June 2010).

I also took a personal lead towards the 2011 riots and helped London businesses who were affected get back on their feet through the High Street Fund (BBC News Online, London businesses hit by riots can apply for £3m funds, 26 August 2011, The Mayor's proposals for devolution, June 2010).

Additionally we have provided £50m for regeneration projects in town centres affected by the disturbances, with the Government providing £20m especially for the areas of Tottenham and Croydon. Proposals for a further £40m from the Outer London Fund are underway, (The Mayor of London, 'Riot regeneration funding, 9 December 2011).

Make it easier for businesses to do business with the GLA group. The London 2012 Organising Committee and Olympic Delivery Authority (Boris Johnson, Backing London Business, p.5).

Promise delivered.

We have made it easier for businesses to work with the GLA group by championing initiatives such as the CompeteFor website started in 2007 (GLA, 'CompeteFor' Website) which allows businesses to bid for City Hall contracts and makes the procurement process more accessible for firms of all sizes. 155,000 businesses are registered and there are 10,500 contract opportunities. 8574 of which have been awarded as of the 8th March. Over 74 per cent of contracts have been awarded to SMEs and 37 per cent of the contracts have been awarded to London businesses as of the 8th March (City Hall, CompeteFor Website).

To date over £270 million worth of Games-related contracts have already been won by suppliers through London through Compete For, (Mayor of London, CompeteFor).

The GLA group has also helped improve the cash flow of small and medium-sized enterprises through the prompt payment of their invoices, with an average of 86.6 per cent of all valid invoices from SMEs paid within 10 working days. (GLA, Delivering Responsible Procurement, February 2012).

In the future we will make sure the LDA adopts business-like financial transparency and reporting principles (Boris Johnson, *Backing London Business*, p.8).

Promise delivered.

In the first week after I was elected as Mayor of London I announced the formation of the Forensic Audit Panel which reported in July 2008 (Legacy London Website, *'Report of the Mayor's Forensic Audit Panel'*).

The report concluded that Ken Livingstone's LDA 'misspent' money 'on a massive scale, say tens of millions' (GLA, *Report of the Mayor's Forensic Audit Panel*, 15 July 2008).

The review of the LDA was conducted by the Forensic Audit Panel which reported in July 2008.

The report concluded that Ken Livingstone's LDA 'misspent' money 'on a massive scale, say tens of millions.'

It also found that there were failings in the LDA's leadership, governance and basic controls which led to the conclusion that the former LDA board was ineffective (GLA, *Report of the Mayor's Forensic Audit Panel*, 15 July 2008).

We will also investigate introducing a target for the GLA and its functional bodies to procure a given proportion of goods and services from local and small businesses (Boris Johnson, *Backing London Business*, p.8).

Promise delivered.

After I investigated, we changed the responsible procurement policy. Although a specific target was not set, we decided on a new policy to ensure that a diverse range of suppliers are encouraged across the GLA group. It is also now incumbent on businesses to communicate when there is an employment benefit with local communities (Mayor of London, *GLA Group Responsible Procurement Policy*).

Prompt payment is also a key plank of this policy to support small businesses. (Responsible Procurement Website).

Making London an attractive place to do business

Pledge

What has been achieved so far

Make business crime a police priority (Boris Johnson, *Backing London Business*, p.9).

Promise delivered.

I was determined to help London's businesses to thrive in as safe an environment as possible.

The MPS now run a number of initiatives including Shop Watch, 646 Safer Neighbourhood Teams in stores and Business and Pub Watch among others (GLA Website, *Focusing on business crime*).

The MPS Policing Plan is also committed to working with businesses to combat crime (MPA/MPS, *Policing Plan 2010-13*).

As a result, business crime has fallen by 3.4 per cent across London. Greenwich, Bexley, Enfield, Kingston-upon-Thames, Lewisham and Waltham Forest have all seen decreases of over 10 per cent (GLA, Press Release, *Mayor welcomes drop in London business crime*, 29 January 2011).

Encourage planners to use section 106 to secure affordable premises for small businesses (Boris Johnson, *Backing London Business*, p.9).

Promise delivered.

The London Plan sets out a new policy to provide and support affordable shop units (GLA, *London Plan*, July 2011).

Scrap the £25 charge which would cost London's businesses thousands of pounds a year (Boris Johnson, *Backing London Business*, p.9).

Promise delivered.

I have not introduced the £25 Congestion Charge. We also now have a flexible Congestion Charge pricing, paying has been made easier through the introduction of an online account system (TfL, Press Release, *Mayor confirms removal of Congestion Charge Western Extension Zone by Christmas and introduction of CC Auto Pay in New Year*, 24 November 2010).

The Western Extension of the WEZ Congestion Charge zone was removed following a consultation in December 2010 (TfL, Press Release, *Mayor confirms removal of Congestion Charge Western Extension Zone by Christmas and introduction of CC Auto Pay in New Year*, 20 October 2010).

Following the removal of the WEZ, a lower than expected increase in traffic driving into and within the former zone and no discernible impact on air quality were reported (TfL, Press Release, *TfL announces initial results following removal of the Western Extension of the Congestion Charging Zone*, 03 June 2011).

Help all businesses avoid Congestion Charge fines by allowing them to pay by account (Boris Johnson, Backing London Business, p.9).

Promise delivered.

In October 2009 I made it easier for Londoners to pay the Congestion Charge by introducing a number of measures, including the introduction of an automated account system (TfL, Press Release, Mayor outlines Congestion Charge overhaul, 15 October 2009).

An Organisation Account allows businesses with six or more vehicles to pay the daily Congestion Charge by direct debit if they are registered for Fleet Auto Pay (TfL, Website, Congestion Charging).

Ken Livingstone made a similar pledge in 2004 but failed to deliver (Ken Livingstone, Manifesto, 2004).

Improve London's transport infrastructure (Boris Johnson, Backing London Business, p.9).

Making progress.

I made investment modernisation and improvement of London Transport infrastructure a key priority of my Mayoralty.

In order to do this I have secured a record £22 billion in the past four years – this includes £6 billion in the Tube and £15.9 billion in Crossrail (HMT, Comprehensive Spending Review, 20 October 2010).

In addition, highways across the city have benefited from over £47 million of investment since 2008 (Mayor of London, Mayor's Questions, 14 December 2011, 4058/2011).

I have secured £4.6 billion in the next four years alone for Tube upgrades (TfL, Business Plan – GLA Budget Update 2011/12- 2014/15, p.10).

We also now have an East London Line extension, creating London's first ever orbital railway (HMT, Spending Review, 22 October 2010, p.23; Mayor of London, Mayor's Questions, 25 February 2009; TfL, Website, London Overground).

Champion London at home and abroad (Boris Johnson, Backing London Business, p.9).

Promise delivered.

I have tirelessly been a champion of London throughout my Mayoralty. Examples of where this positive lobbying brought tangible benefits for the city include the record infrastructure investment that I have secured from the government for projects in London including Crossrail, broadband, smart ticketing, the Northern Line extension to Battersea and the Thames Tideway Tunnel (HMT, Autumn Statement 2010; Crossrail Website, 'Funding').

I have also been vocal in my support for a new airport in the Thames Estuary to help grow London's businesses which has seen the Government announce a consultation into related proposals (GLA Press Release, Mayor of London urges government to act on aviation, 21 November 2011).

The reason I have championed London's causes so persistently abroad is to stand up for the business that make our city a great economic powerhouse. I have been to Brussels to emphasise to them policies which would damage the City of London such as the Financial Transactions Tax and employment directives. (The Telegraph, Mayor of London Boris Johnson takes hedge funds fight to Brussels, 29 Aug 2009)

I am proud that we recently secured investment offers of £10 billion at the World Economic Forum in Davos (The Telegraph, London Mayor Boris Johnson reveals investors £10bn investment offer, 28 January 2012).

We have also invested £2 million in the 'Only in London' tourism campaign which generated £100 million of income to London.

This work has helped to ensure that London remains the most competitive city in Europe in which to do business (Economist Intelligence Unit, The Times, 13 March 2012).

Unlike Ken Livingstone who related that worldwide capitalism kills more people every day than Hitler ever did' and jeopardises our financial services by offering to: 'Hang a banker a week until the others improve' (NME Magazine, April 2000; The Guardian, Ken Livingstone sparks anger with 'Hang bankers' speech, 17 February 2012).

We plan to institute greater independent oversight over Tube and Crossrail investments – to ensure that the mistakes of Metronet aren't repeated and that Londoners get better value for money from their investments (Boris Johnson, *Backing London Business*, p.12).

Promise delivered.

I scrapped the Labour Government's expensive Public-Private Partnership (PPP) and brought the project in-house under TfL (BBC News Website, *PPP deal for London Tube upgrades a colossal waste*, 10 May 2010).

This allows for better scrutiny and control over costs (*The Guardian, Boris Johnson's TfL pushing London Underground PPP down the tubes*, 4 January 2010).

The cost of the Jubilee Line upgrade illustrates how much money can now be saved following the end of the PPP. The original projected cost for the Jubilee line upgrade when the contract was signed at the end of 2002 was £285.3 million. However, the final cost was £721 million, more than double (TfL, Press Release, *Final Jubilee line upgrade cost vindicates decision to end PPP says TfL*, 12 October 2011).

Crossrail will provide an increase of 10 per cent in the capacity of London's rail network with larger increases along the outer London corridors on which Crossrail will operate. For example, the current Heathrow Connect service runs two trains per hour. This will be replaced with four, longer Crossrail trains per hour which will more than triple the passenger capacity of these services on the Great Western Main Line (Mayor of London, *Mayor's Questions*, 16 November 2011).

We will trial orbital bus routes in the outer suburbs to connect key transport hubs such as town centres and railway station (Boris Johnson, *Backing London Business*, p.12).

Promise delivered.

A thorough trial I conducted showed that although the buses were used, they were not very cost effective (TfL, *Surface Transport Panel Report*, November 2009).

However, the East London Transit bus is now running services from Ilford to Dagenham Dock via Barking town centre. The second phase will run from Barking town centre to the Barking Riverside development (TfL Website, *East London Transit*).

We will lobby the Government to invest in additional rail capacity in South London (Boris Johnson, *Backing London Business*, p.11).

Promise delivered.

As Mayor, I have consistently and successfully lobbied for funds for key rail projects in South London, such as work to increase the capacity on the Richmond to Clapham Junction service to Stratford and the completion of the first ever orbital rail from Clapham Junction to Surrey Quays (TfL Website, *Projects and Schemes*).

Providing training that businesses need and Londoners want

Pledge   *What has been achieved so far*

Cut through bureaucracy and consolidate the Adult Skills agendas and funding organisations in London (Boris Johnson, *Backing London Business*, p.4).

Promise delivered.

We have centralised the training and skills provision at City Hall via reforms to the London Skills and Employment Board. This allows for a more flexible approach to the commissioning of training, and is set out in a report in 2008 (LSEB, *London's Future The Skills and Employment Strategy for London 2008-2013*).

The skills agenda has been taken up by the new London Local Enterprise Partnership from June 2011. (Future of London, *New details emerge on London's LEP*, June 2011).

Listen to employers and Londoners (Boris Johnson, *Backing London Business*, p.4).

Promise delivered.

As Mayor of London, I have ensured that I am is accessible to Londoners and employers. Between November 2008 and November 2011 I held seven People's Question Times (GLA Website, *People's Question Time*).

Other platforms have also been embraced to work alongside People's Question Times such as the 3 Talk London events held so far and the 9 Mayor's Consultation meetings held so far on specific issues, including 2 on business and the economy (Talk London Website, GLA Website, *People's Question Time*).

Another example of how my team and I listen to London's businesses is by acting on the results of consultations such as the decision to scrap the Western Extension Zone for the Congestion Charge (Mayor of London, Press Release, *48 hours until the end of the Western Extension Zone*, 22 December 2010).

Quarterly meetings of his London Business Advisory Council alongside annual meetings of his International Business Advisory Council give businesses a further opportunity to raise issues with the Mayor (GLA Website).

This is more than the statutory minimum of 16 POTs Ken Livingstone held over his two terms in office (GLA Website).

Promote skills to Londoners through a single branded service for advice and guidance (Boris Johnson, *Backing London Business*, p.4).

Promise delivered.

The new London Local Economic Partnership will be the single branded service for advice on skills and guidance (Future of London Website, 10 June 2011).

This has allowed us to take a more employer led approach to training as has been highlighted by the creation of 40,000 new apprenticeships with 100,000 being aimed for by the end of 2012 (Mayor of London, Press Release, *Mayor of London aims for 100,000 apprenticeships by 2012*, 27 October 2011).

Protecting Our Local Environment
Manifesto 2008

Mayor Boris Johnson

Champion and support the London's 2011 WorldSkills Competition (Boris Johnson, *Backing London Business*, p.4).

Promise delivered.

WorldSkills was held in 2011 at the Excel Centre in London and saw 150,000 delegates watch 1,000 young people from 57 countries take part in the skills competition.

I attended and thoroughly enjoyed taking part of the 'Have a Go Launch' (My Venue Website, 7 October 2011; The Guardian, *Lessons in Life*, 1 March 2011).

My Progress Report to Londoners on the 2008 Manifesto • Backing London business

49

Protecting and preserving open spaces

| Pledge | What has been achieved so far |

I will protect green belt land and open space from development (Boris Johnson, *Protecting our Local Environment*, 2008, p. 3).

Promise delivered.

The new London Plan, published in 2011, commits to protecting the green belt and other open spaces: 'Growth will be supported and managed across all parts of London to ensure it takes place within the current boundaries of Greater London without: a. encroaching on the Green Belt; b. having unacceptable impacts on the environment (GLA, *London Plan*, p.34 July 2011).

I will amend the London Plan to protect against development on gardens (Boris Johnson, *Protecting our Local Environment*, 2008, p. 3).

Promise delivered.

In 2010 the Government changed the definition of brownfield sites so that domestic gardens are not included and no local authority is obliged to build on gardens if it does not want to (DCLG, Press Release, *Clark – new powers to prevent unwanted 'garden grabbing'*, 9 June 2010).

These changes were reflected in my new 2011 London Plan, under which private residential gardens are no longer classed as previously developed land and boroughs are allowed to introduce a presumption against development on back gardens or other private residential gardens in their Local Development Frameworks (GLA, *The London Plan*, July 2011).

I will invest £6 million in making our open spaces safer and cleaner (Boris Johnson, *Protecting our Local Environment*, 2008, p. 3).

I have also supported domestic gardens through the Capital Growth Project. 1032 food gardens have been unveiled with a target of 2000 spaces by the end of 2012. Grants from City Hall for the gardens range from £200 to £1000 (GLA, *Mayor announces '1000 + community food gardens tendered by 35,000 Londoners*, June 2011).

Promise delivered.

I have dedicated a significant amount of my time as Mayor visiting schemes to improve our open spaces. Under the Help a London Park scheme, 11 parks including Crane Valley Park in Richmond and Wandle Park in Croydon have been awarded £6 million (GLA Website, *Help a London Park*).

I am also investing £390 million in 80 outdoor spaces projects over the next two years (GLA, *Great Outdoor*).

I have been a vocal supporter of the Capital Clean-Up campaign, to make London cleaner and greener for the Olympics 2012 by co-ordinating events from litter-picks to litter enforcement and education activities across the capital. Around 1,700 volunteers took part in nearly 150 events across 22 boroughs during the summer 2011 campaign (Mayor of London, *Mayor's Questions*, 14 September 2011).

I will invest in 10,000 street trees to improve the local neighbourhoods that need them most (Boris Johnson, *Protecting our Local Environment*, 2008, p. 3).

Promise delivered.

I was delighted to plant the 10,000th tree on the 14th of February 2012. 10,000 trees have been planted in areas in 29 boroughs considered to be of greatest need since 2008 (Mayor of London, *Mayor's Questions*, 23 March 2011, GLA Press Release, *Boris marks delivery of his trees and parks promises by planting 10,000th street tree*, 14 February 2012).

I will work with the boroughs to make London cleaner (Boris Johnson, *Protecting our Local Environment*, 2008, p. 3).

Promise delivered.

I have worked constructively with boroughs of all political colours to make London cleaner. The 'Love Clean London' mobile phone application was launched in March 2011 to engage citizens and reduce litter and associated costs. (Mayor of London, Press Release, *Mayor launches assault on 'grime-crime' ahead of Olympic year*, March 2011).

I have been a vocal supporter of the Capital Clean-Up campaign, to make London cleaner and greener for the Olympics 2012 by co-ordinating events from litter-picks to litter enforcement and education activities across the capital. Around 1,700 volunteers took part in nearly 150 events across 22 boroughs during the summer 2011 campaign (Mayor of London, *Mayor's Questions*, 14 September 2011).

In addition, the new non-emergency phone number 101 encourages reporting of fly-tipping for boroughs to take action on these reports (Direct Gov Website, *Reporting non-emergency crimes using 101*).

I will encourage every member of staff in the GLA, TfL, MPA, and LFEPA, to do one day a year volunteering for a green charity (Boris Johnson, *Protecting our Local Environment*, 2008, p. 3).

Promise delivered.

I have encouraged volunteering throughout my time as Mayor. I have given all Greater London Authority staff three days a year leave for volunteering activities. The 2011 annual staff survey showed that 53 per cent of GLA staff undertake volunteering activities either inside or outside work-time (Mayor of London, *Mayor's Questions*, 14 December 2011).

My advisers and directors were also involved in a variety of activities during volunteering week (1–7 June 2010) and on an on-going basis (Mayor of London Press Release, *Mayor goes back to school to urge businesses to get volunteering*, 26 May 2010).

If trials of a new 101 non-emergency number prove successful, we will look at the options for rolling it out across the capital (Boris Johnson, *Protecting our Local Environment*, 2008, p. 8).

Promise delivered.

My pledge has not only met been in London, there is also now a new 101 non-emergency service available across England and Wales, providing members of the public with an easy way to report less urgent crime, such as fly tipping, and speak to local officers (Direct Gov Website, *Reporting non-emergency crimes using 101*).

Making it easier to recycle and reduce waste

Pledge

What has been achieved so far

I will make recycling easier and more convenient through innovative approaches, such as paying Londoners to recycle (Boris Johnson, *Protecting our Local Environment*, 2008, p. 9).

Making progress.

In 2010 a trial of a scheme called Recycle Bank was launched in London. The scheme gives householders shopping vouchers or donations to charity to the value of how much they recycle (The Guardian, 'Boris Johnson acts to boost London's recycle rates', 18 January 2010, Mayor of London, Mayor's Questions, 16 December 2009).

Lambeth is the first London council to trial Recycle Bank using a newly-developed model of the initiative that specifically caters for flats (Let's Recycle Website, *First London RecycleBank scheme launches in Lambeth*, 16 May 2011).

I am keen for this scheme to be rolled out across other London boroughs.

I will work with the boroughs to improve recycling rates and reduce the amount of London's waste that is sent to landfill (Boris Johnson, *Protecting our Local Environment*, 2008, p. 9).

Promise delivered.

Since I became Mayor, recycling rates have increased from 25 per cent in 2007/8 to 32 per cent in 2010/11 (GLA, *Household Waste Recycling Rates*).

This improvement has been helped by initiatives such as Recycle Bank and the ramping up of Recycle for London's programme, which is now being used by most of London's boroughs to help their communications with residents and businesses.

In addition, I have set targets for waste reduction, reuse and recycling that are tougher than the EU Waste Directive targets (Mayor of London, Mayor's Questions, 5 May 2011).

I will support a ban on plastic bags in London (Boris Johnson, *Protecting our Local Environment*, 2008, p. 9).

I have been a vocal supporter of a ban on plastic bags in London. I have held talks with council leaders and the London Waste and Recycling Board on the best way to reduce bag numbers, and have carefully studied the new powers used in Wales. (Daily Mail, *Boris calls for plastic bag ban across London in fight against 'poisonous' waste and litter*, 5 August 2011).

I have written to the Government asking it to consider whether it is using its powers effectively to reduce the number of single use plastic bags in circulation (Mayor of London, Mayor's Questions, 14 December 2011).

The capital's waste strategy sets out my support for locally-driven campaigns, like Greener Upon Thames voluntary reduction scheme, and for the national programme delivered by the Association of Convenience Stores. Options to deliver a voluntary reduction scheme tailored to London's small and independent retail environment are being investigated and I have also written to major supermarkets to encourage them to re-double their efforts (Mayor of London, Mayor's Questions, 16 November 2011).

Making transport more sustainable

Pledge

What has been achieved so far

Promise delivered.

Get London's traffic flowing better, so reducing traffic emissions (Boris Johnson, *Protecting our Local Environment*, 2008, p. 13).

We have taken concrete steps to improve congestion in London. 2,000 traffic light signals have been reviewed since 2009 and a further 1,000 signals are being reviewed in 2011/12 (TfL Website, *Smoothing traffic flow*).

Changes made to over 1,000 traffic light signals in 2010 delivered a six per cent reduction in unnecessary delays at traffic signals (TfL, Press Release, *Londoners to face fewer delays at traffic signals*, July 2010).

A list of 145 signals which could be removed was also published in June 2010 and a further 26 were added to the list in November 2011.

Out of the 204 suggested removals, 22 have already been removed with removal agreed for another 15 and 80 are under discussion with boroughs. It has been agreed between TfL and the boroughs that the remaining 87 signals will be maintained (TfL, Website, *Suggested signal removal list*, Feb 2012; TfL Website, *Smoothing traffic flow*).

Lobby the Government to stop the expansion of Heathrow (Boris Johnson, *Protecting our Local Environment*, 2008, p. 13).

Promise delivered.

Throughout my term as Mayor, I have argued that expanding Heathrow is not in London's best interests due to its geographic location, stating in 2011 that "noise problems and poor air quality at Heathrow have reached such levels that further increases in the number of air traffic movements there are untenable". (Public Sector Travel, *London Plan: Boris rules out Heathrow expansion*, 28 July 2011).

The national Government has now also made clear that it does not support the construction of additional runways at Heathrow, Gatwick or Stansted (Hansard, 6 April 2011).

I am however a strong supporter of greater aviation capacity for London, and have produced two detailed reports on the business case and necessity of London remaining a leading European hub (GLA Press Release, *Mayor urges Government to act on aviation*, 21 November 2011).

Increase the number of hybrid buses when feasible (Boris Johnson, *Protecting our Local Environment*, 2008, p. 13).

Promise delivered.

The hybrid bus programme will see 300 new hybrid buses introduced by 2012 (TfL, *Hybrid buses*).

Make London a genuinely cycle-friendly city by introducing a central London cycle hire scheme and increasing the number of cycle parks (Boris Johnson, Protecting our Local Environment, 2008, p. 13).

Promise delivered.

As a dedicated cyclist, I notice everyday just how genuinely cycle-friendly London now is. I am proud of the fresh thinking, innovative approach that we have taken towards cycling.

The Barclays Cycle Hire scheme was rolled out across central London in mid 2010. (The Guardian, Cycle hire scheme launched in London, 30 July 2010, Mayor of London, Press Release, Mayor's flagship cycling scheme - Barclays Cycle Hire - opens for business, 30 July 2010).

Four Cycle Superhighway routes have also been opened and four more routes will open in 2013 (TfL Website, Cycle Superhighways).

Between 1 April 2008 and 31 March 2010, over 40,000 cycle parking spaces were delivered across London (Mayor of London, Mayor's Questions, 26 January 2011).

We are also working hard to make cycling in London safer by improving junctions on Cycle Superhighways and have recently launched a major review of other junctions (Mayor of London, Mayor's Questions, 16 November 2011; TfL, Press Release, TfL confirms priority junctions for cycle safety review, 7 February 2012).

Use my influence as Chair of the MPA to ensure the police take cycle theft more seriously (Boris Johnson, Protecting our Local Environment, 2008, p. 13).

Promise delivered.

I have ensured that cycle theft is treated more seriously. The Cycle Security Plan produced by TfL, British Transport Police, City of London Police and Metropolitan Police Service was launched in July 2010 sets out what we have done, and plan to do, to prevent and deter cycle theft and criminal damage (TfL, Cycle Security Plan).

One of the Plan's proposed initiatives was the dedicated MPS Cycle Task Force, which was launched in July 2010. In its first year of operation alone, the Task Force made 176 arrests for crimes related to cycle theft and security marked over 12,000 bicycles. In 2010 cycle theft fell by 3 per cent (Mayor of London, Mayor's Questions, 14 September 2011).

Tackling climate change

Pledge

What has been achieved so far

Work to help cut London's carbon emissions by 60 per cent from their 1990 levels by 2025, including collaborating with the C40 group of cities to develop strategies to tackle climate change (Boris Johnson, Protecting our Local Environment, 2008, p. 20).

Promise delivered.

We have several active projects working towards this aim:

The RE:NEW programme, which aims to reduce CO2 emissions from existing homes. 11,000 homes have already been retrofitted, with a total of 55,000 due by end of March 2012.

The RE:FIT programme pilot, held in 42 GLA group buildings, guaranteeing energy savings worth of £1 million per year. 140 organisations have already shown interest in the model to date, with 200 buildings committed to be retrofitted, to the combined value of over £35 million.

The £3million RE:CONNECT programme has created 10 Low Carbon Zones across London, which are on track to deliver a 20.12 per cent CO2 reduction by 2012.

The London Heat Map, an interactive tool that allows Londoners to identify opportunities for decentralised energy projects in London.

The £100 million London Green Fund to invest in low carbon waste, decentralised energy and energy efficiency (Mayor of London, Mayor's Questions, 5 May 2011; GLA, Press Release, New figures show green economy in London is vibrant and bucking downturn, 26 October 2011). The Mayor's Climate Change Mitigation and Energy Team have been working with the C40 Cities to share their expertise on monitoring carbon emissions and to lower carbon emission in London (Mayor of London, Mayor's Questions, 15 June 2011).

Work with the boroughs to encourage Londoners to install insulation in return for Council Tax rebates (Boris Johnson, Protecting our Local Environment, 2008, p. 20).

Promise delivered.

I have worked with London's boroughs to increase the energy efficiency of London's homes. Instead of a introducing a council tax rebate scheme, more effective initiatives have been introduced.

I have committed £7.8 million to RE:NEW – an area-based homes energy efficiency programme which is installing free 'easy' energy efficiency and water efficiency measures such as showerheads and radiator panels in 55,000 London homes by March 2012, as well as referring homes for further insulation and heating measures. This means that every household in a RE:NEW area can receive free energy efficiency measures, no matter what type of home they live in or their income. This is particularly helpful for the nearly 60 per cent of homes in London with solid walls. (GLA, Mayor Answers, 14 December 2011).

I have also frozen my council tax precept for the last three years to ensure that Londoners are protected from tax rises while maintaining London's public services and investing for the future (Mayor of London, Mayor's Questions, 15 June 2011).

I will set a positive example to the corporate sector by upgrading the energy efficiency of the GLA group buildings, and pressing the sector to retrofit buildings with company measures developed and we we have its promises to improve the energy efficiency of its buildings in London (Boris Johnson, Protecting our Local Environment, 2008, p. 20).

Promise delivered.

I have set an example through the pilot of the REFIT programme in 42 GLA group buildings. This delivered guaranteed energy savings worth £1 million per year. An innovative commercial model to support the public sector to retrofit buildings with company measures has also been developed and we we have successfully applied for European Local Energy Assistance (ELENA) funding to accelerate its rollout. (Mayor of London, Mayor's Questions, 5 May 2011).

140 organisations have already shown interest in the model to date, with 200 buildings committed to be retrofitted, to the combined value of over £35 million (GLA, Press Release, New figures show green economy in London is vibrant and bucking downturn, 26 October 2011).

I will promote the development of electricity micro-generation in London and the greater use of on-site renewable energy. (Boris Johnson, Protecting our Local Environment, 2008, p. 20).

Promise delivered.

I have promoted this consistently.

I backed EDF Energy's bid for funding to provide a smart electricity network in London, including increased micro-generation and renewable energy installations (Energy Efficiency News, Micro-generation, 24 June 2010).

The Mayor has undertaken the first ever decentralised energy master-planning exercise across London and is now supporting the commercialisation of large-scale decentralised projects which can heat and power London's existing and new buildings more carbon-efficiently (GLA, Press Release, New figures show green economy in London is vibrant and bucking downturn, 26 October 2011).

I will support the introduction of a Waste Heat Levy and the greater use of Combined Heat and Power in London to improve the efficiency of power generation (Boris Johnson, Protecting our Local Environment, 2008, p. 20).

Promise delivered.

I have persistently supported the Waste Heat Levy, and GLA senior officers have regular meetings with officials in the Department of Energy and Climate Change about introducing one. Under the Municipal Waste Management Waste Strategy, a carbon floor is suggested for waste to energy plants, encouraging boroughs and operators to ensure such plants are operated in CHP mode. Under the London Plan, developers are required to use CHP in new developments where appropriate. The Climate Change Mitigation and Energy Strategy also supports CHP as part of the decentralised energy programme. £3 million of European Local Energy Assistance Funding from the European Commission has been secured to support the commercialisation of large scale decentralised energy projects, including CHP projects (Mayor of London, Mayor's Questions, 14 December 2011).

I will use all the powers at my disposal to push the use of renewable energy sources in London (Boris Johnson, Protecting our Local Environment, 2008, p. 20).

Making progress.

I have already undertaken the first ever decentralised energy master-planning exercise across London and aim now supporting the commercialisation of large-scale decentralised projects which can heat and power London's existing and new buildings more carbon-efficiently (GLA, Press Release, Student inventors can help make London greener with Mayor's £20,000 Low Carbon Prize, 26 October 2011).

I also backed EDF Energy's bid for funding to provide a smart electricity network in London, including increased micro-generation and new renewable energy installations (Energy Efficiency News, Micro-generation, 24 June 2010).

I will offer a Mayor's prize for new research into low carbon technology, to promote innovation (Boris Johnson, Protecting our Local Environment, 2008, p. 20).

Promise delivered.

The Mayor's Low Carbon Prize was launched in 2011 (GLA, Press Release, 24 November 2011).

I announced the winner of the inaugural Mayor's Low Carbon Prize, at a ceremony at City Hall on 7 March 2012. The £20,000 award, sponsored by the Berkeley Group, was a student from Kingston University for his "green key" to supply 'new residents with an electronic key containing up to date information on local services and ideas to help them live more sustainably. (Mayor of London, Mayor's low carbon source-Recognising student innovation).

Building a Better London
Manifesto 2008

Mayor Boris Johnson

Helping more Londoners to afford their own home

Pledge

What has been achieved so far

Help people who do not qualify for Government intermediate housing schemes to benefit from a new 'First Steps Housing Scheme', offering quality homes 20 per cent below the local market rate, built on non-essential Brownfield land released by the GLA estate (Boris Johnson, *Building a Better London*, 2008, p. 6).

Promise delivered.

In September 2010 I initiated the First Steps programme (Mayor of London, Press Release, *Mayor and HCA to help 1,000 families get a foot on property ladder*, 21 September 2010).

I have amended the London Plan to raise the income level required for 'First Steps' eligibility above that set by Government schemes, enabling anyone earning less than £60,000 a year to get on the programme and families earning up to £74,000 seeking a three-bed or larger (GLA, *London Plan*, July 2011).

My First Steps programme includes the First Steps Shared Ownership programme which enables first time buyers buy a home with monthly housing costs at approximately 20 per cent lower than if you were to buy the home outright on the open market or rent it privately (FirstSteps Website, *FirstSteps Buy*).

Around 13,360 people had been helped by the First Steps programme by February 2011. (Mayor of London, *Mayor's Questions*, 18 May 2011).

I am on track to meet the target of delivering 20,000 First Steps homes by 2012 (Mayor of London, *The revised London Housing Strategy*, December 2011).

Create a network of Community Land Trusts (Boris Johnson, *Building a Better London*, 2008, p. 6).

Promise delivered.

I have promoted community-led development in my London Housing Strategy, and ensured through the HCA London Board, which I chair, that a Community Land Trust is delivered on the former St Clements hospital site in Tower Hamlets. The land will be held in trust by the community and some of the housing held within a CLT.

We firmly believe therefore that creating a network of CLTs across London is the most creative and transparent use of public assets owned by the GLA (Boris Johnson, *Building a Better London*, 2008, p. 13).

I am also promoting a CLT on the Olympic Park with proposals invited for a CLT as part of the Chobham Manor development (OPLC, Press Release, *Legacy Company calls on developers to build Olympic Park's first family neighbourhood*).

These mark the prospect of the first urban CLTs in the UK.

241

Making progress.

The target of 50,000 homes was not met by 2011 because of the toughest market conditions in years. However I am on course to beat my target of 50,000 affordable completions by 2012 – a record for any mayoral term (Mayor of London, A Revised London Housing Strategy – Initial Proposals, August 2011, p.16).

Work closely with borough councils to deliver 50,000 new affordable homes by 2011, replacing the 50/50 split with a unit target agreed with each borough council (Boris Johnson, Building a Better London, 2008, p. 6).

I also scrapped the counter-productive 50 per cent target for affordable homes that I inherited from the old London Plan (Mayor of London, Mayor's Questions, 24 February 2010).

Amend the London Plan to increase the building of affordable family sized homes (Boris Johnson, Building a Better London, 2008, p. 6).

Ken Livingstone's 50 per cent target delivered an average of just 32 per cent and frequently presented a barrier to growth and development. (GLA, London Plan Annual Monitoring Report 5, February 2009, p. 33, Table 16).

Promise delivered.

My revised London Plan places greater emphasis on family-sized housing, and 42 per cent of new social rented housing funded in the spending round (2008-11) was for family-sized homes, compared to 35 per cent in the previous spending round (2005 - 08) (Mayor of London, London Housing Strategy, February 2010; London Councils, Leader's Committee: Mayor's Housing Strategy - London Council's Response, February 2007, Recommendation 6).

London is producing more family-sized affordable homes than it has for a decade (GLA, Revised Housing Strategy, December 2011).

Increase the number of intermediate homes by a third in London, helping more low-income and key sector workers into home ownership (Boris Johnson, Building a Better London, 2008, p. 20).

This replaces Ken Livingstone's 70:30 split (GLA, Revised Housing Strategy, December 2011; p. 34; GLA, London Plan, July 2011).

Promise delivered.

Both the London Plan and the London Housing Strategy now have a 60:40 social:intermediate split.

The 2011 revised housing strategy includes a significant proportion of family-sized housing, with new homes designed to the Mayor's larger space standards. (GLA, Revised Housing Strategy, December 2011).

Facilitate a comprehensive audit of all London's empty and 'hidden' homes' to increase the social housing stock (Boris Johnson, Building a Better London, 2008, p. 6).

Promise delivered.

The Empty Homes Audit was carried out by the GLA and the London boroughs in 2010 and provisionally identified 11,088 private sector homes empty for more than one year (Mayor of London, Mayor's Questions, 13 July 2011).

As part of the Targeted Funding Stream investment of £60 million, between 2008-2011 4,145 empty homes were brought back into use and are now occupied (Mayor of London, Mayor's Questions, 16 November 2011).

Provide a further £60 million for the regeneration of empty homes (Boris Johnson, Building a Better London, 2008, p. 6).

This is three times more than the amount of funding provided for empty homes (GLA, Revised Housing Strategy, December 2011, p. 38).

Promise delivered.

As part of the Targeted Funding Stream investment of £60 million, between 2008-2011 4,145 empty homes were brought back into use and are now occupied (Mayor of London, Mayor's Questions, 16 November 2011).

Return the Mayor's Council Tax precept to borough councils transferring their dormant stock to short life housing providers, to help reverse homelessness (Boris Johnson, Building a Better London, 2008, p. 6).

Promise delivered.

In 2011, with my support, the Government launched the New Homes Bonus, which gives bonus payments to councils for homes brought back into use and additional homes (DCLG, Press Release, 1 December 2011).

Amend the London Plan to encourage boroughs to work together towards the delivery of the Thames Gateway (Boris Johnson, Building a Better London, 2008, p. 6).

Publish an online 'Fair Rents Guide' for London (Boris Johnson, Building a Better London, 2008, p. 6).

Promise delivered.

The new, innovative London Rents Map now shows average private sector rents for different types of home across London, ensuring greater transparency for renters and attracting around 73,600 hits since it went live in December 2009 (London Rents Map Website, GLA, Revised Housing Strategy, December 2011).

Promise delivered.

My London Plan 2011 replaced the former London Plan. It consolidated alterations since 2004 and outlines our support of the development of the Thames Gateway and my intention to work with relevant agencies in London and neighbouring regions to support their development. The Plan also encourages relevant London boroughs and sub-regions to engage with relevant agencies beyond London to develop the area (GLA, The London Plan, July 2011).

I have also lobbied for an airport in the Thames Estuary which would drive development in this area (GLA Press Release, Mayor urges government to act of aviation, 21 November 2011).

I have secured funding for Crossrail which joins the Thames Gateway with central London (House of Commons Library, THAMES GATEWAY SNI SIC/3894, 8 March 2011, p.3).

In addition, I have worked with No. 10 to make the Royal Docks an Enterprise Zone, creating thousands of jobs. (GLA, Press Release, London's Royal Docks to become one of country's largest Enterprise Zones, 23 March 2011).

I have also established a Mayoral Development Corporation which will take some of the responsibilities from the Thames Gateway Development Corporation (DCLG, Press Release, 6 February 2012).

242

Make design quality central to the Housing Strategy. (Boris Johnson, *Building a Better London*, 2008, p. 6).

Promise delivered.

My London Housing Design Guide, published in August 2010 aims to end the era of poorly designed, cramped homes, and renew the capital's traditions of design excellence.

This is already being delivered for affordable housing, and new standards are being applied to private sector housing through the new London Plan and Supplementary Planning Guidance. The SPG outlines two levels of standards:

- 'Baseline' standards set the baseline for quality and design that new homes should meet. These are mandatory for all new homes
- 'Good practice' standards are those that go further and will lead to the kind of exemplary housing quality and design the Mayor is committed to achieving.

The standards will apply to all new housing in London. All homes must at a minimum meet all the baseline standards and are encouraged to meet the good practice standards. I expect new homes that are in receipt of public funding to meet the new standards in full (GLA, *Revised Housing Strategy*, December 2011).

Designing developments to combat crime

Pledge

I will make designing out crime a key priority in the London Plan and the Mayor's Housing Strategy to prevent creating poor quality housing where crime flourishes. (Boris Johnson, *Building a Better London*, 2008, p. 29).

What has been achieved so far

Promise delivered.

The London Plan sets out the designing out crime policy, which calls on boroughs and others to create safe, secure and appropriately accessible environments where crime and disorder, and the fear of crime do not undermine quality of life or community cohesion (GLA, *The London Plan*, July 2011).

The Housing Strategy also sets out that new homes and developments should be built to principles that design out crime and fire risks (GLA, *Revised Housing Strategy*, December 2011).

Protecting green spaces and historic views

Pledge	What has been achieved so far

Project ten historic views of St Paul's Cathedral and the Palace of Westminster by reinstating the original viewing corridor under Regional Planning Guidance 3A (RPG3A).

Promise delivered.

Protection of these and other views have been confirmed in the London Plan (GLA, *The London Plan, July 2011*).

Amend the London Plan to protect three additional sites in London, rejecting future planning applications that obstruct views from St James's Park towards Horse Guards Road, the bridge over the Serpentine in Hyde Park to Westminster, and Island Gardens on the Isle of Dogs to the Royal Naval College.

Promise delivered.

These are included in the London Plan's protected views (GLA, *The London Plan, July 2011*).

Call on the Government to adopt the 'Merton Rule' to promote the use of on-site renewable energy.

Promise delivered.

I did encourage Governments to adopt the Merton Rule (Mayor of London, *Mayor's Questions, 16 July 2008*).

The Planning and Energy Act 2008 allows local councils to set targets in their areas for on-site renewable energy, on-site low carbon electricity and energy efficiency standards in addition to national requirements (*Planning and Energy Act 2008*).

Amend the London Plan to urge developers to adopt the Sustainable Code to build low carbon homes for the private sector market.

Promise delivered.

The London Plan has been amended to encourage builders to build more environmentally-friendly homes. It also sets out the expectation that developers will abide by the Government's new Code for Sustainable Homes and achieve the highest Code standards possible (GLA, *London Plan, July 2011*).

Investments in new and existing homes should now contribute to reducing London's carbon emission by at least 60 per cent by 2025 (GLA, *Revised Housing Strategy, December 2011*).

Publish a specific outer London development strategy.

Promise delivered.

I have ensured that London receives its fair share of funding and focus. The Outer London Commission was established to advise how outer London can play its role in London's economic success (GLA Website), its report set out a development plan. (Boris Johnson, *Building a Better London, 2008, p. 31*)

I also appointed Cllr Theresa O'Neill as a dedicated Advisor on Outer Borough Relations on 11 February 2011. She monitors borough activity and regularly meets with outer borough Leaders (GLA Website, Teresa O'Neill, Mayor of London, *Mayor's Questions, 14 December 2011*).

I have ring-fenced money specifically for these areas in my Outer London Fund. Following the submission of over 150 bids in the first and second round of applications, I announced the award of nearly £42 million of funding from my Outer London Fund to 23 boroughs across the capital. (GLA Website, *Outer London Fund, January 2012, GLA Website, Successful bids*)

Amend the London Plan to protect domestic gardens from new development.

Promise delivered.

In 2010 the Government changed the definition of brownfield sites so that domestic gardens are not included and no local authority is obliged to build on gardens if it does not want to (DCLG, Press Release, *Clark - new powers to prevent unwanted 'garden grabbing', 9 June 2010*).

These changes were reflected in my new 2011 London Plan, under which private residential gardens are no longer classed as previously developed land and boroughs are allowed to introduce a presumption against development on back gardens or other private residential gardens in their Local Development Frameworks (GLA, *The London Plan, July 2011*).

I have also supported domestic gardens through the Capital Growth Project. 1032 food gardens have been unveiled with a target of 2000 spaces by the end of 2012. Grants from City Hall for the gardens range from £200 to £1000 (GLA, *Mayor announces 1000+ community food gardens tended by 35,000 Londoners, June 2011*).

Encourage planners to use section 106 to secure affordable units for small, independent shops.

Promise delivered.

The London Plan sets out a new policy to provide and support affordable shop units (GLA, *London Plan, July 2011*).

My Progress Report to Londoners
on the 2008 Manifesto

BackBoris2012.com

Promoted and printed by C Scott on behalf of BackBoris2012 and London Conservatives both of 30 Millbank, London SW1P 4DR

Appendix 2
Election Results

It is a general truism that in elections the candidates come and go, but that the parties remain. As the following results show the London Mayoral Elections are the exception that prove the rule. Rather than it being the political parties' that have remained fixed it is the parties that have changed. And they show just what a mountain Boris had to climb to get re-elected in 2012.

In 2000 the conventional wisdom was that Labour would win and the Conservatives come second. That thinking had to be thrown away when Labour chose Frank Dobson to be their candidates. Ken Livingstone, the long-time Labour leader in London, was piqued and stood as an Independent. Suddenly all the talk was about how this would affect the Labour vote. There were some who thought that a split Labour vote might let the Conservative candidate, Steve Norris, go through the middle to win. In the event Ken Livingstone got a solid 39% of first preference votes, to Norris's 27% and Dobson's 13%, going on to pass the winning post with 57% once second preferences were counted. In 2004 Labour adopted Livingstone as their candidate. Despite this change in the formal political line up, the actual share of the votes did not alter much. Livingstone got 37% to Norris's 29%, and won on second preferences with 55%. Ken Livingstone's vote seemed rock solid and impervious to the shifting slate of political parties in the race.

Enter Boris. This time Livingstone got 36% of first preference votes, much as before. But Boris leapfrogged him by scooping 43% of first preferences and going on to get 53% once second preferences were taken into account. Boris did this, not so much by persuading voters to change their minds as by massively increasing voter turn out. Livingstone actually got 200,000 more first preferences in 2008 than he had in 2004, but Boris almost doubled the Tory vote from 545,000 to 1,043,000. The high profile slogging match of one celebrity against another had galvanised voters. But come 2012 that excitement would wane. A second Boris vs Ken match could not hope to create the excitement of the first. The worry was Boris's voters would not turn out again. How they were persuaded to do so is the story of this book.

Seats on the London Assembly

	2000	2004	2008	2012
Conservative	9	9	11	9
Labour	9	7	8	12
Liberal Democrat	4	5	3	2
Green	3	2	2	2
UK Independence Party		2		
British National Party			1	

The two UKIP member defected to Vertias in Jan 2005 and set up their own party "One London" party in Sept 2005

London Mayoral Election Results 2000

Name	Party	1st Preference Votes	%	2nd Preference Votes	%
Ken Livingstone	Independent	667,877	39.0%	178,809	12.6%
Steve Norris	Conservative	464,434	27.1%	188,081	13.2%
Frank Dobson	Labour	223,884	13.1%	228,095	16.1%
Susan Kramer	Liberal Democrats	203,452	11.9%	404,815	28.5%
Ram Gidoomal	CPA	42,060	2.5%	56,489	4.0%
Darren Johnson	Green	38,121	2.2%	192,764	13.6%
Michael Newland	BNP	33,569	2.0%	45,337	3.2%
Damian Hockney	UKIP	16,234	0.9%	43,672	3.1%
Geoffery Ben-Nathan	Pro-Motorist Small Shop	9,956	0.6%	23,021	1.6%
Ashwin Tanna	Independent	9,015	0.5%	14,766	2.9%
Geoffrey Clements	Natural Law	5,470	0.3%	18,185	

Name	Party	Final Votes	%
Ken Livingstone	Independent	776,427	57.90%
Steve Norris	Conservative	564,137	42.10%

London Mayoral Election Results 2004

Candidate	Party	1st Preference Votes	%	2nd Preference Votes	%
Ken Livingstone	Labour	685,541	36.8%	250,517	15.7%
Steve Norris	Conservative	545,423	29.1%	222,559	14.0%
Simon Hughes	Liberal Democrats	284,645	15.3%	465,704	29.3%
Frank Maloney	UKIP	115,665	6.2%	193,157	12.1%
Lindsey German	RESPECT	61,731	3.3%	63,294	4.0%
Julian Leppert	BNP	58,405	3.1%	208,686	13.1%
Darren Johnson	Green	57,331	3.1%	56,721	3.6%
Ram Gidoomal	CPA	41,696	2.2%	56,721	3.6%
Lorna Reid	IWCA	9,542	0.5%	39,678	2.5%
Tammy Nagalingarn	Independant	6,692	0.4%	20,391	1.3%

Candidate	Party	Final Votes	%
Ken Livingstone	Independent	828,390	55.40%
Steve Norris	Conservative	667,180	44.60%

Summary of the 1 May 2008 Mayor of London election results

Name	Party	1st Preference Votes	%	2nd Preference Votes	%
Boris Johnson	Conservative	1,043,761	43.2% (+14.1%)	257,292	12.9%
Ken Livingstone	Labour	893,877	37.0% (+0.2%)	303,198	15.1%
Brian Paddick	Liberal Democrat	236,685	9.8% (-5.5%)	641,412	32.0%
Siân Berry	Green	77,374	3.2% (+0.1%)	331,727	16.6%
Richard Barnbrook	BNP	69,710	2.9% (-0.2%)	128,609	6.4%
Alan Craig	CPA	39,249	1.6% (-0.6%)	80,140	4.0%
Gerard Batten	UKIP	22,422	0.9% (-5.3%)	113,651	5.7%
Lindsey German	Left List	16,796	0.7%	35,057	1.7%
Matt O'Connor *(withdrew from contest)*	English Democrats	10,695	0.4%	73,538	3.7%
Winston McKenzie	Independent	5,389	0.2%	38,854	1.9%

Name	Party	Final Votes	%
Boris Johnson	Conservative	1,168,738	53.2% (+8.6%)
Ken Livingstone	Labour	1,028,966	46.8 (-8.6%)

London Mayoral Election Results 2012

Name	Party	1st Preference Votes	%	2nd Preference Votes	%
Boris Johnson	Conservative	971,931	44.0% (+0.8%)	82,880	44.74%
Ken Livingstone	Labour	889,918	40.3% (+3.3)	102,355	55.26%
Jenny Jones	Green	98,913	4.5% (+1.3%)		
Brian Paddick	Liberal Democrats	91,774	4.2% (-5.6%)		
Siobhan Benita	Independent	83,914	3.8% (N/A)		
Lawrence Webb	Fresh Choice for London	43,274	2.0% (+1.1%)		
Carlos Cortiglia	BNP	28,751	1.3% (-1.6%)		

Name	Party	Final Votes	%
Boris Johnson	Conservative	1,054,811	51.53% (-1.65%)
Ken Livingstone	Labour	992,273	48.47% (+1.65%)

INDEX

Bretwalda Books Ltd